Born in 1893 in Melbourne and educated at Scotch College, J. P. McKinney led a wandering life in outback Australia until he enlisted with the A.I.F. on the outbreak of World War I. His experiences during five years in the Middle East, France and later in England led him to embark on the reading of philosophy in a search for the basis of what he saw as a modern fragmentation of life and thought. Throughout the next twenty years, though handicapped by war-caused illness and the raising of a family in Depression farming conditions in Australia, he continued to widen and deepen his reading and to educate himself in both philosophy and the philosophy of science from the Greeks to the present day.

On the outbreak of World War II he decided to devote himself wholly to this task, and the rest of his life was spent on it. The publication of a comparatively brief and summary book, *The Challenge of Reason*, he saw as premature, and he soon withdrew it. He wrote a number of articles for philosophical journals in America and England, and *The Structure of Modern Thought*, a fuller statement of his final position, was completed just before his death.

D0844988

CE

THE STRUCTURE OF
MODERN THOUGHT

THE STRUCTURE OF
MODERN THOUGHT

J. P. McKINNEY

1971

CHATTO & WINDUS

LONDON

Universitas
BIBLIOTHECA

Published by
Chatto & Windus Ltd
40 William IV Street
London W.C.2
*
Clarke, Irwin & Co. Ltd
Toronto

ISBN 0 7011 1639 0

B
804
. M 23
1971
cop. 2

© Judith Wright McKinney 1971

All rights reserved. No part of this publication
may be reproduced, stored in a retrieval system,
or transmitted, in any form, or by any means,
electronic, mechanical, photocopying, recording
or otherwise, without the prior permission
of Chatto & Windus Ltd.

Printed in Great Britain by
William Lewis (Printers) Ltd
Cardiff

CONTENTS

CONTENTS

ACKNOWLEDGEMENTS

Thanks are due for permission to quote from the following copyright material: *Doubt and Certainty in Science* by J.Z. Young (The Clarendon Press, Oxford); *Philosophy in A New Key* by Susanne K. Langer (Harvard University Press: copyright 1951, 1957, by the President and Fellows of Harvard College; 1970 by Susanne Langer); and *The Revolution in Philosophy* by A.J. Ayer (Macmillan & Co. Ltd., and St. Martin's Press Inc., New York).

PREFACE

How do we know *what* we know?

This is not a problem that the intelligent layman usually regards as any concern of his. It can be left to the philosopher, he would say.

But there is a problem that today deeply concerns the intelligent layman, though he may not present it to himself as a problem, partly because it is so pervasive that it eludes definition, and partly because there does not seem to be anything he can do about it. This is the problem of communication.

The failure of communication between man and man is the great contemporary 'theme': plays, poems, novels are devoted to exploring – or perhaps exploiting – this modern 'anguish'; a whole philosophy has been written around it. Words (this is the theme) become a screen between man and man, between man and reality – '. . . words are the end, not the beginning, so they are bogus, retaining none of the process of responsiveness; frozen, clotted things'. (Our purpose here is to record the *fact* that this view prevails, not to either agree or disagree with the view.)

Because the problem of communication is so pervasive and so elusive, and because the problem of knowledge is so remote from our everyday concerns, it is not easy to see that the former is a by-product of the latter. But the fact is that the breakdown of communication is an expression of the state of knowledge. 'As physics has developed', remarked Bertrand Russell, 'it has deprived us step by step of what we thought we knew concerning the ultimate nature of the physical world.'

The connection is obvious enough, once stated. Language, words are the medium through which we communicate what we know – as well as, of course, what we feel, and think and hope and desire, concerning what we know — to one another. So that any fundamental change in our ideas of what we know must affect our ideas of language, and this in turn — indirectly and by insinuation rather than by direct observable effect — must react upon the complex and continuous business of communication.

As Eliot's Sweeney said, 'I gotta use words when I talk to you', and when the words and what they are intended to communicate begin to 'slip, slide, perish, decay with imprecision', a situation exists which, though it may be good for poetry — the poet being able, as it were, to live on the waste matter of his own anxiety — imposes an unbearable strain on the day-by-day business of living.

So indefinable is this problem, this chain-reaction breakdown of knowledge, of language, of communication that it does not seem to be capable of any sort of rational explanation. And yet the situation has a clear-cut historical genesis.

Until well into the present century philosophers had no doubts concerning how they knew what they knew. What they were getting to know was Reality, and Reality was a given, determinate fact which caused us to have the sort of experience we did have, and on the basis of this experience knowledge was built up. Knowledge and language presented no real problem. They were simply manifestations of Reality. All that was necessary was to get to know more about Reality, and the method for doing this had been finally worked out by Newton and his successors. All that was left was to fill in the details.

In retrospect, that situation seems innocently idyllic. To-day, under the cool calm gaze of modern physics, that fixed and determinate world of our predecessors has been replaced by a world which is characterized by relativity, probability, discontinuity and indeterminacy. Even without stopping to inquire precisely what these terms mean, it is obvious that the transition from the idea of a *determinate* world, to the idea of it as fundamentally *indeterminate,* must involve a profound change in our ideas of the nature of knowledge. For if the thing we are getting to know is of an utterly different order from what we thought it was, then our manner of getting to know it must be correspondingly different; we are not getting to know it in the way we thought we were.

This, it will be seen, presents a problem that falls in a sort of no-man's land between the philosopher's specialized discussion and the ordinary man's feeling that 'something is wrong'. Regarded in its widest aspect and in its overall relevance, the question, How do we know what we know? is today everybody's concern.

That is the purpose of the following work: to investigate the problem of knowledge, and so of communication, for the light it throws upon the 'modern crisis of feeling and of thought'.

The above emphasis on the effect of modern physics on our idea of knowledge does not mean that we are going to follow the present custom of trying to squeeze some metaphysical significance out of the famous Principle of Indeterminacy. All we are going to do is, having noted the tremendous impact on our lives of the modern revolution in physics, to inquire what corresponding effect might be expected to result from the modern revolution in philosophy.

I say 'might be expected' advisedly, because, as is generally known, the Revolution in Philosophy has not had, and indeed claims that it is not its business to have, any such effect on our lives.

Obviously then, if we are going to inquire into what effect philosophy might be expected to have, we are not going to accept on its face value the image which the modern philosopher has tended to project of himself as 'aloof, indifferent, paring his fingernails', as quibbling while Rome burns.

From this it will also be obvious that the book, though it deals with a very ancient concern of philosophy, the problem of knowledge, is not specifically addressed to the philosopher.

The book is, in fact, a bringing together, a sort of rendering down, of papers dealing with various aspects of the modern revolution of thought, which I have contributed over a number of years to various of those journals in whose calm and sequestered pages philosophers like to commune with one another.

For the benefit of those who might wish to test themselves on some more substantial philosophical fare, I append a list of such papers. But these, though they may provide more mental exercise, will not yield any more enlightenment – if as much – than the following pages will supply. The main difference will be that the papers listed are presented with a full panoply of footnotes and references, as befits the company they keep, whereas here, except for two footnotes, which the reader may ignore if he wishes, what can't be included in the text I have dispensed with.

I claim to have done this out of consideration for the ordinary reader, but perhaps it is really a private gesture of revolt against the tyranny of the footnote, which is even more of a tyranny when the footnotes stand in serried ranks at the back of the book than when they jostle for the reader's attention on every page.

But I have another and quite good reason for reducing references to a minimum. If, making use of a quotation, you give a specific book-page-author reference for it, the impression you naturally give is that what you are concerned with is the particular author's expression of his own personal opinion, and at once you have narrowed your range of reference; somebody has only to say, 'Well, I don't regard *him* as an authority anyway', and the point you are trying to make is lost.

But the sort of points I want to make don't rely on any authority quoted. The quotations I use are simply illustrations of current attitudes of mind. It doesn't matter whether or not you, or even I, agree with the opinion expressed. All that matters about it is that it expresses a standpoint which is a fact of the current thought situation. For this reason, wherever possible I give quotations without any references; I assume that the professional philosopher, if he knows his business, will know the source of the quotation, and the non-professional reader won't care in any case.

Where I have given references it is because a specific criticism of that particular opinion seems to require this – but I probably haven't even succeeded in being quite consistent in this. All very bad form, academically. But this isn't an academic book. My purpose is to keep the discussion as wide-open and general as possible. Hence, quotes without references.

One final word of guidance for the reader. The book is in two parts. The two parts have a different purpose in focus. Part One deals with the problem of knowledge. But it is not an attempt to solve that problem: it is merely an attempt to see what the problem *is*. On investigation it is found that this isn't easy. The problem – a very ancient concern of philosophy – is found to be beset by all sorts of confusions. All sorts of 'solutions' of the problem have been advanced, but these seem to have consisted largely in taking some chosen temperamental stand and pushing into the background whatever didn't agree with this.

The purpose of Part One is to cast a calm and unbiased eye over the confused scene and to bring to the surface and examine these accumulated difficulties, these intellectual skeletons in cupboards, for these are what the problem of knowledge, in its contemporary form, consists in.

This, it will be seen, directly reverses the usual procedure. Instead of discreetly by-passing difficulties, we are deliberately seeking out and emphasizing difficulties; but unless the reader keeps this in mind he may find himself asking in a tone of frustration, 'What is all this supposed to *prove*?' It isn't supposed to prove anything, except that confusions exist and that we can't hope to grope our way out of them until we know what they are.

But to track down confusions is inclined to be itself a confusing task. A rather daunting one too. It would be easy, in a moment of weakness, to give up the attempt, fall back on the comfort of one's own chosen confusion, and let the rest go by default. Well, that is a matter for one's personal

decision. But let me say by way of encouragement that, out
of the accumulating confusions of Part One, a clear view of
the problem of knowledge does emerge, so that in Part Two
we can proceed, from a firm base, to the constructive part
of our undertaking.

List of published papers

Philosophy of Science (July 1952): 'Discussion'

Philosophy of Science (July 1953): 'Comment' (on Professor Kemble's 'Reality, Measurement and the State of the System in Quantum Mechanics')

Philosophy East and West (Oct. 1953): 'Can East Meet West?' (Discussion of Professor F.C. Northrop's 'The Meeting of East and West')

Australasian Journal of Philosophy (Dec. 1956): 'The Status of Theoretical Entities'

Hibbert Journal (April 1957): 'The Philosophical Implications of Logical Analysis'

Philosophy of Science (July 1957): 'The Rational and the Real: Comments on a Paper by Prof. E. Topitsch on 'Society, Technology and Philosophical Reasoning'

The Journal of Philosophy (Sept. 15, 1957): 'Concepts and Meanings: A Footnote to Philosophy'

Philosophy and Phenomenological Research (Sept. 1957): 'Philosophical Implications of the Modern Revolution of Thought'

Philosophy of Science (Oct. 1957): 'Knowledge and Experience: Comment on a paper by Prof. L. von Bertalanffy on "The Relativity of Categories" '

Mind (July 1958): 'Experience and Reality'

Australasian Journal of Philosophy (Dec. 1959): 'Phenomenalism: A Survey and Reassessment'

Indian Journal of Philosophy (Dec. 1960): 'The Nature of Knowledge' (Comment on a paper by Professor K. Popper)

Part One

KNOWLEDGE

INTRODUCTION

1. *'Sheep that look up and are not fed'*

There was a time when philosophy was anybody's business. It was an occupation open to any man of goodwill, reasonable intelligence and earnest intentions.

When Descartes laid the foundations of modern philosophy with his famous 'I think, therefore I am', he was a soldier of fortune. 'I was then in Germany,' he tells us, 'attracted thither by the wars in that country, which had not yet been brought to a termination; and as I was returning to the army from the coronation of the emperor, the setting in of winter arrested me in a locality where, as I found no society to interest me, and was besides fortunately undisturbed by any cares or passions, I remained the whole day in seclusion, with full opportunity to occupy my attention with my own thoughts. '

Such were the homely beginnings of the philosophy of individual experience.

Spinoza, too, was an ordinary man, a lens-grinder. Leibniz was a diplomat and man of affairs. Locke was a physician. Berkeley was a bishop with a fanatical faith in the medicinal virtues of tar-water. Hume was a diplomat and man of letters. And, of course, there was the universal exemplar, Socrates, who was a stone-mason.

It was Kant, stirred from his dogmatic slumbers by Hume's shattering criticism of the principle of Universal Causation, who turned philosophy into a specialized undertaking, with its own peculiar terminology and mode of attack. Anyone can read Hume, given a certain amount of goodwill and concentration; you always know what he means, even if you don't like the sound of it. But with Kant the amateur acknowledges himself defeated. He must leave it to the professional

3

philosopher to decide what it is all about – only to find, if he pursues the matter further, that even the professional is not quite sure.

But it was not until the present century, in particular until the last two or three decades, that philosophy became an occupation quite consciously and deliberately reserved for professional philosophers.

An account of this development is given in outline by Professor Ryle, in his editorial Introduction to *The Revolution in Philosophy,* a series of Third Programme talks issued in book-form.

During the present century, 'Philosophy developed into a separate academic subject, partly detached from classical scholarship, from theology, from economics, and last of all from psychology. The teachers of philosophy at a university came to constitute a faculty and they organized their own discussion groups . . . This new professional practice of submitting problems and arguments to the expert criticism of fellow craftsmen led to a growing concern with questions of philosophical technique and a growing passion for rationative rigour . . . Philosophers had now to be philosophers' philosophers . . . transcendental dictions were becoming unidiomatic at the same time as the technicalities of logical theory and scientific method were stiffening the working parlance of philosophers.'

Professor Ryle adds, 'Already surrendering its historic linkage with mental science or psychology and no longer remembering its former claim to be the science of things transcendental, philosophy looked like losing its credentials as a science of anything at all.'

The six talks that make up the book to which Professor Ryle is writing the introduction are concerned with the 'revolution' in philosophy which resulted from the contemporary philosopher's efforts to meet, at the new professional and technical level, this challenge to his chosen subjects.

For the moment, however, we are not concerned with the effect on the philosopher of this 'revolution' in which he

became involved, but with the incidental effects of the new
and specialized ways of philosophizing on the intelligent layman, who once, even if he did not aspire to be a philosopher
himself, could at least expect to be able to read and understand and gain some benefit from the writings of philosophers.

It is obvious that this new, technical, professionalized
philosophy is going to present the inquiring layman with
some serious difficulties of understanding. But in addition to
this, the professional philosopher, addressing himself now to
his fellow philosophers, is no longer concerned with the sort
of problems that attract the layman to philosophy. In fact,
under the pressures exerted by the new techniques of thought,
the philosopher very soon found himself going through a
revolution within his original 'revolution', in which all the
traditional problems of philosophy which had occupied men's
minds for over two thousand years, were declared to be
'pseudo-problems', with which the philosopher need not
further concern himself.

What becomes of the intelligent layman and his search for
help and guidance now? In the closing essay of the series that
Professor Ryle edited, Professor Warnock says — and as the
claim was not struck out by the editor, we may assume that
he voiced the prevailing mood: 'If . . . there are some people
who still wish to complain that philosophy does not meet
their requirements; that they look up like hungry sheep and
are not fed; it may perhaps be proper to ask them why
philosophy *ought* to meet their requirements. Hungry sheep
should not expect to be fed, simply because they are looking
up, for they may be looking in the wrong direction.'

That is the answer the philosopher gives to our question
as to the effect of the modern revolution in philosophy on
the hopes and needs of the inquiring layman. A rather uncompromising answer. The layman may not find it very much
to his taste. He might feel impelled to complain that, if, as
Professor Warnock suggests, he is looking in the wrong
direction for an answer to his questions, then surely it is
the business of the philosopher to at least give him some

indication of the direction in which he should look. For, after all (he might say), isn't the philosopher one trained by society to do its thinking for it? He can't just opt out with a shrug of the shoulders and huddle away in a corner with his own chosen problems; he must acknowledge *some* responsibility to society.

There may be some truth in all this, but as the philosopher shows no sign of admitting that there is — he is even inclined to claim, today, that he not only needn't provide answers to the layman's questions, but he needn't provide any answers to any questions — it would perhaps be better to face the facts. And the fact of the present situation is that, in a world of accumulating doubts and uncertainties, the intelligent layman is 'on his own'. He cannot call upon anybody else to do his thinking for him.

. . . He cannot call on anybody else. That is to say, he cannot call on anybody but himself . . . And the implication of that is, to say the least of it, challenging. For the implication is that, if the inquiring layman wants some light in the midst of his present encompassing gloom of doubt, then he must seek that light for himself. If, being hungry, he looks up but is not fed, then he must stop looking up and set about seeking his own nourishment.

Well, we have faced up to our situation. The philosopher won't help us; we must help ourselves. If we want an answer to our questions we must do our own philosophizing.

But — the question at once presents itself — having accepted the challenge of our situation, how are we to proceed? How are we even to begin?

2. *Different ways of philosophizing*

It might seem that if we are going to try our hand at doing our own philosophizing, we should start off by asking, What is philosophy? But I don't think so.

That, of course, is the usual approach. Books on philosophy, or at any rate those addressed to the layman, usually start off by asking and trying to answer this question. But throughout the ages the answers have varied.

At first it was assumed that philosophy's business was to present a Grand Scheme of the Universe, a sort of Ultimate Truth, compulsive by reason of its very universality. The final abandonment of so ambitious an undertaking — it lingered on into the early decades of the present century — naturally left a sort of intellectual vacuum in its wake.

But an intellectual vacuum is intolerable to thinking man. Thinkers of a certain temperament tended to fill the vacuum with a philosophy of methodical pessimism. Only on the foundations of unyielding despair, it seemed, could the soul's habitation be safely built.

But that was a passing mood. The development of new logical techniques offered a way out. These were the new techniques of thought, referred to by Professor Ryle, which were to contribute toward the professionalization of philosophy.

The new logic proved to be a powerful instrument of analysis. Philosophy had once proudly claimed for itself the task of synthesis, the building up of a comprehensive world-picture. It now saw its task as methodical and ever more penetrating analysis. The modern philosopher was no longer building a world-picture out of elements of thought as the traditional philosopher had regarded himself as doing. He was now reducing an already-given world-picture by progressive logical analysis to its elementary basis, to the ultimate units on which it would be found to rest.

This change-over from *synthesis*, the building up of a world-picture, to *analysis*, the breaking-down of a world-picture, represents, we can see, a pretty drastic revolution in men's idea of the business of philosophy. It represented, for one thing, a highly articulate repudiation of all forms of metaphysical speculation.

The traditional philosopher had set himself the task of

accounting, in purely conceptual terms – Time, Space, Substance etc – for the world of matter and motion in which he found himself. The view of the modern philosopher, as expressed by Bertrand Russell, was 'Instead of supposing, as we naturally do, that . . . *matter* is what is "really real" in the physical world . . . we must regard matter as a logical construction, of which the constituents will be just such evanescent particulars as may, when an observer happens to be present, become data of sense to that observer.'

In other words, what has been, for the traditional philosopher, an absolute World-in-itself of physical objects in motion in terms of time and space, which was the *cause of* our experience, was now to be regarded as a *construction from* the data of our experience. And the task of philosophy now was *logical analysis*, the methodical reduction of what had been regarded as physical objects to their elements in the sensory data of the individual who happened to be observing them.

As A.J. Ayer put it in *Language, Truth and Logic*, that brilliant but as it turned out rather too impetuous expression of the new mood of thought, ' . . . must not the metaphysician begin, as other men do, with the evidence of his senses? And if so, what valid process of reasoning can possibly lead him to the conception of a transcendent reality?' – a reality, that is, that transcends the evidence of his own senses.

But this question, aimed at the very basis of traditional metaphysics, was soon to give rise to an interesting question concerning the procedure of analysis itself: What is the nature and outcome of logical analysis? What was the philosopher's purpose in pursuing this new philosophical task of logical analysis?

And once this question had been raised, once attention was drawn to the *outcome* of the new task of philosophy, it was realized that though, theoretically, 'things', as logical constructions from sense data, should be capable of being analysed (in however recondite and roundabout a way) into such sense-data, such analyses were not in fact being produced.

This struck a blow at the very basis of the new way of philosophizing, which had been entered into with such confidence and enthusiasm as a cure for old ills and a source of new insight.

Another change in the philosopher's idea of the nature of philosophy was on the way. This was the 'revolution in philosophy' referred to by Professor Ryle, a sloughing off of the 'troublesome legacy of discredited theories', as one contributor to Professor Ryle's symposium expressed it.

But to meet the requirements implied in the phrase, 'the revolution in philosophy', it would seem that we would need to know, not only *that* certain theories – of analysis and of meaning and truth as verification – were now discredited, but *why* they were discredited; not only that they had failed to work, but how and why they had failed to work. All that was known was that, having been effective in destroying one way of thought, these theories had proved to be inadequate as the basis for a new way of thought, and so had to be abandoned.

The change over from the traditional view of philosophy as the *synthesis* of a world-picture, to the view of philosophy as the *analysis* of a (given) world-picture, and from the view of the world as the independently existing *cause of* experience, to the view of the world as a *construction from* experience – this was a revolution with its successive steps fully worked out and documented. Philosophers knew, not only that the old way of thought wouldn't work, but *why* this was so. But when, in its turn, the new way of thought failed to work, all they knew was that something was wrong, and, not knowing what this something was, the only way out seemed to be to scrap the whole enterprise, with all its confident hopes and claims, and look round for something else to do.

Luckily something else was at hand. Wittgenstein, in his earlier work, had wanted to show how experience, language and reality were related. Realizing that he had failed in this, he started again on the basis: Well, they *are* related – that's how things are. Give the grocer a shopping list with 'five apples' on it, and he knows what to do. Don't let us ask 'What is the meaning of "five" and how does he know this meaning, and how does the writer of the list know that he will know?' No such thing is in question here. Haven't we already tried to answer those questions and found ourselves bogged down and defeated? Don't let us get into that muddle again. Don't let us fall into the old philosophical trap of being bewitched by words – what does 'meaning' mean? as if it had *a* meaning, as if there weren't all sorts of meanings, all sorts of uses of the word 'meaning'. Let us simply assume that the grocer acts as we have described. Explanations must come to an end somewhere, unless we are to get caught up again in all those problems we were once so sure that we had finally solved. And anyway, such problems are meaningless. Aren't such activities as commanding, questioning, recounting, chatting as much part of our natural history as walking, eating, drinking and playing? And we don't ask about *their* nature and origin.

Perhaps if philosophers, armed with their new techniques of thought, hadn't set about their task of demolition with such confidence that they were right and all previous genera-tions of thinkers – not simply wrong, but stupidly wrong, the realization that they too were somehow wrong might not have had such a catastrophic effect on them. It seemed that they must either admit that they were no better or wiser than those whom they had so heartily condemned; or, in a gesture of self-defence, declare the whole corpus of problems which had engaged men's minds for two thousand years to be pseudo-problems, not worthy of a philosopher's interest or attention; and, as a safeguard against any further set-backs. set up, as a new ideal, a philosophy of non-commitment, in which no questions were to be asked and no answers given. In this way Wittgenstein, whose own philosophical odyssey had so closely reflected that of a whole generation of thinkers, became 'the most powerful and pervasive influence upon the practice of philosophy in England.'

So, in the light of this brief glance at the philosopher's

various attempts to say what philosophy is, what it is about, it would seem that it would not be worth our while prefacing our own philosophical enterprise with an attempt to decide on our own definition of philosophy. At the end of our enterprise, we might find ourselves in possession of some sort of answer. Until then, it seems that it will be better to leave the question in abeyance.

Perhaps, indeed, it might be better not to describe our venture as philosophizing at all. Perhaps we should say, more modestly, that we are simply going to try our hands at thinking things out for ourselves, the professional philosopher having abandoned us to our own resources.

And for a start, we want to know what was the cause of the failure of the philosopher's undertaking, which, in turn, caused his failure of nerve. All we know is that, for some reason, his efforts to analyse the given world-picture into its basis in sensory experience, and his effort to use the data of sense as a basis for the operations of the Verification Principle, both failed.

Indeed, stated in this way, we can see that this was not two failures, but one. And it concerned the effort to establish the relation between reality and sensory experience. It seemed to be beyond dispute that we all must begin with the evidence of our senses; and logically it seemed to be proven that the world of matter was 'a logical construction, of which the constituents will be just such evanescent particulars as may, when an observer happens to be present, become data of sense for that observer'. And yet, when the philosopher tried to trace the steps from the observer's sensory data — however broadly he interpreted these — to the given body of knowledge, no such relationship could be established.

The paradoxical situation was, as we can now in retrospect see, that the knowledge any individual possessed must be drawn from the data of experience, but no individual's experience was adequate to account for the body of knowledge he was actually found in possession of.

Either this was a complete and insoluble mystery, which

11

could only be rationally dealt with by denying its existence and refusing to look far enough to see that it did exist — a sacrificing of reason in the attempt to preserve reason — or, somewhere in the period covered by the foregoing account, a false assumption had crept in, and was bedevilling thought. If so, the clue we want lies snugly embedded in that account.

Chapter I

A NEW LOOK AT AN ANCIENT PROBLEM

1. *The biologist takes over from the philosopher*

So far we have considered only the contribution of the philosopher to the problem of knowledge. But it is an interesting fact that, at the point where the philosopher repudiated the problem, and with it the concept of knowledge itself, a new investigator entered the field.

The philosopher got as far as to show that, *in principle*, the world of our everyday experience is an experiential complex, a construction from the data of experience. But he found himself unable to work this out in detail. And then, into the gap left by this failure, stepped the physiologist, with a different approach to the ancient and intractable problem.

The philosopher, as we have seen, approached this problem by way of the logical analysis of concepts, such as *thing* and *world*. He regarded himself as an empiricist because he was seeking for the experiential basis of such concepts. But hard-headed and rigorous as his procedure appeared to be, this submitting of concepts to logical analysis was a purely intellectual enterprise; it was an abstract sort of empiricism.

If we pose the problem of knowledge to ourselves in its simplest form, we naturally ask: Here am I in possession of a body of knowledge – how did I come into possession of this knowledge? The obvious answer is: By way of the messages delivered to me through my nervous system; for it is clear that, from my simplest reaction to my environment to the most complex piece of information conveyed to me by the spoken or written word, whatever I come to know must reach me through the instrumentality of my sensory equipment.

It is the individual's nervous system, and its culminating point, the brain, that the physiologist is concerned with. So, by the very nature of his approach to the problem of knowledge, as we have just stated it, it would seem that he is in an ideal position to give an answer to the question that defeated the philosopher.

By contrast with the philosopher, the physiologist's approach is strictly empirical. Not the logical analysis of the concepts the individual is found to possess, but observation of and experiment on the individual's nervous system, is to be the source of the physiologist's conclusion. It is of interest then that whereas the philosopher ended with a blunt repudiation of the inquiring layman and his needs and aspirations, the physiologist not only feels confident of solving the problem of knowledge, but regards himself as doing so in a way that is of the utmost significance to the layman.

I hope that I shall be able to show you that by further study of these matters [the workings of the brain] we may see the connection between our doubts, longings, and highest aspirations and the processes that have gone on in animals for hundreds of millions of years, perhaps with the eternal processes of the stars. These are high aims; but would you expect less from the study of man's unique feature, the brain?

These words are taken from the opening chapter of Professor J.Z. Young's *Doubt and Certainty in Science* (an amplification of the 1950 Reith Lectures). They are certainly a far cry from the philosopher's 'Why *ought* philosophy to meet their requirements?'

Approaching the problem which had led the philosopher into a logical impasse, Professor Young says:

The method I am going to suggest as a working basis is to organize *all* our talk about human powers and capacities around knowledge of what the brain does. When the philosopher studies the way in which people think, let him consider what activities this represents in the brain: for certainly there is some. When the theologian studies the fact that human beings tend to organise their activities around statements about gods, let him consider the activity that this involves in the brain. When the educationist and psychologist follow the ways in which the child grows to his mature powers and later perhaps goes astray, let them consider the processes of the development and decay of the activities of the brain.

Comparing the brain to a gigantic government office or to a calculating machine, he says:

> How would this office be organized, how would it convert the information it received, the sensations entering by way of the nervous system, into orders for the governing of the territory it controls? Everything, surely, would depend on its having arrangements by which all relevant information could be brought together to produce the right answer to every question put to it. This is just what happens in the nervous system. The sense organs transmit information to whichever departments of the brain can use it. But how does the brain bring this information together, so as to send out the right orders to the territory it is responsible for in the body? To find this out we must return to the comparison of the brain with calculating machines. Information reaches the brain in a kind of code, you remember, of impulses passing up the nerve-fibres. Information already received is stored in the brain either by sending impulses round closed circuits, or in some form corresponding to a print ... The information received in the past forms the machine's rules of action, coded and stored away for reference ... Similarly, the brain is constantly relating the new impulses that reach it to the information already stored away in its tissues.

It may be noted that in any comparison of human brains with calculating machines the question of course arises: Man puts the code into the machine; how does the code get into man? There is a curious feature of Dr. Young's treatment of this problem that may be noted in passing. He asks, 'How does the brain bring this information (delivered by the senses) together so as to send out the right orders?' For answer we are referred to the man-made calculating machine, which is a device for sorting out information according to a code, i.e., the code built into it by man. The peculiarity of this is that the physiologist seems to be saying that the human brain receives its code in the same way as the machine, which receives its code from the human brain.

However, what immediately concerns us is the general conclusion of the physiologist's discussion. And to our surprise, and despite his specialized experimental approach as against the philosopher's reliance on logical analysis, the physiologist is brought to substantially the same conclusion as the philosopher: the conclusion, namely, that what we call the world is an experiential construction.

And this is surprising because, whereas the physiologist has promised us a solution of the problem of knowledge, the philosopher, having arrived at this same conclusion, was forced to acknowledge that it offered no such solution; in fact accepted it as showing that this was an insoluble pseudo-problem. This was the reason for his drastic repudiation not only of the problem of knowledge, but of the concept of knowledge too; and finally for his repudiation of the layman and his hopes and aspirations.

The physiologist, on the other hand, regards this conclusion not only as solving the problem of knowledge, but as doing so in a way that fulfils the aspirations of the inquiring layman even beyond his expectations.

We might be tempted to say: Well, let us accept the physiologist's offering, since he offers us what we want. But on consideration, there is something rather disturbing about the situation that confronts us. We can hardly rest content with a situation in which the logical and the experimental approaches to the problem of knowledge lead (a) to the same conclusion and (b) to diametrically opposed interpretations of that conclusion.

It would seem that, as a preliminary exercise in our effort

to think things out on our own account, we had better see what we can make of this disconcerting confusion of outlooks.

As a first step, let us look again at the physiologist's statement of his conclusion and his justification of it. We do so with the conviction that something is wrong somewhere, though we are quite open-minded as to where the trouble lies.

2. *The individual and the world*

Under the chapter heading, 'The Establishment of Certainty', Professor Young writes:

> In one of his poems A.E. Housman expresses a feeling we sometimes have; a feeling of being lost in the Universe, of not *belonging* there:
>
> > I, a stranger and afraid
> > In a world I never made.
>
> A world I never made? But the researches outlined in the last two lectures show that the brain of each one of us does literally create his or her own world. To explain this we must answer the question: How does each brain set up its own characteristic rules?

This idea, that each of us sets up our own world-picture, is not peculiar to Professor Young. The same conclusion has been arrived at by other investigators. Sir Russell Brain, in *The Nature of Experience,* says, 'The perceptual world, therefore, if I may use the term to describe the whole realm of our perceptual experience, is a construct of the percipient's brain.' And E.O. Adrian, in *The Physical Background of Perception,* quotes K.J.W. Craik in *The Nature of Explanation* (giving us two instances in one) as speaking of the individual's mind 'making a working model of reality.'

According to Professor Young, this building-up of a world-picture or body of knowledge, from the data of experience

17

'. . . is a process which we may consider as beginning with each human being at the moment when, as a new-born babe, his eyes open onto the world. From that moment the incoming stimuli begin to leave their mark on the brain, its rules begin to be established.' Again, he speaks of 'the store of rules in the brain, rules learnt by the long years of exploring with the eye during childhood.'

This account of the matter does not seem to present any difficulties. Even at the commonsense level it is clear enough that each of us enters the world in a state of nescience. The brain is like a clean sheet of paper on which experience has not yet written its messages. From then on, as we develop, the knowledge we attain to is a direct expression of our ever-widening experience. All must come to us, as individuals, through our sensory equipment, even, as noted earlier, the spoken and written words with which our elders direct our education.

If the individual lacks some normal capacity for experience — if his sensory equipment is deficient in some way, if for instance he is born blind — to that extent his knowledge will be deficient. The individual builds up his picture of the world from the data of his experience, and his capacity for experience is the measure of the world he comes to live in. As Sir Russell Brain says, 'The physical world, therefore, is what we infer about the causes of our perceptions, and since it is a product of inference it is a symbolic representation of the structure of events occurring in space-time.'

But though this is superficially straightforward and common-sensical enough, on consideration we may note what looks like a doubtful point. It seems that, if the individual's sensory equipment is in some way deficient, then the knowledge he ultimately possesses will be deficient in that sense and degree. But, though it seems to follow from this that all we know is a direct expression of our individual capacity for experience, nevertheless the obvious fact is that each of us, as an individual, knows more than our own experience is capable of accounting for.

I know, in some sense of the word 'know', that there is a place called Spain. But I have never been to Spain. What I know of Spain — and I know a reasonable amount — I do not know on the basis of any direct sensory experience of my own. And this applies to my knowledge of places and facts about other parts of the world. Indeed, though I speak confidently of 'the world' in this way, my own actual sensory experience does not cover sufficient of the world to yield the comprehensive picture that the word 'world' naturally conveys.

In other words, consideration makes clear that much of the knowledge I possess has not been derived from my own individual experience. Is this the fact that the philosopher ran up against when he tried to analyse the world with which we are all familiar into a system or series of sensory data? His logical analysis seemed to prove to him that what we call the world is an experiential construction; but when he tried, either to reduce the world *to* sense-data, or to build up the world *from* sense-data, he found the task beyond him. He found himself landed with the paradox that the world was an experiential construction — his logic guaranteed that — which had not been, because — as again his logic guaranteed — it could not be, built up from the actual data of experience.

The physiologist, on the other hand, has no hesitation in saying that the world-picture which we all possess *has* been built up from the data of experience. Let us see then what is the basis of the physiologist's assurance.

We have already glanced, above, at the case of a person born blind, whose knowledge is in that sense defective. Professor Young cites the interesting case of a person who, having been born blind, has later gained his sight by way of a surgical operation. This is clearly a case that should have something significant to tell us in relation to the problem of knowledge.

'What would such a person see: what would he say, on first opening his eyes on the new world?' asks Professor Young. 'During the present century the operation has been done often enough for systematic and accurate reports to be collected.'

What do these reports have to tell us relevant to our present inquiry? Professor Young quotes them in support of the thesis that 'the brain of each one of us does literally create his or her own world'.

Unfortunately for our efforts to find some secure basis for our enterprise of thinking things out, the case of the blind man, cited by Professor Young, does not, on examination, prove what he presents it as proving. On the contrary, it seems that if it proves anything, it proves the opposite of Professor Young's thesis.

This is disappointing, but the basic rule of an enterprise such as ours must be 'Let's face the facts as we find them.' And the unfortunate fact is that the solution of the problem of knowledge seems to have eluded the physiologist just as it did the philosopher.

But let us look at Professor Young's presentation of the case of the blind man who gains his sight. If nothing else, it will be an exercise in thinking things out.

3. 'A stranger and afraid'

What would a person, who had been born blind and later received his sight by way of an operation, see, what would he say, on first opening his eyes on the (to him) new world?

Professor Young's answer is, 'The patient, on opening his eyes for the first time, gets little or no enjoyment; indeed he finds the experience painful.'

This need not surprise us. After all, being plunged into the world of sight is like a kind of birth, though it is a birth that takes place, for the individual, at a high level of consciousness. But that isn't the important point for our present purpose.

He reports only a spinning mass of lights and colours.
He proves to be quite unable to pick out objects by

sight, to recognize what they are, to name them. He has no conception of a space with objects in it, although he knows all about objects and their names by touch. 'Of course,' you will say, 'he must take a little time to learn to recognize them by sight.' Not a *little* time, but a very, very long time, in fact, years.

Once this is stated it hardly surprises us, though we might not otherwise have thought of it. But it is the reason for his difficulty, as pointed out by Professor Young, that is the really interesting point.

His brain has not been trained in the rules of seeing. We are not conscious that there are such rules; we think that we see, as we say, 'naturally'. But we have in fact learned a whole set of rules during childhood . . . Many of our affairs are conducted on the assumption that our sense organs provide us with an accurate record independent of ourselves. What we are now beginning to realize is that much of this is an illusion; that we have to learn to see the world as we do . . . These most interesting observations on the difficulties of people born blind show that we have to learn from others how to see.'

Reminding ourselves that what we are examining is the relevance of these facts — for we are not questioning that they *are* facts — for the thesis that 'the brain of each one of us does literally create his or her own world', let us see what this thesis actually says.

In the first place, as we have already remarked, it reaffirms the conclusion to which the philosopher was brought by his logical analysis of concepts such as *thing* and *world*: the conclusion that the world is a construction from the data of experience. But we can now see that the physiologist carries this conclusion a stage further. For he claims, not only the world is a construction from the data of experience, but that it is a construction that each one of us makes directly from the data of our own experience.

What at once strikes us is that this latter claim recalls the difficulty we noted above that, in actual practice, the

21

conception I have of the world goes beyond anything that my own experience would be capable of accounting for. So, although the physiologist's account of the matter, as we have just examined it, seemed straightforward and commonsensical enough, nevertheless there is evidently something wrong somewhere.

With this in mind, let us look again at the case of the man born blind who receives his sight. He is unable to recognize what we call 'the familiar world', because the world he now looks out on is, to him, startlingly unfamiliar.

We might be tempted to think of him looking out in surprise at a world of trees and houses and people and clouds and motor cars — all the everyday furniture of the earth. But what he actually looks out on is a bewildering confusion of light and shade and colours. In fact even this is no doubt too specific a description of what he sees. Perhaps it would be more correct to say simply that what he sees is an indeterminate and bewildering confusion.

The reason for his bewilderment is that, owing to his blindness, he has never learned the rules for 'seeing' — rules which we, because we have always had our sight, are quite unconscious of, though we continually use them for the interpretation of our moment-by-moment visual experience.

The plight of the ex-blind man, in fact, throws a significant light on the problem of knowledge. What we call seeing a tree is not just a simple matter of a tree standing there in its pristine integrity, waiting for me to project my eyesight at it and see it. The difficulties of our ex-blind friend shows that there is much more in it than that.

An act of seeing involves not only a projection of my eyesight, by which certain sensory data impinge upon my nervous system, but also an act of interpretation. And this act of interpretation involves, not only the application of certain rules of interpretation, by which I classify and arrange the given data, but the possession of a concept, in this case 'tree', to which, by way of the rules, I can relate the given data.

What happens when I 'see' a 'tree' is that I say, in effect,

22

'These visual (and other) data of which I am now conscious belong under the concept *tree*.'

The system of concepts and the rules of interpretation I am quite unaware of, because, since I first began to absorb them with my mother's milk (so to speak) they have been gradually built into my system of nerve reactions.

I am unaware of the concepts and the rules because their use has become habitual to me. Not so with our ex-blind man. Not having acquired the use of the system of rules for dealing with visual data, being suddenly faced with such data he is unable to cope with them. He has had the concept *tree,* but this has been associated only with other kinds of data, tactile, auditory, etc.

So the ex-blind man's plight draws our attention quite dramatically to the fact that what we, blessed with all our faculties since infancy, confidently refer to as the World — with a majuscule to emphasise its objectivity and complete independence of us and our experience — this is, in fact, the expression of a bold and comprehensive act of interpretation of data. In other words, what the word 'world' refers to is, as the philosopher's logic disclosed, an experiential construction.

So the case of the ex-blind man cited by the physiologist seems to support the thesis, common to both the physiologist and the philosopher, that what we are referring to when we use the word 'world' is a construction from the data of experience.

But, as we have seen, the physiologist goes a step further than the philosopher in the assertion, not only (a) that the world is a construction, but that (b) it is a construction which each one of us makes from the data of our own experience.

We have just seen that the case of the ex-blind man supports the thesis common to both philosopher and physiologist, that the world is an experiential construction. But the question now arises, does it support the physiologist's further thesis, that each of us is responsible for our own world-picture, our own experiential construction?

This question is suggested by the fact that, as already noted, there seems to be *some* difficulty in the physiologist's claim. And yet, on the other hand, it seems to be a matter of demonstrable fact that each one of us, as an individual, is necessarily dependent for what we get to know on the working of our own sensory system, and this is no doubt the basis of the physiologist's claim that we all create our own world-picture.

And yet, isn't there also the fact that, somehow, each one of us, as an individual, is able to transcend, in the knowledge we are actually found to possess, the limitations of our own experiential data?

Let us see if an examination of the physiologist's second thesis, that each of us creates our own world-picture from our own experiential data, throws any light on this contradictory situation.

4. *The individual and his experience*

A little while ago we remarked that an answer to the question, How does the code get into the man, how does the individual come by the system of rules and concepts for the interpretation of his moment-by-moment experiential data?, would be the solution of the problem of knowledge.

The physiologist's answer to this question is implicit in his thesis that each one of us creates our own world. 'To explain this,' he says, 'we must answer the question: How does each brain set up its own characteristic rules?'

What is here presented as a question awaiting an answer can be seen to be itself the answer to a previous, implicit, question. In asking, How does each brain set up its own characteristic rules? the physiologist is in effect making the statement, 'Each brain sets up its own rules', and then asking the question, 'How does it do so?'

The point of breaking up the physiologist's original question

24

in this way, into a statement and a question, is that, until it has been shown *that* the individual does set up his own system of rules, what looks like an account of how he sets up his own rules could be really an account of something quite different; an account, for instance, of how he enters into an already established set of rules. The difference would be that, in the latter case, he would not be generating the rules *out of* his own experience, he would be using a given set of rules for the interpretation *of* his experience. The two different accounts of his procedure would imply two very different views of the nature of knowledge.

This makes it necessary to take a closer look at the claim that each individual sets up his own characteristic rules for the interpretation of his moment-by-moment experience. And when we take this closer look we are at once struck by the fact that there is a significant sense in which the set of rules the individual is found to possess cannot properly be described as characteristic of him as an individual. For the very purpose and outcome of the procedure of bringing his private experiential data under interpretative rules is to make it *communicable*.

Professor Young has himself emphasized the importance of communication. Asking, 'What then are the special characteristics of modern man?' (he might as well have made this a question concerning *man* as distinct from the other members of the animal world), he answers 'Surely the chief one is that of co-operation between individuals. Man's large brain is used to develop an intricate social system, based mainly on communication by words.'

Evidently, then, the important outcome of the individual's interpreting his subjective experience in terms of a set of rules is that his experience is thereby rendered communicable. That is to say, instead of being doomed to live in a private world of his own, he is able, by communicating with his fellows, to live in a common world.

And this, in fact, is what he does do. Even if it is true that each of us, by virtue of our necessary reliance on our own sensory equipment, creates our own world, it is equally true that the world that each of us creates turns out to be, in essential features, the 'same' world as all our neighbours create.

That is obvious — overlooking for the moment that 'same' may be suspected of rather begging the question at issue. But on consideration, the point at issue is just the fact that, though each of us is, theoretically, confined within the limits of his own experience, we nevertheless, on this purely subjective basis, have arrived at the objective conception, 'same world', as the common focus of the experience of all individuals.

The obvious fact is that we do communicate with one another, we do somehow create the 'same world', the same body of knowledge. In fact, what we call knowledge *is* common knowledge — that is what the word 'knowledge' means. What isn't *common* isn't knowledge, in any accepted sense of the term: the pink rats that the D.T. sufferer sees running along the rail of the bed are not knowledge.

So it would seem that the set of rules by means of which we all arrive at this *common* world on the basis of our *private* experience, cannot be characteristic of each of us, as individuals. If we are going to use the word 'characteristic' we would have to say that the world, and so the rules that are used for its creation out of experience, are characteristic of all of us, of man rather than of men.

So we are back to the question, which the physiologist's statement of the case tended to obscure: How did the code — the set of rules for the creation of a common world out of individual experience — get into man?

As far as we have gone, it seems that we can say that it is very doubtful if we each create our own world from our experiential data; even if it could in some sense be said that we do, it is even more doubtful that we each create our own set of rules to use for the transformation of our private data into common, communicable knowledge.

With this in mind, let us look again at the ex-blind man

and his difficulties, to see if he can help us to sort out our own difficulties.

5. *We take a look at the physiologist's argument*

A man who had been blind since infancy was travelling to London by sea for an operation to give him his sight. The vessel he was on ran into a storm and was wrecked. He was washed up, a lonely survivor, on a small island. Luckily (luckily for our discussion, that is) enough stores were washed up with him to keep him alive. In addition, by scrambling among the rocks on the shore at low tide -- though he was of course adept at feeling his way about, it was not easy for him in these strange surroundings — he was able to supplement his diet with oysters, which abounded. One day, unfortunately (or fortunately for our discussion) he slipped, fell, struck his head on a rock and was rendered unconscious. When he regained consciousness, a terrifying experience awaited him. The blow on the head had given him his sight, and he found himself alone in a strange, confused and bewildering world, to which he was without any clue. How did he get on in this lonely predicament?

If what the physiologist has to tell us of the difficulties of those who have been under observation in hospital after recovering their sight is correct — and we can take it that it is — our lone castaway is faced with a practically impossible task.

Such a person, we are told, sees only 'a spinning mass of light and colours. He proves to be quite unable to pick out objects by sight, to recognise what they are, or to name them. He has no conception of a space with objects in it, although he knows all about objects and their names by touch.'

This is the situation of the patient in hospital, when, after his operation, the bandages are removed and he experiences vision for the first time. The difference between the patient in hospital and our unfortunate castaway on his island, is that the former is surrounded by people — doctors, nurses, his friends and relatives — all willing and anxious to initiate him into the new world that has opened up to him; whereas our castaway faces his bewildering problems with no-one to depend on but himself.

The patient in hospital has the assistance of those who already know the rules for the interpretation of visual data — they know how to translate the spinning chaos of lights and colours into the forms of communicable knowledge. And yet, even with their solicitude and guidance, the patient has the utmost difficulty in adjusting himself to the world of sight.

> 'The patient', the physiologist tells us, 'often finds that the new sense brings only a feeling of uncertainty, and he may refuse to make any attempt to use it unless forced to do so . . . However, such people can gradually learn; if sufficiently encouraged they may after some years develop a full visual life and be able even to read . . . [But] unless he is quite clever and very persistent he may never learn to make use of his eyes at all . . . '

— he may never learn to 'see' the world which is familiar to those of us who have been born with all our faculties.

It is clear that the operation which has given the patient his sight has not solved his problems — it is really only the beginning of his problems. But now compare his situation, surrounded by people, already familiar with the rules of interpretation, who are ready to help and encourage him, with the plight of our lonely castaway; the plight, that is, of literally creating his own world of things set in a permanent framework of time and space, out of the spinning mass of lights and colours that has suddenly burst upon him; in fact, before he can even start to do this, of first exploring this indeterminate chaos and setting up his own characteristic rules for its interpretation.

If we now remind ourselves that the case of the man blind since birth who receives his sight is intended to establish the thesis that each of us, starting from infancy, builds up our own world-picture from our experience, we find ourselves brought to the conclusion that it does *not* establish this. On the contrary, the difficulties that the patient in hospital has to surmount, and the impossibility (by contrast) of the lone castaway's situation, suggests that if each one of us had been faced with the task of building up, from our own experience, the complex world-picture we are actually found to possess, the task would have defeated us.

In other words, accepting, as of course we must, the fact that we do possess this complex world-picture, the case of the ex-blind man proves (if it proves anything) that none of us, as individuals, could have arrived at this world-picture on the basis of our own experience. And in fact the physiologist might be said to have prepared us for this conclusion when he said, as quoted earlier, 'These most interesting observations on the difficulties of people born blind show that *we have to learn from others how to see.*'

In other words, the case of the ex-blind man shows us that, as individuals, we do not set up our own world-picture on the basis of our experiential data interpreted in terms of our own 'characteristic rules'. We learn from others, from infancy onwards, an already established set of rules, and with these we interpret our private experiential data in such a way as to bring these under the concepts of the common world-picture, thus transforming *subjective* experience into *objective* knowledge.

We are thus faced with the curious situation that what was intended to prove the physiologist's thesis, on the contrary disproves it. But this makes it necessary to ask, how did it come about that the physiologist chose an illustration, which, setting out to prove that we each create our own world-picture, in fact proves the opposite? I think it was because he did not realize that he was presenting a *dual* thesis. And so because his illustration proved the first part of his thesis — that the world is an experiential construction — he took it for granted that it proved the whole thesis — that this is a construction which we each make from our own experiential data.

Does this mean that after all the physiologist doesn't do any more for us than the philosopher did? No, I don't think so.

The philosopher had anticipated the physiologist in formulating the conclusion that what we call the world is an experiential construction. But then, failing to see *how* this construction had been derived from experience, he threw over the whole problem as an insoluble mystery.

The physiologist, stepping into the breach, carried the inquiry the step further that the philosopher had failed to take, with the explicit claim that the world is a construction which we each arrive at on the basis of our own experience.

The physiologist then, as we have seen, proceeded to prove by the reference to the ex-blind man, (a) that what we call the world *is* an experiential construction, and (b) that no individual would be capable of deriving this construction from his own experience.

We can now answer the question whether, after all, the physiologist hasn't landed us in the same dead-end that the philosopher ended in. The answer is, No.

Taking a detached view of the physiologist's approach to the problem of knowledge we see that his failure to prove all that he set out to prove constitutes a positive contribution to the problem, as against the philosopher's purely negative and defeatist conclusion. For what the physiologist has shown is that *what we call the world is an experiential construction which has not been drawn from the experience of any one individual.*

And this, a moment's reflection will make clear, is a most important clarification of the ancient and troublesome problem of knowledge.

6. *A new look at the problem of knowledge*

The question may suggest itself: Are we justified in interpreting the physiologist as proving something which conflicts with what he himself regarded himself as proving? He set out to prove that what we call the world is an experiential construction which each individual derives from his own experience. We have now interpreted his argument as proving the contrary of this.

It might be argued that the physiologist should know best what he means and that the conclusion we have drawn from his argument is illegitimate. But, as we have seen, rather to our surprise, the physiologist himself supports our interpretation when he tells us that 'we have to learn from others how to see'; from others, that is, who are already in possession of the rules of seeing, the rules by means of which private data are transformed into public knowledge, the rules of the common world-picture. We don't each build up our own world by means of our own rules; we have to learn from others how to interpret our experience.

The interest of this is that it presents us with a direct reversal of the idea, from which the physiologist started, of each of us building up our own world-picture from our own data. We now have the idea of the individual as interpreting his own private data in terms of an already created world-picture and its appropriate system of concepts, expressed in language.

In this connection Professor Young says, 'There have been many speculations about the origin of language,' and, by way of solution of this problem, 'I want to follow the simple suggestion that a name or a sentence functions as a tool to produce an appropriate reaction in another person.' But this, of course, though a useful account of how language works, is not an account of the origin of language.

Professor Young goes on, 'The words appropriate to each object, action, or situation are first learned by hearing them and uttering them . . . Each human brain learns a set of rules for producing words. It also learns to react appropriately to the word signs given by others.'

Still this is not an account of the origin of language; it is an account of how an individual learns an already established language. But though it doesn't tell us what it purports to tell us, what it does, incidentally, do is, emphasise that language, and the system of concepts embodying the common world-picture, is something which the individual has to learn; he doesn't create it, he is taught by others. And if this should seem so drastic a departure from the original thesis that we must be mistaken in our interpretation, the physiologist himself leaves us in no doubt whatever when he says, 'But biology has shown us to what an extraordinary extent our ways of observing and speaking are not our own but . . . are inherited and learned,' and 'We now have enough facts to enable us to picture quite fully the inheritance of our system from our parents. We can follow how, by education, elaborate rules of action grow up in our brains.'

The physiologist has not only failed in his attempt to give an account of the origin of language, but this failure has involved him in a reversal of his original account of the origin of knowledge. Knowledge, which at first was said to be the individual's own creation, is now said to be, not something that he creates, but something – an already created something – which he must learn.

But there is a further difficulty about the physiologist's account of knowledge that is worth glancing at, as it seems to point to an aspect of the problem which it would be as well for us to bear in mind.

When he is thinking in terms of his original individual-experience view of knowledge, Professor Young speaks of ' . . . a process that we may consider as beginning in each human being at the moment when, as a newly born baby, his eyes open on the world,' and of 'rules usually learnt by the long years of exploration (of the world) with the eyes during childhood.'

At the end of this book, when he has in mind the other

view of the individual as entering into an already established common world-picture, he says 'At best what we are producing is a system of the universe as conceived by man . . . '

What is regarded, in the first instance, as an objective world which the individual explores and gets to know (on the basis of his own experience), is later regarded as a system of the universe 'as conceived by man'. There is an interesting shift here between two views, one of an Absolute World which is the cause of experience, and the other of the world — more precisely, what we call the world — as a man-made structure or conception.

We are now presented, not only with *two* conflicting viewpoints, but with two *pairs* of conflicting viewpoints. In the first place we have been given two conflicting views of knowledge. We are now given two conflicting views of the subject-matter of knowledge — the World, or world (or 'world').

This is sufficient to warn us that our inquiry is going to lead us into a land of many confusions, which will no doubt threaten to overwhelm our discussion as we proceed. The best we can do is to keep our heads, accept facts as we find them, and trust that, as the confusions fall away, things will begin to fall into their own shape and pattern. And if we should occasionally feel tempted to give up and turn back, we must remind ourselves that there is no turning back; those old tracks are now overgrown and obliterated. That way lies the wilderness of doubt that we are trying to extricate ourselves from.

One precaution at least we can take, and that is to deal, as far as possible, with one confusion at a time. Adopting this tactic, let us concern ourselves with the change-over that gradually takes place, as the physiologist's account of knowledge progresses from the individual seen as building up his own world-picture, to the picture of him as entering, from infancy onward, into an already-established world-picture.

That there is a genuine, and it would seem significant, vacillation of viewpoint here is indicated by the fact that in the last pages of his book Professor Young returns to his original standpoint, which, as we have seen, his reference to the ex-blind man has disproved. 'Each individual,' he finally says, 'thus forms his own way of life, his own order and rules . . . '

The one thing that emerges clearly out of this conflict of viewpoints is that the individual arrives at the world-picture or body of knowledge he is finally found to possess, not by a simple exchange of impressions between himself and 'the world', but by submitting his moment-by-moment experiential data to the interpretation of a set of rules.

Of these rules, the physiologist says, 'The difficulty at present is that we cannot see what form the rules take;' and, of the idea of the rules as embodying a set of 'models', 'I cannot pretend to be able to develop this idea of models in our brains in detail.'

The difficulty here would seem to arise from the conflict between the two views of the origin of these rules, on the one hand that the individual creates them, and on the other hand, that he inherits and learns them; that is, between the view that the knowledge an individual possesses is a direct function of his own experience, and the view that it is not a function of his experience.

'Nevertheless,' says Professor Young, 'there is reason to think that some kind of anatomical organization is at the bottom of the secrets [of the individual's acquisition of knowledge]. Study of the way the nerve cells and their processes are related and connected seems to me to be one of the ways of trying to solve the problem.'

The 'problem' he has in mind obviously is that of showing how the individual creates his own world-picture, with its governing rules, out of his own experience. But if the physiologist's other view is correct, that the individual enters into an already-established world-picture, then the study of the working of the individual's nervous system would not solve the problem of knowledge, but would simply show how the established body of knowledge is transmitted to the individual by those already in possession of it; or else show the individual utilizing this body of knowledge for the interpretation of his own moment-by-moment experience, in order to transform subjective data into objective, communicable knowledge. In neither case is the individual creating the body of knowledge he thus participates in.

There is the same difficulty here that we noted just now in regard to language: a tendency to treat as an account of the origin of language what is, in fact, an account of how, having (somehow) originated, it is learned and used by the individual.

7. *The problem of knowledge as we now see it*

The problem of knowledge as it now presents itself seems to consist of this, that it is not possible to get from the *private* world of experience in which the individual is necessarily confined by the very fact of his individuality, to the *common* world-picture he is found to participate in, and which both *antecedes* and *transcends* his experience. The individual's experience is found to be incompetent to account for the common world-picture; no relationship of cause and effect can be found between them.

But we know that the movement in the other direction, from the common world-picture to the individual experience, is (somehow) possible. A cause-effect movement in this direction is clearly demonstrable, because the individual does participate in the common world-picture; it provides the system of rules in terms of which he organizes his private experience. We may not be able to say *how* the individual is inducted into this common world-picture, this already established system of rules for the interpretation of experience — remembering that even the instruction he receives from his elders must reach him by way of his private sensory equipment, i.e., by way of sensory data that are private to him — but we know that he *is* so inducted.

But, on consideration, we know more than this. We know, in general terms, what is happening when the individual is being so inducted. Under the instruction of his elders (whose words reach him, necessarily, as the data of his private experience) *the individual is building up in his growing consciousness his own replica of the common world-picture.*

At this point there is an almost compulsive urge, for the philosopher at any rate, to raise an emphatic objection, which we had better take a look at before we go on. Here, for instance, is the German philosopher Gottlob Frege, who has had such an influence on English philosophy, insisting on the impossibility of there being any such relationship between the sense data of different individuals as would constitute a common world-picture, much less a replica of it.

For it is impossible to compare my sense-impression with that of someone else. For that, it would be necessary to bring together in one consciousness a sense-impression belonging to another consciousness. Now even if it were possible to make an idea — [there is a complication here in the (apparently unconscious) change from 'sense-impression' to 'idea'] — disappear from one consciousness and, at the same time, to make an idea appear in another consciousness, the question whether it were the same idea in both would still remain unanswerable . . . it is impossible for us as men to compare another person's idea with our own . . . No other person has my pain. — [back to sensation here] — Someone can have sympathy for me but still my pain always belongs to me and his sympathy to him. He does not have my pain and I do not have his sympathy.

There is clearly something wrong with this latter contention, because, though it is obvious that, in one sense, my pain necessarily 'belongs' to me, the fact of somebody sympathising with me on account of my pain indicates that there is a sense in which it is shared by him. And his sympathy, too, though it may be said to 'belong' to him, at the same time is shared by me in the sense that it is sympathy *for* me, which is addressed *to* me, and which I am able to accept and appreciate.

Frege also speaks of the impossibility of sharing an idea. But here, even more than in the case of sensation, the facts refute him. Because the fact is that we have the word 'idea', and this word, as it is commonly used, means a certain sort of experience which is shared or is capable of being shared between individuals (of the same cultural group). The word 'idea' does not mean something that has to 'disappear' from one consciousness before it can 'appear' in another. If we were to continue this (inappropriate) form of expression, we would have to say that it is the essential nature of an idea that it can be in two or more consciousnesses at once. In fact, it is precisely the function of an idea to act as a medium for transforming private sensations into public, communicable knowledge.

'But,' the propounder of the above argument will at once protest, 'what sort of thing is this that can be in two places at once?' Again of course, the form of expression used is inappropriate, but the protest serves to pinpoint the question at issue, which is: What is the nature of this *idea* which acts in this way as an intermediary between individuals who, by their very individuality, seem to be inescapably imprisoned in their own subjectivity? For that is the dual fact; that individuals seem to be imprisoned and yet by virtue of the *idea*, they do communicate.

Frege was in effect denying that the word 'idea' has any meaning; he was claiming that there is nothing — and by nothing he seemed to mean *no thing*, no physical entity — that the word stands for. But words don't only stand for physical things, they stand also for experiences. An 'idea' clearly does *not* stand for some sort of physical thing, but just as clearly it *does* stand for some sort of experience. For obviously, if men had never had the sort of experience that they mean by 'idea', then the word 'idea', the concept *idea*, would never have arisen in the human consciousness. Correspondingly, the fact that we have the word 'idea' indicates that we do have the concept *idea*, and hence men must have had this peculiar kind of experience.

37

Frege's argument rests on what has been called a 'category mistake'. Part of his difficulty is that he is thinking of ideas in inappropriate terms. But fundamentally his mistake — a very common one — is that he is saying, 'What I can't understand I refuse to admit the existence of.' Because he can't understand the origin and functioning of the sort of experience that is called 'idea', he says in effect, 'Men don't have any such experience.' But this is obviously nonsense, because men *have* the idea *idea* and so must have the experience to give rise to the idea, and in any case can be seen around us actually having that sort of experience, inexplicable as it may at present seem. Indeed, Frege's own effort to persuade us that there is no such experience as 'idea' rests, contradictorily, upon the assumption that we, to whom his argument is addressed, do have the experience 'idea', thus enabling him to communicate to us his idea that we have no such experience.

So the peculiar situation is that if Frege's contention were correct, if we were each imprisoned, in the way he suggests, within our own experience, then Frege himself would not be putting forward an argument to persuade us that this was so. What he is trying to do is to prove that such a means of communication could not be established in the first place. What he does prove, or rather demonstrate, in the act of presenting his argument to us, is that, despite the difficulties amounting, seemingly, to impossibility, to which he refers, we do share our experiences; i.e., we do all participate in what must be called a body of common experience; we *do,* somehow, share the same idea; we share for instance the same idea 'same idea', as Frege necessarily assumed in denying that we do.

Curiously enough, this standard argument, which has the effect of inhibiting any attempt to understand knowledge, by concentrating on only one aspect of the knowledge situation, has as its more recent counterpart another standard argument, which produces the same inhibiting effect by concentrating on the other half of the knowledge situation. This argument consists of the attitude, 'Of course we have knowledge, and men do break through their subjectivity and communicate.

But there is nothing mysterious or impossible about this, there is nothing to puzzle us, as long as we start off by simply accepting the fact that men act as they do.'

Both arguments rest on the attitude: The best way to deal with a problem you can't see an immediate solution of is to deny that the problem exists. The first argument says, 'There is no problem of communication, because communication is impossible.' The other says, 'There is no problem of communication because we *have* communication and that is all there is to it.' It seems worth remarking that if medical science had been guided by the attitude of denying the existence of any disease it couldn't see a cure for, it wouldn't have proved very beneficial to mankind.

We may begin to suspect that the approach to the problem of knowledge, perhaps because of its ancient lineage, and the extent and ineffectiveness of men's efforts to solve it, has become beset by all sorts of confusions and obstructions that will trip us up if we let ourselves become involved in them.

So, ignoring these objections, our own discussion proceeds from the fact that the individual builds up, under the verbal instruction of his elders, which comes to him as data private to himself, his own replica of the common world-picture: this is the fact to be explained; and we know that it *is* (somehow) such a replica, because when he uses the terms of the world-picture he thus builds up, those to whom he addresses himself (as Frege addressed us in the above argument) respond in the way that he intends. If he says, 'Look at that tree,' they have the experience 'tree' as he intends, and not the experience (say) 'dog' or 'house' or 'mountain'.

The individual builds up his own replica of the common world-picture: the significance of this is that it is just such a two-way procedure that the physiologist was trying to describe to us: the induction of the individual into the common world-picture, and the interpretation by the individual of his private experience in terms of the common world-picture into which he has been inducted.

Once we have got this clear we can see that there is a significant sense in which the physiologist was right when he claimed that the individual does create his own world-picture from his own private data. But he was also right in saying that the world-picture that the individual thus creates is not his own but is inherited and learned.

I think that there can be no doubt that it was the physiologist's failure to recognise and reconcile these two aspects of knowledge, individual experience and common experience, that was the cause of the difficulties that beset his attempt to solve the problem of knowledge. We can see this if we tabulate the movement of his thought as follows:

p.61. 'The brain of each one of us does literally create our own world.'

p.154. 'Our ways of observing and speaking are not our own but are inherited and learned.'

p.160. 'Each individual forms his own way of life, his own order and rules.'

We create our own worlds, we don't create our own worlds, we do create our own worlds: there must be a reason for this peculiar swinging of thought between two apparently contradictory viewpoints. And we can now see that there is. Each view, taken alone, seems not only natural but true to the facts. The individual *is* dependent on his own experiential resources; these resources *are* insufficient to account for his knowledge without guidance from some source external to his experience, and this guidance he *does* receive from his elders.

It was the very confusions of the physiologist's account, as compared with the philosopher's evasions and rationalizations when he came up against these difficulties, that helped us to clarify our view of the problem of knowledge.

At the same time, these confusions must make us look uneasily at the physiologist's comment, 'What could we not achieve if we only understood more about this computing machine of ours and how to give it the rules best suited to realize the ends we desire?'

This is a rather frightening prospect in itself. Isn't the world at present torn asunder by the efforts of rival ideological groups determined to set up the sort of rules that will help 'us' to achieve the ends that 'they' desire? Heaven protect us, in the present state of human affairs, from new techniques for manipulating the individual mind.

This, of course, is not what the physiologist meant. He had in mind those 'doubts, longings and highest aspirations' and their connection not only with man's animal past, but with 'the eternal processes of the stars'. But unhappily these ultimate and lofty considerations would not prevent new techniques of mental manipulation from being put to the most debased immediate ends, ends which at one stroke would render these ultimate considerations irrelevant, and in any case unattainable even if relevant.

But that is only an aside. The real objection to this reliance on the study of the brain is that as the physiologist himself has shown, the rules in question are not a product of the individual brain, our 'calculating machine'. They are the governing principles of that already established body of knowledge, our common world-picture, which, in a way that neither we nor the physiologist have attempted to explain, is available to the individual for the organization of his private experiential data.

If we want to know more about the system of rules and how it works, we must first know how it has been arrived at. This is the problem of knowledge, the question, *what is the origin and nature of a body of knowledge which, though not derived from the individual's own experience, is available to him for the organization of his experience?*

By following up the physiologist's difficulties we are now face to face with the core of the problem of knowledge. And that is better than wandering, like hungry sheep deserted by their shepherd, in a waste-land of doubts and confusions. We haven't *solved* the problem of knowledge, but

41

we now know what the problem *is*. And we know not to mistake an account of an individual being inducted into the concepts of the common world-picture, for an account of the origin of that world-picture. The beginning of knowledge in the individual is not the beginning of knowledge.

Chapter II

THE WORLD WE KNOW

8. *Outgrowing the garment of thought*

Our look into the difficulties that beset the physiologist's attempt to solve the problem of knowledge having paid something of a dividend, it seems as if it would be worth our while taking another look at the philosopher's difficulties in the light of what we now know.

The view of knowledge that prevailed up to somewhere in the first quarter of the present century – the 'traditional' view as opposed to the 'modern' view – was perfectly simple and straightforward. It has been called the 'spectator-spectacle' view of knowledge.

This view assumes that there are two elements in the knowledge situation, a spectacle and a spectator, something experienced and someone who experiences it: a World – with a capital W to indicate its objective status – presenting itself for inspection, and someone to inspect it and record the result of the inspection, this record being knowledge.

Knowledge, of course, is only knowledge if it is true. And the truth of knowledge, on the spectator-spectacle view, consists in its correspondence with the given facts.

This is the view we naturally adopt as we go confidently and successfully about our daily affairs. In fact it is just this sense of a simple, direct, meaningful relationship between ourselves and that which we know, which man has somehow abstracted out of the flux of experience, that enables us to go about our affairs so confidently and successfully. Without this sense of permanence and meaningfulness life would be much more confusing and difficult.

There is a perfectly good reason for the dominance of

43

this traditional spectator-spectacle view over our minds. It is a view of knowledge and truth which is embedded in our language. We speak of 'the World', 'that thing', 'a tree', and those modes of speech – and many others of course – imply the *objective existence* of whatever we are referring to; its existence, in its own right and independently of us or our experiences, as the thing that it just naturally is.

So natural is this way of looking at things to us that we might be inclined to wonder how it ever came to be questioned, or even if it wouldn't have been better for us if it had never been questioned.

But philosophically speaking – and that is the role we have committed ourselves to – it is just as much a misdirection of thought to brood over the possibilities if the traditional view had not been questioned, as, it having been questioned, it is to dwell on the 'mistake' of our predecessors in having held it.

All that matters is the facts: and the first fact is that this is the way thought has progressed.

And the second fact is that the correspondence-view of knowledge seems perfectly natural and comfortable only as long as it remains an attitude of mind in which our thoughts move freely, like fish in water. But as soon as we try to make this view of knowledge explicit – and this, too, is part of the development of thought – we begin to be uneasily aware of elusive difficulties hovering in the background.

But, let us repeat, it is a view which is so natural to us, so conformable to our habits of thought and ways of speech, because it *is* our habit of thought, our way of speech. This consideration will help guard us against thinking that we are *criticizing* the traditional view of knowledge, when, in the course of operating with it, we are brought to the point of thinking about it, and then to the point of becoming aware of the difficulties inherent in it.

For this, as we have seen, is what happened early in the present century. St. Augustine is said to have remarked of Time: 'If nobody asks me what time is, I know, but if I am asked I know not.' Similarly, the modern philosopher knew what the World was, until he began to ask himself what it was, and then he found that he knew not; or rather that he now knew something so different to what he had always assumed, that he had difficulty in adjusting himself to the new view which his own inquiries had brought about: the view that the word 'world' means not World, but world-picture, a construction from the data of experience.

Actually, we can see that, startling as the change appears to be, it was in fact implicit in the traditional spectator-spectacle, correspondence-theory of knowledge. On that view, on one hand stood the World, waiting to be reported on, and on the other hand stood the spectator, making his report, recording his knowledge, his picture *of* the World.

But we can see that what he *knew* was this picture. The picture was immediate to him, it was his at first hand. The World was (we can see) mediated to him, it was mediated to him through his picture, it was his at second-hand, so to speak.

It was natural, because of the established habits of thought and speech, to speak of the spectator's picture of the world, but we can see that there was some sort of leap of faith in this. For what the spectator *had* was the picture, or more precisely, the report, based on experience. Because of his inherited ways of speech and thought, he quite naturally tended to think of this report being of experiences caused by the world: he saw the objective World as causing the subjective experiences, thus:

$$\text{World} \longrightarrow \text{Experience}$$

But in fact the starting-point, for him, was necessarily experience, and the knowledge situation actually stood:

$$\text{Experience} \longrightarrow \text{World}$$

He saw the World as preceding the experience, but, for him, the experience necessarily preceded the World. It was just *because* his experience was so immediate to him that he was

45

KNOWLEDGE

unaware of it. He was unaware of experience just because (as we might say) he was looking *through* it; just as we are unaware of our spectacles just because they facilitate our seeing.

But, of course, this being so, what was called the World, the spectacle of which he was the spectator, was not, strictly speaking, an objective something 'out there', the independently existing *cause* of his experience. It was (somehow) a *function* of experience, a deduction, or we might say, a construction, from experience.

And this is what the twentieth-century philosopher found himself saying, drawing out the implications of the traditional spectator-spectacle view of knowledge.

It was a perfectly straightforward development. Here was an old and familiar way of thought, the basis of our cultural heritage. It not only facilitated the organization of experience, but, by its use, we were progressively enlarging and enriching our capacities for experience.

This enlargement and enrichment of experience involved a progressive practical exploration of the possibilities of our accepted view of knowledge. At first the view of knowledge was enlarging experience. But clearly, this very process itself must in time reach a point where this progressive enlargement of experience begins to bring its own pressures on the accepted framework of knowledge.

Hitherto, the framework of knowledge, the spectator-spectacle standpoint, has been so natural as to be simply accepted without question. But, in response to the new pressures, it comes to be examined.

It is now, for the first time, held consciously. It becomes a theory of knowledge. From being an unconscious instrument of thought, it becomes now a subject of thought. The unconscious spectator-spectacle view of knowledge becomes the consciously-formulated Correspondence Theory of Truth. The question then arises, what is the nature of this correspondence between experience and fact which (somehow) constitutes knowledge. The rest is the story of modern thought.

It has been, we can see, a perfectly straightforward

development . . . But no, this is not quite correct as an account of the situation. The modern philosopher didn't see himself as drawing out the implications of the traditional view of knowledge. He saw himself as *criticising* that view, as sitting in judgment on it and pointing out its errors.

This standpoint, of course, had quite a respectable philosophical history. Hadn't Kant pioneered the modern movement of thought a century and a half earlier with his *Critique of Pure Reason?* It is a short step from a *critique*, a critical evaluation of thought, to a *criticism*, in which you are sitting in judgment on your predecessors.

But once you have adopted the attitude of criticism, the attitude of sitting in judgment on your predecessors, you are in the peculiar position of doing the right thing — working out the implications of the view of knowledge which has so far guided the development of thought — but you are doing it for the wrong reasons.

The right thing for the wrong reason: that means that you will have things right, but never quite right. And the further you go, the less right things will be, until they get so wrong that there seems to be no way out of your difficulties, you seem to be caught up in an insoluble problem. And insoluble problems are precisely what the philosopher, the modern philosopher anyway, will have nothing to do with.

9. *'I know that things exist'*

What we call the world is a construction from the data of experience: even when it has become clear to us that this 'modern' standpoint has always been implicit in the 'traditional', that is, our normal and natural view of knowledge, we find difficulty in adjusting ourselves to so drastic a change in our thought-processes.

But surely, we feel impelled to insist, with the confidence born of our philosophical innocence, there isn't just knowledge or experience. There must be knowledge and experience *of* something. Can't I in fact prove this by simply holding up my two hands, touching one with the other and saying 'here is one hand' and 'Here is another hand'?

However, our purpose at the moment is not to argue for or against this revolutionary new view of knowledge — the change from World as *cause of* experience to 'world' as *construction from* experience — but simply to note how revolutionary it is, and in what specific sense it is revolutionary. By keeping our heads and refraining from taking sides, we may end up with some sort of insight into the significance of this revolutionary development in which men became involved, without any deliberate and conscious intention of their own, around the turn of the present century.

We needn't feel ashamed of our difficulty in assimilating so drastic a change. We will find that the philosophers who have been instrumental in bringing it about have themselves had difficulty in reconciling themselves to its full implications.

But on the view that what we call the world is an experiential construction, and not a World-in-itself, philosophers were in general agreement. Bertrand Russell, writing of 'The Ultimate Constituents of Matter', said forthrightly '. . . we must regard matter as a logical construction, of which the constituents will be just such evanescent particulars as may, when an observer happens to be present, become data of sense to that observer.' And again, even more uncompromisingly, 'I maintain that there are no propositions of which the "universe" is the subject; in other words that there is no such thing as the "universe"!'

And another logician (Quine) has said, 'The totality of our so-called knowledge and beliefs, from the most casual matters of geography and history to the profoundest laws of atomic physics or even of pure mathematics and logic, is a man-made fabric . . .' And 'We can improve our conceptual scheme . . . but we cannot detach ourselves from it and compare it objectively with an unconceptualized reality': that is, we cannot know Reality-in-itself, but only our man-made conceptual scheme.

But perhaps (it might be thought) the philosophers and logicians have simply been trapped into this strange stand-point by some quirk of their logic. But that isn't so, for haven't we just seen that what they are saying is simply the implication of the traditional view? The physicists, too, approaching the problem from their own specialized stand-point, have been brought to the same conclusion. Einstein, for instance, says, 'We are accustomed to regard as real those sense perceptions which are common to different individuals, and which therefore are, in a measure, impersonal . . . The conception of physical bodies, in particular of rigid bodies, is a relatively constant complex of such sense perceptions.'

Finally, two views from another philosopher (Ayer) will help to throw an interesting light on the development we are considering. In an early work he says, 'We express the fact that to speak about material things is, for each of us, a way of speaking about sense-contents, by saying that each of us "constructs" material things out of sense-contents . . .'

This is perhaps rather elusive. In the first place he says that when the individual speaks about material things he is really speaking about sense-contents. Ayer is here drawing attention to the implication of the traditional point of view at which we have already glanced, i.e., that it is the experiential data that are immediate to the individual, what are called material things being derived or inferred from these. He then goes on to say that we express this fact by saying that the individual 'constructs' material things out of his sense data.

I think we can here see thought groping its way uncertainly from the things-in-themselves of the traditional view to the new view of things as experiential constructions. We can see the philosopher (I think) trying to find a formula that will state the revolutionary new viewpoint without any obvious commitment to its more drastic implications. He is not saying explicitly that things *are* experiential constructions, he is saying, cautiously, what we say when we say that they are.

I think we can say that at this stage, though the philosopher sponsored the 'tough' modern view that the traditional idea of things-in-themselves as the objects of knowledge was 'wrong', he felt uneasily that the full implications of this new view might deprive him, as an empiricist, of anything for knowledge to be knowledge of.

But, however that may be, it is of interest as an indication of the inner tensions set up by the movement of thought, to find Ayer saying some years later, 'Surely I know for certain that these physical objects exist? And if I do know this for certain, I know it on the basis of my sense-experiences . . . At the present moment there is no doubt, so far as I am concerned, that this table, this piece of paper, this pen, this hand, and many other physical objects exist. I know that they exist, and I know it on the basis of my sense-experiences.'

If in the first quotation Ayer was uncertain about accepting the full implications of the new 'world-as-construction-from-experience' point of view, he is here in full retreat from that view and its implications and harking back to the comfort and assurance of the earlier view, that things, his table, paper, pen, etc., are 'real existents' 'out there', which he is getting to know on the basis of his own sensory experiences.

This attitude to the implications of the new viewpoint is not peculiar to Ayer. We have already noted Russell's pronouncement that the world of matter is a construction from some chance observer's sensory data. Later we find him saying 'Philosophers from Thales onward have tried to understand the world . . . I cannot feel that the new philosophy is carrying on this tradition.'

The shift of thought from World-as-cause-of-experience to world-as-construction-from-experience was a more drastic and revolutionary change than those who helped to bring it about were at the time aware of. Their idea of themselves as criticising their predecessors and exposing their errors had the effect of obscuring from them what they themselves were doing. It obscured from them their own errors, and so, when these errors began to bedevil their own thought-processes, as they necessarily did in time, it was not possible to get a clear view of the real nature of their difficulties.

To sort this situation out it will pay us to take a closer look at the movement of thought in which the philosopher was now caught up.

10. *The historical genesis of the philosopher's problem*

The knowledge situation as we now see it consists of two elements or factors: a common element, a world-picture having universal validity, and an individual element, an element of individual interpretation in terms of this common world-picture.

In the history of thought, the common element seems to have been the first standpoint adopted in the attempt to account for knowledge. But the success, over the past three hundred years, of the physical sciences, with their emphasis on the world as revealing itself directly to our senses, has had the effect of shifting interest from the common element to the element of sensory experience.

But in this new form, the problem of knowledge does not at once present itself as an attempt to establish the relationship between a common world-picture and sensory experience. Historically speaking, problems don't emerge in that clearcut form. Men grope their way toward a new standpoint; they have committed themselves to it before they succeed in clearly defining it in their own minds. Indeed, such a definition is usually a matter of hindsight rather than of foresight. But it will be seen that, if we have fallen into the attitude of *criticizing* prior ways of thought, such hindsight is not easy to exercise; it is not easy to see our present insights as resting upon what we have come to regard as the 'mistakes' of our predecessors, 'mistakes' which we see ourselves as correcting.

However, the immediate point is that the problem of knowledge, as it now developed under the influence of the physical sciences, presented itself as the defining of the relationship between 'experience' and 'the World'. At first the World seems to be the one clearly defined and absolute term in the knowledge-situation. 'Experience' seems more elusive. If it is defined at all, it is defined — or merely accepted as being definable — in terms of the World and its objects and phenomena. They, as the sort of things they are seen to be, seem to account sufficiently for the sort of thing experience is: how better could you account for the experience, *tree*, than by giving as precise an account as possible of the tree which causes the experience? At this stage things are primary and absolute, experience is secondary and derivative.

While this is just a generally accepted standpoint it does not seem questionable. But as soon as men begin to make it explicit — and that is what both the philosopher and the physicist are doing; making explicit and precise the ideas which the mass of men hold vaguely and imprecisely — a certain modification of the original standpoint obtrudes itself. Tentatively at first, and at last boldly, it is said that 'The world is not that totality of *things*, it is the totality of *facts*.'

Now, quite definitely, but not yet wittingly, thought is poised midway between the two factors in the knowledge situation, as this has been traditionally conceived; between the World and experience. For, though a fact is still, in the familiar sense, a fact of the World, it is also, in a not quite so familiar but not wholly unfamiliar sense, a fact of experience.

It is now only a step from talking about the World as the cause of experience, to talking about experience itself. But the step is not a direct and simple one. Philosophers don't take it at once. In fact, as our inquiry, even as far as it has gone, has shown, they have considerable difficulty in taking it at all. Or rather, they take it, once the first timidity is over, with an almost lighthearted abandonment, but then, beginning to realize its implications and its difficulties, they are once again overcome by timidity.

But this is a gradual development — so gradual that they are able to rationalize their timidity into a new way of philosophizing. When the philosopher first finds himself talking, not now of things as the cause of experience, but of experience itself, he does not at once, as we might have expected, begin to talk about sense-data. Rather the basic element of knowledge, from the new, experiential point of view, is regarded as being the sentence or statement or proposition in terms of which the individual expresses what is regarded as his most immediate and direct experience of the World. (Much controversy is devoted to the question which of these is the basic element, but that need not detain us.)

Taking the proposition (or other equivalent) as expressing the individual's most direct and immediate contact with the World — (note that it is still the World that the philosopher is thinking in terms of, though his thought has, in fact, moved over to the other, the experiential, factor) — it is natural to regard a simple proposition (say) 'I see a tree', or 'That is a tree', as in some way a *picture* of the fact, or state of affairs, which it is 'about'; in something the same way that a picture or succession of pictures of a motor smash, is a reproduction or copy (in a different medium) of the actual smash itself.

But does a proposition 'picture' a fact? This soon begins to seem doubtful. At first it is boldly claimed that the word 'picture' is being used in the ordinary sense. But it then transpires that, in this claim, 'ordinary sense' is not being used in the ordinary sense.

When the picturing view of language proves too difficult to work out in detail, the next natural step is to seek a *structural* relationship between language, the individual's statement or proposition, and the World. A proposition, to be true, must, it seems, somehow correspond to the structure of the facts it reports. But what is the nature of this correspondence? How does a sentence, i.e. a series of man-made conventional noises or marks on paper, correspond to a state of affairs in the external World?

The world is, it now seems, a complex of just such 'states of affairs'. By a subtle transition, the World — now perhaps, more appropriately, the world — becomes whatever is this general state of affairs: 'the world is whatever is the case.'

Thought, as a result of its reduction or analysis of the

World to a set of basic propositions reporting an individual's immediate experience, is now poised between two points of view, (1) that the World is, in the original traditional sense, an independent 'something out there' that is the cause of the sort of experience we have; and (2) that it is a complex of or construction from the various states of affairs or facts that are represented in the propositions of individual experience.

This distinction does not at once become explicit. For a time, thought continues to move between the two standpoints. But gradually, with the progress of the analysis of basic propositions, difficulties begin to present themselves, to overcome which these propositions come to be regarded not as true reports of absolute facts, but as conventions, as something that men have (somehow) mutually agreed to accept and work with.

But this leads to difficulties, too. It begins to appear that something more fundamental than these so-called 'basic propositions' is required on which to rest the structure of knowledge. Indeed, it seems clear, on reflection, that a proposition of the form, 'I see a tree', is not itself the expression of an elemental piece of individual experience. It becomes clear that further analysis is required to reveal the true basis of knowledge.

And so, under further analysis, the propositions of individual experience give place to the data of sensory experience. Sense-data now become the elements out of which knowledge, our world-picture, is to be constructed, or reconstructed. Things — trees, mountains, houses — are seen as complexes of sense-data where previously they had been, first, things-in-themselves, self-subsistent constituents of the absolute World, and then, states of affairs or complexes of states of affairs.

Things now become 'inferences' from sense-data. The thing that I see is an inference from my sensory experience of that thing. The World is the total complex of these inferences. Here, it will be seen, the vacillation between two viewpoints, the traditional 'World as cause of experience', and the emergent 'world as construction from experience', is beginning, as might be expected, to entangle thought in peculiar difficulties. Things are now no more than inferences — in a more extreme form of this view, 'illegitimate inferences' — from the individual's sense-data.

But this, it will be seen, implies the question, 'What is now to be regarded as the cause or origin of the sense-data?' The difficulty is that the sense-data are now regarded as the cause of the thing, which is itself the cause of the sense-data. It can be seen that this is not only a case of circularity, but that it is an echo of the difficulty, which is here becoming acute, that thought is now working with two alternative conceptions of its subject-matter: the World as something 'out there', and the 'world' as something 'in here', an experiential construction.

As the present century advanced, this general difficulty was beginning to present itself in various contexts and in various technical forms — which itself made the basic difficulty elusive to explicit formulation. Philosophers were in the position of trying to solve a problem without knowing what the problem really was.

There was indeed a very strong temptation not to want to solve the problem, or even recognize it. The peculiar situation gradually arose that, as current developments began to entangle thought in ever-increasing difficulties, there seemed to be a certain advantage in maintaining both viewpoints, as alternative refuges when the difficulties (due to the vacillation of thought between these two viewpoints) threatened to become embarrassing. The World continued to be a handy back-stop in cases of emergency, while things, under progressive analysis, became first 'inferences from sense-data', and then 'illegitimate inferences from sense-data'.

Once things had been reduced to such illegitimate inferences or 'mere fictions', it became logically improper to speak of things at all. The philosopher must now speak only of 'logical constructions' from sense-data.

But obviously this could only be a resting-place. If there was to be no talk of 'things', why talk of 'logical constructions from sense-data'? It became clear that it was the sense-data themselves that the philosopher was concerned with.

It is of interest that the physicists found themselves going through a similar procedure of reduction, which took the form, 'Why talk of electrons? Why postulate an electron to account for your observations? Why not talk in terms of the actual observations themselves – or at any rate in terms of the mathematical formulae in which your observations are expressed?' It was in this way that Quantum Theory developed into a powerful tool of thought.

For philosophers, sense-data now became the basic units into which the World had been reduced by progressive analysis. All that now remained was to *prove* the analysis by re-constructing or synthesising the World from these basic data. This was the problem of tracing the relation of sense-data to Reality, the solution of which problem 'would be just about the most notable advance in philosophy that could be made.' A problem before which, as we know, the philosopher was to admit defeat, or rather, to stand defeated without admitting it; the problem, as stated by the physiologist, of how 'the brain of each one of us does literally create his or her own world'; a problem which, as the physiologist also showed, is *insoluble in the terms in which it is stated.*

11. *'Between two worlds'*

The word 'knowledge' implies a relationship, a trans-action. That was one of the difficulties that we saw the philosopher becoming involved in when he had reduced the things of our familiar world to a momentary conjunction of an individual's sense-data; there seemed to be nothing left for knowledge to be knowledge of. The difficulty was that 'knowledge', in implying a relationship, thereby implies at least two elements or factors to be related. The problem facing the tough-minded philosopher was to formulate the modern view of knowledge – the view of things as constructions from experience – in such a way as to still leave knowledge as a transaction, instead of just a static individual attitude of mind.

Traditionally, no such difficulty arose, of course. Knowledge was knowledge of the World. The World, as the sort of thing it just naturally was, caused us to have the sort of experience we did have, and on the basis of this experience we built up our body of knowledge. Knowledge was a relationship between a knowing subject and a thing known. It was a transaction between the individual and the World about him; or, more precisely, between the World as active cause of experience, and the individual as passive recipient or recorder of experience.

But as soon as the World-as-cause-of-experience has become the world-as-construction-from-experience (leaving on one side for the moment the question of *how* it has been so constructed) one of the original factors — and it is what had been regarded as the initiating factor, at that — in the transaction called knowledge is no longer operative.

What has happened is that the word 'world' has been redefined. It once meant 'self-subsistent thing out-there which causes experience'. It now meant 'construction from experience'. And the important point, methodologically speaking, about this redefinition of the word 'world' is that, in any context in which the word occurs, it will now no longer mean what it was originally taken as meaning.

And the significance of this is, as already noted, that the word 'world' — all words, in fact, but in particular so all-embracing a word as 'world' — is bound up with the whole set of our minds, with the way we think.

A word such as 'world' holds together, and maintains in a common focus of significance, a whole range of experiences. How it does this we are not at the moment considering. All we are concerned with is the fact that it does do this. All words do this, to repeat, some more than others, but all in some degree, else they don't function as words.

So, having redefined a structurally important word like 'world', the question arises — even apart from the far-reaching implications of the new definition itself — how are we to talk about this new world-as-experiential-construction? How, indeed, are we even to state our redefinition without involving ourselves in contradiction?

For consider the statement: 'The world is a construction from the data of experience.' This is our redefinition of the word 'world'. But in the very statement of the new definition we have had to use the word we are trying to redefine. But until we have redefined it, and not only that, but have assimilated the new definition to our thought-processes, we are still necessarily using the word in its original sense.

In our discussion so far, I have tried to avoid this difficulty, or at least cover it up, by stepping tactfully from 'World' to 'world'. But this is only a subterfuge. The fact is that so far we have been in effect saying, 'The World which is the independently-existing cause of our experience is a construction from our experience'; and this is an obvious contradiction. We can't have constructed from experience the world which has first caused the experience from which we do the constructing.

Let us take a look at a working instance of this elusive difficulty. Here we have Ayer (in his later phase) disproving the claims of 'phenomenalism' (the technical name for the view that things are experiential constructions). Speaking of 'a more general difficulty, which is, I think, fatal to phenomenalism', he says:

> if the phenomenalist is right, the existence of a physical object of a certain sort must be a sufficient condition for the occurrence, in the appropriate circumstances, of certain sense-data . . . And conversely, the occurrence of the sense-data must be a sufficient condition for the existence of the physical object . . . The decisive objection to phenomenalism is that neither of these requirements can be satisfied.

Simply stated, if the things-as-experiential-constructions view is right, then (according to Ayer's argument) the existence of a physical object should produce certain sense-data and the presence of certain sense-data should guarantee the existence of an appropriate physical object.

But what is a 'physical object'? If phenomenalism is right, a 'physical object' is a conjunction of sense-data. That being so, would we expect a certain conjunction of sense-data to produce that conjunction of sense-data? Or, given a certain conjunction of sense-data, would we take this as guaranteeing the existence of that conjunction of sense-data?

But this, of course, is not what Ayer meant. By 'physical object' he meant 'independently-existing-cause-of-experience', in the traditional sense. But that being so, he was not discussing what should result if phenomenalism was right. He was saying, in effect, 'If there are such things as physical objects, as I believe there are, then phenomenalism can't be right.' In other words, he was not disproving phenomenalism, he was simply sticking to the traditional view of things as the self-subsistent causes of experience.

What was merely the expression of a personal prejudice looked like an argument because Ayer was using two different senses of 'physical object', the traditional and the modern, in the one context.

If what were once thought of as Physical Objects *are*, in fact, conjunctions of sense-data, then that is what they are, and no argument can be based on them as Physical Objects.

What we see in the above 'argument' is an attempt to hold the modern view without getting involved in its implications. It is an attempt, in fact, to hold a modern view of knowledge while retaining the world-in-itself as providing a familiar, old-fashioned guarantee of our acts of knowing.

The 'mistake' our predecessors made was that they didn't realize the implications of their thought-processes. We, today, are in the process of working out those implications, and having difficulty in facing up to them. The tendency is to try to pick and choose, accepting only those implications that are not too disturbing to our habitual ways of thought.

Strangely enough, it seems to be those 'tough-minded' thinkers who were most forward in instituting the revolution of thought, that was to deprive the ordinary man of the support and comfort of the familiar world, who themselves find the greatest difficulty in giving up that same comfort. But the outcome is simply that thought is stranded between a traditional view, which it has outgrown, and a new view, into which it is not allowed to enter.

12. *Two uses of the word 'knowledge'*

Another feature of the word 'knowledge' at which we have already glanced is that it implies something which is common to all individuals (of the same cultural level). What is private and personal to the individual, his toothache or his emotion of delight on looking at a sunset, is not knowledge in the accepted sense of the term. These things only become knowledge if he can give expression to them, however tentatively or incompletely, under some one or other of the concepts of the generally accepted conceptual scheme that we call knowledge.

This presents another difficulty for those who would reduce knowledge to a momentary conjunction of individual sense-data. Not only does this fail to make contact with that which knowledge is said to be knowledge of, but, in its privacy and individuality, and hence incommunicability, it doesn't seem capable of even yielding knowledge.

The fact is that there are two distinct, though closely related, uses of the word 'knowledge'. In one sense it refers to the conceptual scheme which is shared by all members of the cultural group, to which, as the common mode of communication, the individual must adjust himself if he wants to understand and be understood. If he has a toothache and wants somebody else to do something about it for him — either sympathize or make an appointment with the dentist — it won't do for him simply to pace up and down and groan. He must bring his private experience under the forms of the common conceptual scheme and say, 'I have a toothache.'

The other, different but closely related, sense of the word

'knowledge' refers to this private bringing of one's subjective data under the common conceptual scheme in the act of knowing. To know is not just to have a private experience. The mystic, of course, may speak of 'knowing God', in some private ecstasy in his cell, and this is a perfectly legitimate use of 'know'. But it is only legitimate and meaningful because of the other common working use of the word, of which the mystical use is a variation.

And this common workaday use of the word consists, not simply in the individual's experiencing certain data, but in an act of judgment in which he sees the given data as belonging under a certain commonly held conceptual form. He translates his private language of groans into the common, and so communicable, form, 'I have a toothache', or, experiencing certain visual, tactile etc. data, he says, 'That is a tree.'

It is clear that these two factors, the private experiential data and the common conceptual scheme, have equally important roles to play in the knowledge situation. Kant expressed this when he said, 'Thoughts without content are void; intentions without conceptions, blind.' Sensations that have not been brought under conceptions are not knowledge; concepts which relate to no possible experience, are empty, or would be, if such conceptions existed.

The modern philosopher, wielding his Verification Principle as an instrument for the purification of our thought processes, has in fact declared many of our commonly used concepts to have no relation to any possible experience, and so to be meaningless. But by experience he meant specifically sensory experience. Any term that couldn't be reduced to a conjunction of sense-data came under this ban.

But this tremendous simplification of the problem of knowledge gave rise to another interesting problem. If there is found in common use a term which has no counterpart in any possible experience, then how did that term arise in men's minds? Where did it come from? How did they come by it? The fact is that if you assert that there are such non-experiential terms — and in saying that a term is meaningless, you have asserted that it exists, even though only as a meaningless term — you are committing yourself to some extra-experiential metaphysical or mystical source of such terms. And this, of course, is precisely what the Verification Principle was intended to dispose of.

But in any case, as we have seen, the Verification Principle itself proved to be tainted with metaphysics. And in addition, pure sensory data, to which all knowledge was to be reduced in the procedure of verification, proved to be inadequate as a source of knowledge. Here a cleavage of standpoints, which has characterized the whole development of systematic thought (philosophy) came to a head.

In any attempt to account for knowledge, the two elements or factors in knowledge just discussed provide a choice of starting-points. One takes one's stand either on the *common* factor, the established conceptual scheme, or on the element of individual experience. And the choice one makes seems to be largely a matter of temperament, or of specialized interest, as we saw in the case of the physiologist, who emphasised the 'individual experience' element with, however, supporting reference to 'common' experience.

For those with a rationalistic or (in a very broad sense) idealistic or 'Platonic' turn of mind, an approach to the problem of knowledge by way of the common factor, the established conceptual scheme, seems the most satisfying. For them the sweep and comprehensiveness of the conceptual scheme seems to represent the essence of knowledge. Sensory experience, the touch and sight and sound of things, is secondary, derivative, even, in an extreme view, unreal and false. Only that which is true is knowledge, and truth resides only in the body of concepts which is universally and necessarily true in the sense that it is valid for all individuals on all occasions. By contrast, mere sensory experience is transient, contingent and riddled with error.

There is a comprehensiveness and grandeur about this approach to knowledge which, to certain temperaments, is compulsive. To those of another cast of mind, however, it is simply self-delusion on the grand scale. For, transient and contingent and humble — as compared to the grand sweep of the Platonic view — as our sensory experience may be, it is our most direct, immediate and immediately significant kind of experience. It is the necessary foundation of all knowledge. If man were without his conceptual scheme he would still have his sensory experience. But deprived of his sensory experience, the conceptual scheme, if it then existed, would be useless to him. Finally (on this view) it is sensory experience that puts us in direct contact with . . .

But at this point we, living in this twentieth century, find ourselves hesitating. Direct contact with what? The World? The world? Or just with sensory experience itself?

The fact is, neither of these standard ways of accounting for knowledge will work. If, determined to be hard-headed and down to earth and no damned metaphysical nonsense, you start from sensory experience, you can't get to the body of common knowledge, the established conceptual system, that we all actually possess.

On the other hand, if you start from the established conceptual system, though you can show how this scheme gives meaning to the immediate flux of sensory data, you find yourself faced — if you are honest, as a philosopher should be — with another problem, the problem of accounting for the given conceptual scheme which holds this legislative sway over the in-themselves-unorganized deliverances of our senses.

Starting from the given body of concepts, you can give an account of knowledge, but you cannot account *for* knowledge; though, because your account of knowledge carries (necessarily) such an aura of authority, you may easily think that your account *of* does account *for*. And you are encouraged to make this mistake by the fact that, if you start from sensory experience, you can't get to knowledge at all.

It seems that the account of knowledge in terms of the given conceptual scheme must be the right one: it must account for knowledge because it is the only approach that

F

leads to knowledge. But the reason for this is that what we call 'the conceptual scheme' is the same thing that we mean by 'knowledge' (in one of the two senses discussed above). Starting from the one we achieve the other, because the one *is* the other. We have 'solved' the problem of knowledge by assuming the point at issue, which is: *What is the origin and nature of this conceptual scheme, common to all of us, which gives meaning to our in-itself transient and contingent sensory experience?*

13. *Accepting facts as we find them*

We have seen that by logical steps, which to even a non-philosophical understanding were straightforward enough in a general way, the philosopher passed through the successive stages of talking about:

Reality or the world of things
'States of affairs' or 'whatever is the case'
Propositions about 'things' or 'states of affairs'
Basic propositions' about immediate sensory experiences
Logical constructions from sense-data
The sensory experiences, or sense-data, themselves

The actual historical development was not quite as straightforward as that. It had to accommodate contributions from various thinkers, approaching the task from different angles, with different technical and — let it be admitted — temperamental equipments. There was not, in fact, one straightforward movement of logical analysis. There were various more-or-less self-contained movements, the most significant point about which was that, though each was following its own independent impulse, they were nevertheless all converging toward the same general outcome. The above schematic presentation gives an overall picture of the whole movement.

This general outcome was that the Absolute Reality of traditional thought had been reduced to the status of a construction from the data of sense. What had traditionally been accepted as a something independent of *all* experience was now seen as an experiential construction. But, though the steps which have led from Reality, or the World of Things, to sense-data seem, as above outlined, logically justified, nevertheless, for a mind not trained in the niceties of logical thinking, the final conclusion of these steps presents a serious difficulty. With the best of intentions we just can't assimilate the idea of a thing – the pen I am writing with, the chair I am sitting on, the room I am working in – being, not, as I naturally assume, a substantial something existing in its own right, independently of the fact that I happen at the moment to be experiencing it, but a logical construction, a mere complex of sense-data, an abstraction depending for its very existence upon its being experienced. Such an idea simply does not 'click' with our accustomed ways of thinking.

We might be inclined, then, to turn to the contemporary philosopher and ask, 'What precisely do you mean when you claim that the world is a construction from the data of sense?' But to this the contemporary philosopher at once replies, 'You're mistaken, I don't make any such claim.' Taken aback we say, 'Oh, so you say that the world is *not* a construction from the data of sense?' 'No,' retorts the philosopher, 'I don't say anything of the kind'; at which of course, we are completely nonplussed and bewildered, and begin to fear that our discussion has gone astray somewhere and led us into error.

But then, just in time to save us throwing in our hand in despair, we remember that contemporary philosophy is the philosophy of non-commitment: the philosophy of asking no questions and making no mistakes. Nevertheless, we say to ourselves, after such a drastic upheaval in the basic stand-point of philosophy, an upheaval which has plunged both philosophy and culture generally into the 'modern crisis', the philosopher can't be in the completely negative position of having no opinion whatever about the outcome of this revolution.

So we say to him: But if you don't say that the world *is*

an experiential construction, and if you don't say that it is *not* an experiential construction, what do you say about the status of the world in modern thought? To which the philosopher replies: 'Contemporary philosophy does not concern itself either with explaining or with describing the world, but only with the way in which we speak about the world.' And he may add that 'to philosophize is not to talk about things, it is to talk about talk.'

And if, in our philosophical innocence, we should insist, 'But you once claimed that the world is a construction from the data of sense, didn't you? Why did you give up that idea?' the philosopher gives the final and crushing retort that to ask such a question indicates a complete lack of understanding of the present interests of philosophy.

So there seems to be nothing for it: uneasy as we may feel about our familiar substantial world having dissolved into a mere experiential construction, we will have to put up with it for the time being, in the hope that our own inquiry will presently throw some light on the question. That means that we must go ahead on our own account, taking facts as we find them, and turning them over carefully to see what their implications may be.

So, accepting the fact that philosophers, before they 're-tired according to plan', had been brought, by successive logical steps, to the view at which we have just glanced, that what we call the world is an experiential construction, we proceed to note the difficulty involved in any attempt to express this change of viewpoint — we have, in fact, already glanced at this point.

We found that in any such statement we were caught in an elusive contradiction. It didn't seem possible to say that the 'world' was no longer to be regarded as the sort of thing it had traditionally been thought to be, without, in the process, using 'world' in the traditional sense of World, and so affirming what we were intending to deny. But if, taking the plunge and accepting the modern view with all its implications, we say, 'The word "world" means "experiential construction" ', we seem to deny the essential nature of knowledge as a transaction, a relationship, between two factors. In redefining the word 'world' we seem to have at the same time deprived 'knowledge' of any real meaning.

That, so it seems, is the essence of the dilemma that arises out of the transition from the traditional to the modern view. But you don't solve a dilemma by clinging to one horn of it and shutting your mind to the other. There is only one cure for a dilemma such as this, and that is to see how it came about, to see what is wrong. A dilemma is not a fact-in-itself: it is a symptom. It is a symptom that our thinking has gone astray somewhere. So let us take another look at the matter.

The difficulty the philosopher was caught in concerned the nature of 'world' (or World or world). Traditionally, 'world' had been the cause of experience, which in turn was the cause (so to speak) of knowledge, thus:

World ———→ Experience ———→ Knowledge

If now 'world' collapses into experience, all you have is experience — pure experience, experience-in-itself, not experience of anything — as the 'cause' of knowledge. Knowledge is, in effect, epitomized experience. So if the experience into which 'world' has now been absorbed is not experience of anything, neither (so it seems) is knowledge knowledge of anything. So it seems that only by retaining World can we retain knowledge.

So far we don't seem to have done any more than make the original dilemma more explicit. Have we succeeded in sorting out all the elements in the situation? On looking back, we see that we haven't. We started from the statement that the difficulty the philosopher was caught in concerned the nature of 'world'. But this is not all. More precisely, it concerned the nature of *world* as the subject of *knowledge*. So we see that in the transition from World-as-cause-of-experience to world-as-experiential-construction, it is not only the nature of 'world' that is involved. It is also the nature of knowledge.

In fact, if we consider the matter for a moment, the change in question *is* a change in our ideas of the nature of knowledge. And it is *not* a change in our ideas of the nature of the world. This is clear from the fact that we are not talking about the nature of the World. The word 'world' has been redefined as meaning 'experiential construction'. When we use the word 'world' it is (the modern view tells us) this experiential construction that we are talking about.

So the philosopher has not been saying, 'The World is not the sort of thing our predecessors thought it was,' — as we have seen, that wouldn't be saying anything, it would simply be involving ourselves in an elusive contradiction. What he has been saying, in effect, is, 'Knowledge is not the sort of thing our predecessors thought it was. They thought it was knowledge of "the World", that it was based on our experience of "the World". But we now know that what they called "the World" is in fact a construction from experience.' And that, we can see, is a quite different, and highly significant, proposition.

We know that here is one case where the philosopher's fear of the implications of the modern standpoint he was enunciating led him astray. He was afraid that the idea of the World as an experiential construction amounted to a denial of knowledge, and so he clung to the World, appeasing his intellectual conscience by reducing it to a lower case w. And in fact, even when he claimed, non-committally, that he was not concerned with the world, but only with the way we talk about the world, he was still caught up in the traditional mode of thought which his logical analyses had undermined.

But, as we can now see, what superficially looked like a denial of knowledge was, in fact, the beginning of a new insight into the nature of knowledge. But by clinging to the World — 'surely I know that these physical objects exist, doesn't my sensory experience guarantee this?' — he cut himself off from following up this insight, that is, from coming to grips with the revolution of thought in which he was involved. He committed himself to trying to maintain a relationship between knowledge and 'world', whereas what in fact he was doing was, working out the relationship between knowledge and experience.

Actually, what he was concerned with was the question, *How has knowledge been derived from experience?*

And our discussion so far, in particular our examination of the physiologist's difficulties, has shown us that the first part of the answer is, *knowledge has not been derived from the experience of any one individual.*

14. *Unpicking the fabric of thought*

We are now beginning to get a clearer view of the difficulties that beset the path of the philosopher as he set about working out the implications of the traditional view of knowledge, the spectator-spectacle view which is built into the structure of our everyday modes of thought and speech and action.

What the philosopher was proceeding to do was to submit to intellectual scrutiny an ancient fabric of thought with which were bound up all our moods and values as men living in a community of culture; turning back thought upon itself to see how, as thought, it functioned; in what relationship it stood, as man's mode of communicating, to his mode of experiencing; in effect, to *analyse* the common conceptual scheme we call knowledge and so trace it back to its source in experience.

We can understand that such a procedure — literally, an inquiry by thought into the nature of thought, an inquiry in which thought is to be both the subject and instrument of inquiry — must present a peculiar challenge and peculiar difficulties to those who are caught up in it.

We can see, too, that the challenge and the difficulties of such a procedure — the taking apart of thought to reveal its underlying structure — must increase as the undertaking progresses, and will become acute at the point where the *nature* of what we are doing, and the *outcome* of our doing it, begin to emerge into consciousness; *the point, that is, where a cumulative intellectual effort begins to pay a dividend in new understanding.*

The peculiar difficulty here is that we cannot grasp the outcome of what we have been doing until we have grasped the nature of our procedure, but it seems to be only through a clear view of the outcome that we can understand the procedure. Such a climacteric situation challenges us to a supreme effort of honesty; and tempts us to a calculated effort of evasion.

But in any case we know that the philosopher's difficulties in making the transition from World-as-independently-existing-cause-of-experience to world-as-construction-from-experience were complicated by the fact that he saw himself as the critic of prior ways of thought, setting himself up as the tough-minded debunker of the traditional, that is, the generally-accepted, point of view.

In fact, as we can now see, he was working out the implications of that point of view. And in doing this he was not 'debunking' it — he was explaining and accounting for it.

But when the philosopher's procedure was seen as a 'debunking' of the accepted standpoint, the things of our everyday experience became 'fictions', 'fantasies', 'delusions', 'illegitimate inferred entities'; they became 'nothing but' conjunctions of sense-data. One by one the basic concepts of our structure of ideas were shown to be 'meaningless', 'having no basis in any known experience.'

It was at this point that the philosopher, having debunked the ordinary man's world by reducing it to a mere momentary conjunction of sense-data, found that this familiar world could not be reconstituted *from* the sense-data into which his analysis had resolved it; the procedure worked in one direction but could not be made to work in the return direction: it wouldn't *prove*.

Obviously something was wrong. This was a moment that might have led to a painful but therapeutic soul-searching, a critical scrutiny of motives and methods. The philosopher's reaction was to throw over the whole problem, and with it the hopes and aspirations of the ordinary man which his procedure, now proved to be mistaken, had so thoroughly undermined. Problems which his mistaken procedure had failed to solve were dismissed as 'pseudo-problems' with which he need not concern himself. As to the ordinary man and his affairs, the philosopher's attitude was, why *ought* he concern himself with such matters?

What the philosopher had in mind, of course, was the perfectly legitimate claim that it is not the business of philosophy to comfort and console us. Its business is to search for truth, to follow the search no matter where it may lead.

But, of course, the flaw in the philosopher's case was that he himself had already abandoned the search for truth; at first inadvertently, by not realizing what was the nature and outcome of his procedure of analysis; and then deliberately, when, finding that the standpoint from which he was undermining the traditional common man's world-view wouldn't work, he threw over the whole problem.

And now, having seen what the philosophers were *not* doing — they were not debunking an established way of thought — let us see in closer detail what they *were* doing, and why it went wrong in the way it did.

What the philosophers were *actually* doing, as distinct from what they thought of themselves as doing, was, working out the implications of the traditional standpoint. And the implication that emerged was that what had been regarded as the Absolute World was in fact an experiential construction. But — as this was their point of crisis — this, the logical outcome of their inquiry, proved to be logically unworkable: experience, the experience of any individual to whom they might turn, proved incompetent to do what was demanded of it.

Facing up to this dilemma, what we now want to do is, to carry out the reappraisal of motives and methods which the philosophers themselves failed to carry out.

71

Chapter III

EXPERIENCE AND 'REALITY'

15. *The projection of experience*

If we were to ask the philosopher what had been the cause of the failure of the philosophic enterprise he had entered into with such confidence in the early part of the century, he would say, 'The fault lay in a too rigid and too narrow conception of analysis.'

But analysis is just analysis, the methodical reduction of some given whole to its constituent elements. There is physical analysis such as is practised by the chemist, and there is logical analysis, as practised by the modern philosopher. What is meant by speaking of 'a too rigid and too narrow conception of logical analysis?' This must refer, not to the *procedure* of analysis, as an instrument of philosophic inquiry, but to the *outcome* of analysis.

It would seem that the failure of the philosophic enterprise — the failure that was to precipitate the 'revolution in philosophy' — was not due to the procedure of analysis but to the philosopher's ideas as to what he was doing with the procedure of analysis.

If now, we were to press the philosopher further and ask, What *were* you trying to do with the procedure of analysis? his answer would be, I was trying to trace the relation between sense-data and Reality. As one philosopher expressed it 'The resolution of this puzzle would be just about the most notable advance in philosophy that could be made.'

But it was precisely this advance that the philosopher first confidently thought that he had made and then realized that he had failed to make. And what we are here trying to do is, to pin-point the cause of the failure.

73

The philosopher's proposed equation seems a perfectly straightforward one on the face of it. We all, if we are normal beings, experience sensations; if we didn't, we would not achieve Knowledge, we would be 'cut off from Reality' as the phrase goes. So it seems clear enough that these sensations, or in philosophic terminology, 'sense-data', are the necessary source of our Knowledge of Reality.

The modern empiricist's conception of Knowledge as Knowledge of a Reality which men got to know through their experience of it stemmed, of course, from the Newtonian Revolution of thought, in which men turned from the kind of speculation carried out by mediaeval thinking, to a programme of observation of, and experiment on, the real world about them. As Bacon expressed it, 'For we are building in the human Intellect a copy of the Universe such as it is discovered to be, and not as man's own reason would have ordered it . . . we declare that those foolish models and apish imitations [of the mediaeval thinkers following in the footsteps of Aristotle] which men have woven into their Philosophies must be utterly given to the wind.'

This was the conception of Knowledge, as a picture, derived from experience, of the universe 'as it is discovered to be and not as men's own reason would have ordered it', which became the basis of modern empiricism. It was the structure of knowledge, thus arrived at, that the philosopher proceeded to analyse to disclose the relation between experience, the data of sense, and Reality, the objectively-existing cause of experience.

And in the outcome, his analysis was to show, not a relation between sense-data and Reality, but that 'reality' was after all, not Reality-as-such, but reality-as-man's-own-reason-had-ordered-it.

It is not easy to get this situation into a proper focus. The philosopher set out to establish the relation between sense-data and Reality. He failed to establish this relation; instead he was brought to the conclusion that what, in keeping with the traditional view, he had assumed to be Reality-as-it-existed-independently-of-experience was in fact a construction from experience.

This, it will be seen, completely reversed the traditional standpoint. Analysis had shown that when we used the word 'world' or 'reality', we were necessarily referring, not to an independently-existing 'something out there' which was the cause of experience, but to a function of experience, or say a *projection* of experience; it was necessarily 'world-as-experience' and not 'world-in-itself', as our habits of speech suggested, that we were talking about.

The traditional idea, embodied in our habits of speech, as to what the term 'world' referred to, was not, of course, due to some 'mistake', which the modern thinker was correcting. On the contrary, what analysis was revealing *was* that this was how, as a matter of historical fact, thought had developed: by this process of projecting the transient and largely unconscious fact of experience outward, as it were, onto a screen as a permanent picture, which was then reflected back into thought as an objective organizing principle — thought setting up its own terms of organization as the 'fact', 'world causes experience.'

Indeed, looked at in this way, we can see that, far from being a 'mistake' due to the inadequacy of language, this setting up of the concept of an objective World of Reality, on the basis of subjective experience, is man's outstanding achievement, made possible by the symbolic system we call language.

But this, at this point, is an aside. What we are interested in is the fact that the analyst, starting from the traditional assumption as to the nature of the Reality he was dealing with, was brought to a conclusion which invalidated this assumption. He *didn't* reach the conclusion he expected to reach (as to the relation of sense-data to Reality); he *did* reach a conclusion which negated the assumption (as to the nature of 'Reality') on which his procedure of analysis had rested.

And this was not all. For the immediate implication of

this unexpected conclusion was that he had not been concerned with a relation between sense-data and Reality-as-such, but with a relation between sense-data and the experiential construction 'reality'; and this, it can be seen, is an entirely different matter.

It is easy to understand why so confused and contradictory an outcome of what had seemed to be a straightforward inquiry, was not easy to accept or even to get into an objective focus that would make it possible to see what was the real cause of all the trouble. But that is what we now want to do.

The question that now presents itself is this: If the philosopher had *not* been tracing a relation between sense-data and Reality, then this was not, as he thought, what he had failed to do: he could not have failed to do what he was not in fact doing. But he *had* failed; somehow, the procedure of analysis could not be made to work. Then what was the nature of this failure?

The essence of that failure would seem to have been this: Though it had been shown that what we call reality was a construction from the data of sense, it could not be shown *how* the data of sense gave rise to such a construction. The philosopher's dilemma was that the data of sense were shown, by his analysis, to be incompetent to account for the sort of construction which his analysis had shown reality to be.

We begin to see, in this complex situation, the reasons for the philosopher's ready acceptance of a 'new way of philosophizing'. But we may glimpse, too, another actuating motive — largely unconscious no doubt — for the philosopher's retreat from the challenge presented by the outcome of the analytical procedure. That procedure had been acclaimed as a charter of deliverance of the human mind from the age-old dominance of metaphysics, with its emphasis on 'a power outside us'. But if, as analysis now showed, the data of sense were incompetent to account for the knowledge we possess, might not this line of thought, if followed through to its

logical conclusion, bring in by the back door the metaphysics that had been so recently shown out by the front
door? It would hardly be surprising if a challenge such as
this should prove too tough even for — or perhaps particularly for — the tough-minded debunker of metaphysics.

But, for our part, having glanced at the difficulties cent-
ring round Reality as one term in the philosopher's Reality-
sense-data equation, our next concern is to take a look at
sense-data.

16. *The status of sensory data*

There is a final consideration concerning 'Reality' which,
as well as being of interest in itself, will serve to introduce
the subject of sense-data. This is something so obvious that it
would be easy to dismiss it as being irrelevant to the sort of
problem the philosopher is dealing with. But in fact it is
itself sufficient to account for the failure of the attempt to
make the data of sense, the reactions in an individual's nervous
system, add up to the knowledge the individual is actually
found to possess.

The fact is that the knowledge possessed by the individual
is not, in the sense assumed, *his* knowledge. The term 'Knowledge' means or refers to something which is not peculiar and
private to the experiencing individual, but is *common* to all
individuals (of the same cultural level). This body of knowledge is common in the specific sense that all the individuals
of the group have been inducted into it from infancy onward.

Some linguists have gone so far as to claim that the common
system of concepts, imposed on us at an age when we are
unable to resist it, thenceforth allows us only a distorted
view of Reality. We needn't pause here to examine the two
assumptions implicit in this claim, (a) that we have some
independent view of Reality, against which it is possible to
evaluate our commonly accepted picture, and (b) that the
individual, if left to himself from infancy onward, would

arrive at this 'true' picture of Reality.

The immediate point of interest is that it was not possible to show how the individual *constructed* the knowledge he possessed from his experiential data, because the individual was in fact *interpreting* his experiential data in terms of the common system of categories which he had learned from his elders.

But to this simple and obvious account of the matter there is, or at any rate there is generally accepted as being, an equally simple and obvious objection. Each one of us, it would be said, necessarily and inescapably, by virtue of our individuality, receives our instruction from our elders through the intermediary of our private nervous system. The words, etc., in terms of which their instruction is conveyed to us reach us in the form of sensory data which are private and peculiar to us as individuals. So the body of knowledge, the world-picture, we arrive at is, and can only be, our own private construction from our own private data; each of us lives in a private world of our own.

From this fact, it would be claimed, there is no escape. And yet it seems to be equally inescapable that, as the linguists have pointed out, the world-picture each of us arrives at is dictated by the categories of the common world-picture into which we have been inducted from infancy onward.

Here then, are two apparently inescapable yet contradictory facts, (a) that the gap between sense-data and the common-world picture *is* crossed, else we wouldn't have the common world-picture, and (b) that each individual is confined within the limits of his own sensory data and so the gap can't be crossed.

But there are two aspects of the standard philosophical position (b) which make us hesitate to cling to *that* horn of the dilemma of modern thought. The first is that, though the individual's sense-data are said to be the only source of his knowledge, analysis has shown that his sense-data are not competent to account for his knowledge. There is evidently something wrong here, though it is not immediately obvious what.

The other aspect of the standard philosophical position leads us to a discussion of the nature and status of sense-data.

Though the philosopher insists upon the necessary privacy of the data of sense as in effect precluding the possibility of a body of common knowledge, it is of interest that this negative argument is only used, as we might say, obstructively. Any discussion that starts from the fact that we *have* such knowledge, can be brought to a halt before it really gets started by this insistence on the necessary privacy of the ultimate data of sense.

It might be wondered, then, how the philosopher has succeeded in talking about knowledge at all. But the fact is that when the philosopher talks, as we might say, constructively — as opposed to negatively and obstructively — about knowledge, when he talks about the sense-data that are the necessary basis of knowledge, he is no longer referring to these movements in a private nervous system.

The fact is that the term 'sense-data' has two philosophic uses. We see the difference between these two uses when we consider the philosopher's reference to 'a sense-datum'. Obviously *a* movement in a nervous system, a single nervous impulse of the kind a physiologist might register on his experimental equipment, would not be regarded as capable of constituting knowledge. If by 'sense-data' we mean these neurological ultimates, then we would not speak of 'a sense-datum'.

What then is a sense-datum?

By 'a sense-datum', as the ultimate unit of knowledge, the philosopher means the sort of experience that is expressed in a proposition stating the simplest kind of contact the individual has with the world (= World). Such propositions are called 'basic' or 'protocol' propositions. Examples would be 'I see a dog', or, if we wanted to be more precise, 'I see a canoid patch of colour.' Or, if we were being more fussy still, we would not only state the details of the seeing in full, but also the fact that the seeing was occurring, at what time and place, and to whom, thus: 'Otto's protocol at 3.17: (Otto's word-thought at 3.16 was: [In the room at 3.15 there was a table perceived by Otto]).'

But this sort of effort after precision would seem to have no end, this side of madness. Indeed, it reminds us of the story of the lunatic artist who, escaping from his asylum, set up his easel and started to paint the scene before him. But having completed his picture, he realized that there was something missing in it. Yes, of course. *He* was painting the picture but he wasn't included in the picture. So he stepped back, set up another canvas — luckily, like Monet, he had taken out a full supply of canvases with him — and now painted a picture of himself painting the scene before him. But again, as soon as it was finished, he saw that it was incomplete. There was nothing for it but to step back again and start a new canvas, showing himself painting a picture of himself painting a picture of the landscape. When overtaken by his keepers he was still painting frantically, but by now was including in his pictures the rejected canvases that littered the landscape.

Like the over-conscientious painter, the philosopher is no nearer to a solution of his problem of knowledge, no matter how he refines his basic reports of the individual's contacts with the world. This is so because these are not reports of the elements of individual experience out of which a body of common knowledge has been constituted. They are reports of an individual experiencing in terms of that already constituted body of knowledge. They do not show us an individual building himself a private mansion of ideas in which to dwell in solitary contemplation of the world about him. They show him moving about on the ground floor of an already constructed family mansion, our common world-picture, which he has come into possession of as part of his cultural heritage.

Consider 'That is a dog', or 'I see a dog'. This is a direct report of the simplest kind of perceptual experience. And of such experience, Bertrand Russell has said in *An Inquiry Into*

Meaning and Truth, 'I must start from *momentary* episte-mological premises. To do anything else is to evade problems which is a part of the business of theory of knowledge to consider . . . All theory of knowledge must start from 'What do *I* know?', not from 'What does mankind know?' For how can I tell what mankind knows? Only by (a) personal obser-vation of what it says in books it has written, and (b) weigh-ing the evidence in favour of the view that what is said in books is true.'

Again, in *Human Knowledge: Its Scope and Limits,* Russell has emphasized the individual basis of knowledge: 'Individual percepts are the basis of all our knowledge, and no method exists by which we can begin with data which are public to many observers.'

This we can recognize as a variation of the argument that *all* I know must be a function of *my* private data — the disturbances in my nervous system — and so (if the argu-ment is carried to its logical conclusion) there can be no such thing as common knowledge, the sort of thing that mankind knows.

But of course we have knowledge, and so it would be non-sense to carry the argument to its logical conclusion. Instead, the starting-point of my knowledge is taken as being a report such as 'I see a dog', from which 'I pass, by elaborate and doubtful inferences, to *public* knowledge.'

But a statement such as 'I see a dog' *is* public knowledge, the sort of thing 'mankind knows'. It is claimed that we can't start from what mankind knows, but this is what the above account does start from. It is said we cannot start from what is common to many observers. But 'I see a dog' *is* common to many (actual or potential) observers. It is private exper-ience which has been made common to many observers by being reduced — better, elevated — to terms of the common conceptual system. This is seen in the attempt to analyse the conceptualized experience, *dog,* into 'canoid patch of colour', which while getting rid of 'dog', increases the dependence on the common conceptual system.

Even a statement such as 'I have a pain', a direct report of a private and highly personal sensation, belongs to 'what mankind knows'. In bringing this sensation under the common concept *pain,* instead of merely groaning, it is raised to the status of common knowledge.

It can be said that any sensory experience that is expressed in the form of a proposition is already a piece of public knowledge. Accounts of knowledge in terms of 'basic propositions' don't start from an instance of private knowledge, they start from a private instance of public knowledge. They start from an instance of an individual experiencing certain sensations in his private nervous system, interpreting these in terms of the body of public knowledge into which he has been inducted by his elders, and then reporting, 'I see a dog.'

If he had not been so inducted, he would not be able to report 'I see a dog', as the case of the ex-blind man made clear. He wouldn't 'see' a 'dog'. He would merely have certain indeterminate sensations, but would be unable to interpret these in terms of the common concepts 'dog' and 'see', or even 'a' and 'I'.

The attempt to account for knowledge cannot start from 'what do I know?' because what I know is already an instance of the thing we call knowledge. And the thing we call knowledge is not what I, in incommunicable privacy, know, but what 'mankind knows'. Knowledge *is* common knowledge, i.e. what mankind knows, and it is this body of common knowledge, providing the system of organizing principles in terms of which the individual transforms his indeterminate moment-by-moment experiential data into determinate communicable form, that 'theory of knowledge' is trying to account for.

To start from 'momentary epistemological premises' such as 'I see a dog' is to miss the very problem which, as the philosopher's analysis of the traditional standpoint has made clear, it is the business of 'theory of knowledge' to consider; the problem, that is, of *how a body of determinate common knowledge, valid for all individuals for the interpretation of their private experiential data, has been derived from such private experiential data.*

17. *Two kinds of sense-data*

Having rejected the sense-datum — the simple kind of knowledge that is expressed in a 'protocol statement' — we are left with sense-data — the impulses in a nervous system — as the ultimate units from which knowledge has been constituted.

These are the ultimate data of knowledge in the sense that they have not yet been determined within any conceptual system. They are the indeterminate and discontinuous — discontinuous as between individual and individual — elements out of which the determinate picture of a common world of continuous phenomena is to be constituted.

At this point we must be careful not to get our problems confused, as seems so fatally easy in any discussion of knowledge. What we ultimately want to know is how this determinate, continuous, objective world-picture has been generated out of these subjective, indeterminate, discontinuous data. This, the real problem of knowledge, is constantly confused with the quite different problem of how, this common world-picture having (somehow) been arrived at, it is transmitted from one generation to the next.

Let us be clear then, that in now discussing this problem of the transmission of the common world-picture from generation to generation, we are doing no more than clearing the ground for a discussion of the problem of knowledge. We are simply trying to get a clearer view of the nature of that problem before starting to discuss it.

For a start then, we must remind ourselves of an important fact that we noted earlier, namely, that the process by which the individual is inducted into the common world-picture consists in his (somehow) building up in his growing consciousness his own replica of that world-picture.

He is not, as it seems so easy to assume, building up his

own world-picture from his own data. He is building up a world-picture which is the common possession of his cultural group. He is *entering into* an established world-picture, not *building up* his own private world-picture.

Having got this clear, we are brought face to face with the essence of our problem. The problem is: how does the individual build up this common world-picture on the basis of data (the instruction of his elders) which necessarily come to him as the private and peculiar movements of his sensory system?

We may recall here Frege's claim, that my sensations are mine and yours yours, and — according to Frege, who expresses the accepted idea — never the twain shall meet.

But we know that (somehow) the twain do meet; we all do participate in this common world-picture, this given body of knowledge. Obviously, then, something is wrong here. Somehow, some assumption must have crept in which runs contrary to the facts.

What, then, has been assumed about the nature of these data from which the individual is to build his replica of the common world-picture? Well, there is one assumption, though it seems to be so natural that it is not easy to recognize it *as* an assumption.

On consideration it will be seen that it has been assumed that all the data the individual receives are of the same kind or order.

Indeed, this is implicit in the claim that the individual is dependent for all he gets to know, on the deliverances of his own sensory equipment. This implies that there is nothing in these deliverances, these sensory data, that could lead to his building up what we have called a common world-picture. In other words, all his data are assumed to be of the same order.

This assumption has never been questioned, because it has not been recognized *as* an assumption. But, having recognized it as an assumption, let us ask — knowing that the individual *does* arrive at the common world-picture: Could it be that these elementary data are *not* all of the same order? Could it be that some of them contain an extra 'something' that makes just the right amount of difference, the difference that accounts for the individual's acquisition of knowledge?

At once, of course, the hard-headed positivist is on the alert. All this sounds precisely the sort of thing he is determined to have nothing to do with. But the trouble with hard-headed positivists is that they are never prepared to be hard-headed enough. Like their counterpart, the tender-minded idealists, they want to pick and choose as to which facts they will take account of (each of course having a leaning toward a different sort of fact). But the result often is that the hard-headed thinker by-passes an important fact just because, at first glance, it doesn't look like the sort of fact he is in favour of. In other words, he suffers from being only half-heartedly hard-headed.

In the present instance, he will refuse to go a step further until he is told precisely what is implied by a kind of data which is 'different' by virtue of possessing a 'something extra'. The answer, as it happens, is quite simple. The data in question are verbal data, or what we call words, these being the medium through which the individual is inducted by his elders into the accepted body of knowledge.

But to this there is an immediate and crushing retort, this question of words and meaning being one to which the modern philosopher has devoted a lot of time and thought. 'What is this mysterious "difference" that you attribute to verbal data?', it will be asked. 'Is it some essence of language you are talking about? Some ghost-like aura that the word carries about with it as its "meaning"? Well, the plain fact is that there is no essence of language; language is just a man-made conventional system. And words are simply tools, like the hammer, the chisel, the glue-pot in the carpenter's kit. Tools do what they are used to do, words mean what they are used to mean. As far as the individual is concerned, words are just sounds that come to him as auditory data, just as any other sounds do. There is no mysterious "difference" that sets them apart from other data. There is no escape from this. The individual, by virtue of his physical and psychic individuality, is confined within the limits of his own experiential data, and these data are, *for him,* all of the same order.'

We've all become accustomed to this tough, no-damned-nonsense kind of argument. A term like 'meaning', it is suggested, necessarily implies 'mysterious essences', 'occult forces' and all that 'metaphysical mumbo-jumbo'. If, in this scientific age, you still want to cling to that sort of thing . . . But if you don't, well then (so the argument runs — or rather suggests) the only alternative is to face the facts, and see meaning as nothing but . . .

Well, let us face the facts.

Someone says, 'Listen to that dog barking.' You listen and hear a dog going, 'Woof, woof, woof.' These are both sounds, the sound of the words, and the sound of the bark. Both reach you by way of your private sensory system, and so both are data which are private to you. They are both the same *kind* of data, i.e. auditory. But it is quite obvious that they don't have the same *value*. There is an essential difference between them.

But we can be more specific than this. Consider the case of a cat, hearing the sound 'that is a dog barking', and then actually hearing a dog bark. In the first case the cat remains unaffected, in the second case he promptly climbs the nearest tree. The difference in his behaviour indicates that there is a definite difference between what we call the 'verbal' and the 'natural' data.

For the cat, one set of data — the sound of the dog's bark — has a value; the other — the sound of the words, 'That is a dog barking' — has no value. For the human individual, on the other hand, both sets of data, the 'natural' and the 'verbal', have a value. That is to say, all animals, man included, experience natural data, but verbal data are peculiar to man.

But the question is: What *is* this difference? — we can *recognize* it but can we *say* what it is — can we *describe* it? Well, no doubt we could, if we cared to go to enough trouble.

86

But it is unnecessary to do so. Men, becoming aware of the peculiar *value* of the *verbal* data, have already adopted a term to mark its distinction from the *natural* data. This is the term 'meaning'.

But, the tough-minded objector might now insist, that doesn't get us anywhere; isn't 'meaning' precisely what we want an explanation of? The answer to this, of course, is no. 'Meaning' is not precisely what the objector wanted an explanation of; 'meaning' is precisely what he was trying to persuade us to dismiss from our minds. We have already examined the reason for this peculiar attitude. He once thought that he had finally explained 'meaning'. Then he found that he hadn't, whereupon he declared that there was nothing to explain anyway, meaning was nothing but . . .

Well, in these terms, 'meaning' is nothing but the peculiar value that distinguishes *verbal* from *natural* data, the sound 'That is a dog barking' from the sound, 'Woof, woof, woof.'

But there was no need for all this positivistic panic in the face of the (so far) unaccountable. Even as far as we have gone, there is nothing mysterious about this difference between the two kinds of data. It can be reduced — for those who can only feel happy with a 'nothing but' type of explanation — to terms of simple behaviour. This was demonstrated by the cat, who behaved in one way to one set of data and otherwise — or not at all — to the other. The difference is 'nothing but' a difference of behaviour.

Which, of course, is not the whole story. But all that concerns us at the moment is that there are these two kinds of sensory data that the individual receives, 'natural' data and 'verbal' data, and not just one kind, as was too hastily assumed.

Perhaps we might venture the further comment, that the one kind of data, the one we call *words,* is heavily 'plugged' in the process of educating the growing individual, as against the other 'natural' kind, that he encounters more or less by chance as he grows up.

In fact, if the sound 'That is a dog barking' were plugged in the same way in relation to the cat, he could be conditioned to climb the tree without hearing the actual barking of the dog, as Pavlov demonstrated.

So the fact that the knowledge the individual finally comes to possess has reached him by way of his own sensory equipment does not present the difficulty that had been attributed to it. Though all his data are sensory data, and as such private to him, not all sensory data are of the same kind. And some are of the kind that leads to what we call knowledge.

This, to repeat, does not solve the problem of knowledge; it only serves to clarify it. It points to the question, What is the nature of this peculiar value that the verbal data possess, and how has it been arrived at?

But before going on to discuss that, there is still a point to be cleared up, concerning the real nature of the philosopher's failure and his consequent retreat from philosophy. We saw earlier that he was mistaken regarding the 'Reality' whose relation to sense-data he was trying to establish. We have just seen that he had taken too simplified a view of sense-data. We will now see that there was a still further misconception concerning sense-data.

18. *The cause of the philosopher's failure*

Our purpose in carrying out our own reassessment of the philosopher's motives and methods, from the point where the philosophic enterprise he had entered upon so confidently in the early decades of the century had to be written off as having failed, was to lay bare, if we could, the real cause of that failure.

For it is not enough simply to say 'We thought we had finally solved all the traditional problems, but we were wrong.' Failure having been the unexpected outcome of so bold an enterprise, it then becomes urgently important to know precisely *why* the enterprise failed. And this the philosopher has not told us, or himself either, for that matter. He has simply taken up a new philosophic stance and shrugged off the past and its problems as 'just the troublesome legacy of discredited theories.'

And no attempt could be made to inquire into why these theories — the theory that propositions about physical things could be analysed into propositions about sense-data, and that such propositions could be verified by reference to the sense-data of the individual making the proposition — had become discredited. Any paper dealing with the subject would inevitably run up against the comment that this was 'past history' or 'out of touch with current issues'. Indeed, the present discussion will no doubt meet with the objection that few philosophers would today subscribe to the extreme, tough-minded, positivistic, anti-metaphysical attitudes to which we have constantly referred. And the fact is that these stand-points have proved to be so naive as to be untenable, and in their turn, have become part of the growing scrap-heap of discredited theories.

Nevertheless, though theories become discredited and re-pudiated because they are found to be unworkable, they are able to linger on, as unacknowledged but obstructive attitudes of mind, because the real cause of their unworkability has never been brought to light. A philosopher who will slap down one argument with the comment that 'all that is past history', will counter another argument with just the attitude he claims is past and done with; and this privilege of having it both ways is one of the reasons, we might suspect, for the present resistance to any move to turn back the pages and see what went wrong in the first place.

That is what all our discussion has been trying to get at: the essential cause of the philosopher's failure. As we noted earlier, if the philosopher had been asked, and if he had answered honestly, the question, 'In what way did your enterprise fail?' he would have replied, 'I failed to establish the relation between sense-data and Reality.'

The philosopher himself would have thought of this as a failure of *sense-data* to account for Reality. But, as we have seen, an important part of the difficulty concerned the factor which he referred to as Reality. Refusing, or at any rate neglecting, to take account of the full implications of his own procedure of analysis, he continued to see himself as concerned with Reality-as-such in the traditional sense, though in fact he now knew that what he was dealing with was 'reality as an experiential construction'.

So, as a preliminary correction, we have seen that contrary to what he thought he was doing, but in agreement with what his procedure showed that he was doing, he was trying to trace the steps, not from sense-data to Reality-as-such but from sense-data to reality-as-experiential-construction.

The difficulty with sense-data was that, though our sensory experience seems to be our only direct, and so only reliable, source of knowledge of the world about us, and so to be the necessary basis for any straightforward (i.e. non-metaphysical) account of knowledge, nevertheless, in actual practice, no individual's sense-data can be made to add up to the knowledge he possesses.

More explicitly, the difficulty is that if, as assumed, the individual's sense-data are his only source of knowledge, then there must be some principles of inference by which he gets from the data, the actual sensations in his nervous system, to the knowledge expressed as (say) 'That is a tree' or 'I see a tree.'

But if our aim is to give a purely experiential account of knowledge, then these principles of inference must themselves have been derived from the individual's experiential data, i.e., they must have been *inferred*. But then they must have been inferred according to certain principles of inference . . . which in their turn . . .

The fact is that though the individual's sensory data seem to be his only mode of contact with the world about him, any account of knowledge as inferred from these data seems to lead to that logician's nightmare, an infinite regress, the only way of escape from which seems to be by way of some extra-experiential, i.e. metaphysical, principle of interpretation, which is precisely what the tough-minded positivist has repudiated in favour of an empirical account of knowledge.

But when we take another look at the above statement of the problem of knowledge, we see that, in its reference to the individual's contact with the world about him, it is a treatment of the problem in terms of Reality or the World.

So obviously the first thing we must do is, restate the problem, thus: By what system of principles does the individual infer from his sense-data to the world-as-experiential-construction?

But when we do this, we are struck by the fact that this experiential construction which the individual is said to infer from his private data is not a construction which is private and peculiar to him. To come under the heading of what we call knowledge, the construction he arrives at must conform to the picture of the world that is held by those about him. If he says, 'I see a tree', where nobody else sees anything, or sees something quite different, he would be said to be suffering from a delusion, not to be making a unique contribution to knowledge.

So when we speak of the individual inferring knowledge from his private data, we mean that he is inferring from *private data* to *common world-picture*.

And this, we now begin to see, is where the empirical account of knowledge runs into trouble. For the problem can now be seen to be: By what system of principles does the individual infer *common* knowledge from his *private* data?

And it can be seen that, if there is a difficulty in tracing the steps from private data to private knowledge, there is an even greater and more peculiar difficulty in tracing the steps from private data to public knowledge. It is the problem, in effect, of how I am to build up from data which are peculiar and private to me a body of knowledge which shall be universally and necessarily valid, i.e., which shall be legislative for all those about me; and not only this, but shall be recognized by them as being so valid. This, it can be seen, is a very awkward problem, much more awkward than the problem as originally stated. Nevertheless, the fact is that the individual — any individual we like to turn to — does possess a body of knowledge, and this body of knowledge *is* valid for all those about him. This may seem strange until we realize that it is simply another way of stating the demonstrable fact that the individual *participates* in a body of *common* knowledge. But this at once gives rise to the question, How did he come to participate in this body of common knowledge?

And as soon as we have put the question in this form, the answer is obvious. We have, in fact, already looked at the answer more than once. The individual participates in the established body of common knowledge, because he has been inducted into it from infancy onward as part of his cultural heritage.

Indeed, once we have this clearly before our minds, we can see that there is really no difficulty about the question we looked at just now, as to how the individual, starting from his own private data, the sensations in his nervous system, arrives at a body of knowledge which shall be legislative for all those about him. This is because, having been inducted into the categories of the common world-picture, these categories are legislative for *him*. It is by interpreting his moment-by-moment data in terms of these common categories that he raises his purely private experience to the level of communicable knowledge.

And now at last we can see the cause of the failure of the positivist's experiential account of knowledge. We can see why both his procedure of analysis and his Verification Principle, which were to solve all problems and elucidate the nature of truth, could not be made to work.

The problem of knowledge, as the positivist presented it to himself, was: *How does the individual infer the knowledge he comes to possess from his sense-data?* And the question could not be answered, the individual could not be shown to be inferring knowledge from data, because, in fact, he was *interpreting data in terms of an already established body of knowledge.* It was not possible to demonstrate the inferential steps by which the individual proceeded from

A (sense-data) to B (knowledge) because he did not proceed from A to B as assumed.

There is no difficulty in seeing that the individual (1) is inducted by his elders into an already established body of knowledge, a given system of categories, a common world-picture, and (2) that he thenceforth utilizes these categories for the interpretation of his moment-by-moment data: any elementary book of psychology will state this fact and once stated it is too obvious to be denied. The only difficulty seems to have been in recognizing that *this* explains the failure of the positivist's account of knowledge, which precipitated the crisis in philosophy. The individual could not be shown to arrive in the manner assumed at the knowledge he was found to possess, because that was not how he arrived at that knowledge.

The 'crisis in philosophy' and the 'revolution in philosophy' that followed from it took their rise in the philosopher's failure to solve a problem, which, in the form in which he presented it to himself, was insoluble because it ran counter to the facts which it was trying to account for.

But we must be careful at this point not to think that, in discovering the reason for the philosopher's failure to solve the problem of knowledge, we have ourselves arrived at the solution of that problem. A moment's reflection will make clear that the fact of the individual being inducted into the common world-picture by his elders, doesn't solve the problem, it simply — but at the same time very significantly — carries us a step nearer to getting a clear view of the problem.

19. *The crisis in philosophy*

Let us take a look at a modern statement of the problem of knowledge:

All persons who have learned to speak can use sentences to describe events. The events are evidence for the truth of the sentences. In some ways, the whole thing is so obvious that it is difficult to see any problem; in other ways, it is so obscure that it is difficult to see any solution. If you say 'It is raining', you may know that what you say is true because you see the rain and feel it and hear it; this is so plain that nothing could be plainer. But difficulties arise as soon as we try to analyse what happens when we make statements of this sort on the basis of immediate experience. In what sense do we 'know' an occurrence independently of using words about it? How can we compare it with our words, so as to know that our words are right? What relation must subsist between the occurrence and our words in order that our words may be right? How do we know in any given case, whether this relation subsists or not? Is it perhaps possible to know that our words are right without having any non-verbal knowledge of the occurrence to which they apply?

This outline of the problem of knowledge is from Bertrand Russell's *Inquiry into Meaning and Truth*. What we at once note is that the difficulties he refers to arise when it is assumed that 'We make statements of this sort on the basis of immediate experience'. And the meaning of this is made clear when he says, in a passage we have already glanced at but which is worth quoting from again:

Thus, even in regard to what is distant in time and space, what we consider ourselves to know depends, not for its truth but for our knowing it, upon sensations of our own. I think it may be said without exception or qualification that every piece of empirical knowledge (knowledge of matters of fact) that a given person possesses, he would not possess but for some sensation or sensations in his own life.

We can understand why Russell was brought to the conclusion that 'the problem of knowledge remains very obscure and very difficult to deal with'. But, further, we can understand *how* this conclusion was forced on him. It was because of the assumption that the knowledge a given person possesses must have resulted from 'some sensation or sensations in his own life'.

This is put forward as an incontrovertible proposition. And it is, in what it *says,* obviously incontrovertible. − This is what seems to make the problem of knowledge so defeating that many modern thinkers have taken the heroic step of declaring that there isn't any 'problem of knowledge', there are only various uses of the word 'knowledge'.

But in what the proposition *implies,* it obviously, though not quite so obviously, is *wrong.* It is wrong in the sense, which is obvious once you have seen it but which can easily be missed unless you look for it, that it assumes that all the individual's sensations, all the sensory data which are the necessary condition of his achieving knowledge, are of the same order of value. This overlooks the essential fact that certain of these data, the ones we call verbal, have a unique value of their own, which is precisely of the kind to give rise in the individual to what we call knowledge, i.e. to *common* knowledge.

We need not be surprised that Russell says further: 'It appears from our analysis of knowledge' − (knowledge regarded, that is, as derived directly by each individual from the data of his own experience) − 'that, unless it is much more restricted than we suppose, we shall have to admit principles of non-demonstrative inference which may be difficult to reconcile with pure empiricism' (that is, that we shall have to regard knowledge as the metaphysician did, as governed by principles which themselves transcend experience).

Russell, it will be seen, does not shrink from the conclusion that there are more things in heaven and earth than his philosophy − the view, that is, that the knowledge any individual possesses is a simple function of his own experience − is capable of accounting for; though no doubt the principles he thinks it necessary to admit would be those of Logic, not those of the metaphysician's Mind or Spirit.

Let us now look at another statement of the problem of knowledge. Professor Ryle writes:

It seems, on the one hand, very hard to avoid saying that hearing, seeing, tasting could not happen unless appropriate sense-impressions were received; and yet also very hard to give a coherent account of what such sense-impressions are, or how the having of sense-impressions is connected with, say, our hearing a conversation or our seeing a tree.

We can recognize this as another version of the by-now-familiar problem — actually, we now know, pseudo-problem — of tracing the steps from an individual's sense-data to Reality-as-such. The writer goes on:

> In the case of genuine perception (the actual seeing of a tree as distinct from having the hallucination of seeing a tree) we are inclined to say, we both have sense-impressions, produced or stimulated in the normal ways, and also contribute something of our own, namely . . . the interpretation or significance, without which we should not have perceived, say, an oak-tree.

This too we can now recognize: it is an instance of the individual interpreting his momentary data in terms of the replica of the common world-picture which he has built up in his private consciousness under the tuition of his elders. That the writer does not see the situation in this light, however, is clear when he goes on:

> Yet the moment we start to press this tempting idea we are landed in familiar difficulties. Colours as we see them and sounds as we hear them seem at once to collapse into internal reactions or states of ourselves. The oak-tree is not really green and the tenor's voice is not literally shrill. The sense-impressions which were supposed to make perceptions of trees and choirs possible finish by becoming screens between ourselves and trees or choirs. The sensible qualities of things in the world cease to be qualities of those things and become, instead, momentary states of our own minds or nervous systems.

Here again the same kind of difficulty arises, and for the same reasons. 'The sense-impressions' — i.e. the sensory data of an individual here and now — 'which were supposed to make perceptions of trees and choirs possible' — i.e. which were supposed, mistakenly we now know, to provide the basis from which the individual made inferences to trees and choirs — 'finish by becoming screens between ourselves and trees and choirs' — between, that is, the individual confined within the limits of his own data, which are all of the same (natural) order, and Reality-as-such.

But of course there are no screens between us and trees and choirs because we *know* these things, else we wouldn't be able to talk about them. By an act of interpretation we translate our immediate sense-data into these familiar things; but the interpretation is not 'our own', it is something that we have been taught, something which, if we had not been taught it, we would not be able to apply.

These two approaches to the problem of knowledge serve to indicate the persistence and the pervasiveness of the view that the knowledge that any individual possesses is a simple function of his own sensory data. We can understand why a problem — actually a pseudo-problem — which, as formulated, is unanswerable, has had a paralysing effect on thought.

If we stick to individual sensory data, it does not seem possible, as Professor Ryle insisted, to get from this purely subjective starting-point to Reality considered as existing independently of experience. And yet, if we accept the need for some act of interpretation to bridge the gap between private data and Reality, how can we avoid admitting, as Russell did, some principles of inference that are not drawn from experience, so leaving the way open to a return of metaphysics?

There seemed to be no way out of this predicament, except by way of some sort of formula, that would (i) dispose of metaphysics for all time, to protect philosophy against *that* threat, and (ii) provide the philosopher with a 'new way of thought', a new territory for philosophy to manoeuvre in, free from any intrusion of the ancient and intractable problems.

The credit for bringing about this 'revolution in philosophy' goes principally to two thinkers, Wittgenstein and Ryle.

Professor Ryle's *The Concept of Mind* can be said to have performed the remarkable feat of providing a new formula for philosophy by the same procedure with which it reduced the lingering remnants of metaphysics to dust and ashes.

The target of Professor Ryle's attack was the kind of abstractions which earlier thinkers had spelt with a capital letter to indicate their transcendental status; in particular that principal planet in the metaphysician's firmament, Mind, together with its satellite concepts, Intellect, Idea and Thought. These, Professor Ryle argues, are vacuous terms. They do not refer to some sort of supra-experiential entities, they are 'nothing but' kinds of human behaviour. There is no such thing as (say) Intellect. There are only certain observed ways in which people carry out certain activities.

When, for instance, I am said to 'express a thought', there is not some 'occult' happening in some private area of my body called my 'mind' which actuates me to say (for instance) 'That is a tree.' There is not one thing, a 'thought', and another thing or set of things, the words used to express the 'thought'. This is clear, Professor Ryle argues, from the fact that, if I am asked to give an account of this supposed separate entity, my 'thought', all I can do is repeat the words which I first used to 'express it'.

There are, then, no 'thoughts' as mysterious entities in my private 'mind', there are only the words I use on any given occasion, in which I am said to 'express the thought'.

Thus baldly stated, the doctrine does not sound as plausible as Professor Ryle's skill of presentation and persuasive wit make it. But the interesting thing about this reduction of these abstractions to 'words in use' is that, at one stroke, it finally disposes of metaphysics and provides philosophy with a new outlook and field of operations, where the ancient and troublesome problems can find no foothold.

If the traditional problems of philosophy are 'nothing but' instances of words in use; if, as Wittgenstein put it, 'the method of formulating these problems rests on the misunderstanding of the logic of our language', then philosophy is 'nothing but' the study of 'words in use'. It will be realized that, at a time when thought had run into a dead end — the impossibility of getting from an individual's sense-data to Reality — from which it did not seem to be able either to retreat or advance, to have accomplished these two aims by the one formula was a philosophic achievement of the first magnitude. We needn't be surprised that *The Concept of Mind* has been accepted as one of the formative philosophical works of the present century.

To an unbiased view, it may seem astonishing that problems which have exercised the minds of the great thinkers of the past two thousand years have finally proved to be susceptible of so simple and obvious a solution: they were not problems, they were just linguistic 'muddles mistaken for problems'. This, and the fact that this solution emerged so opportunely at a time when the modern thinker's early claims to have reached an 'unassailable and definitive' treatment of these problems had to be abandoned, will make us feel the need to look a little more closely at this 'new way of philosophy'.

And when we do so, one thing that will at once strike us is that the effectiveness of the 'words in use' doctrine as a counter to the claims of metaphysics depends on its pragmatic down-to-earthness. In place of an abstract thought, which when examined dissolves into the words used to express it, we are to deal with an actual instance of an actual individual using certain words here and now; we are to deal directly with publicly observable verbal *behaviour*.

But this might seem to suggest the question: Do my private utterances, stamped as they would seem to inescapably be by my peculiar 'subjectivity', provide a sufficient basis for what we call knowledge? Ryle's purpose in laying the emphasis on my public verbal behaviour is to counteract the conception

Universitas
BIBLIOTHECA
Ottaviensis

of 'thoughts' as essentially private, and so unobservable, and so unverifiable happenings in an individual's inner consciousness. Instead of my unobservable thoughts there is my observable vocal behaviour. The question arises, though: Is my vocal behaviour, the sounds I utter, though observable, any less private to me than the 'thought' they stand for?

But this has not been overlooked by Ryle. He points out that, though the words I use are, in one sense, peculiarly mine, there is another sense in which they reach beyond this subjective limitation. 'The very fact,' says Ryle, 'that an expression is made to be understood by anyone shows that the meaning of the expression is not to be described as being, or belonging to, an event that at most one person could know anything about.'

In other words, the words I use, though by the fact of being used by me they are *my* words, at the same time have the property or power – it is in fact by virtue of such property or power that they *are* words – of disposing those who hear me to react in the way intended by me. This is the significance of the statement that they have been 'made to be understood by anyone', that is to say, they have been made as having, not just some validity peculiar to me, but common validity.

But the difficulty now is that the consideration which saves my vocal behaviour from being as private as the 'thought' it expresses – the consideration which transforms my *vocal* behaviour into *verbal* behaviour – at the same time raises, in a new form, precisely the sort of questions that 'words in use' was intended to short-circuit. The difficulty centres around the simple word 'made'.

'Made to be understood by anyone, by everybody': it was my private utterances that were made to be generally understood in this way. Made by whom, to perform this common function? Made by me? But that won't do; it still doesn't carry us outside the closed privacy of my subjectivity, indeed it carries us further back into that privacy and makes the 'making' still more of a mystery. But if not made by me to be

100

commonly understood, by whom made? And in that case, how so made? And how, my vocal utterances being made to be understood in this unexplained way, did I come to know them as utterances that would be commonly understood, and know that others also so know them, so that I could use them (and they could use them) in full confidence of being understood?

I think that the key phrase 'made to be understood by everyone' serves to indicate that such plausibility as the doctrine of 'words in use' has — apart from the fact that it met an urgent intellectual need — is due to its being an oblique statement of the procedure by which the individual subsumes his private experiences under the categories of the common world-picture.

But in any case, the fact seems to be that the word 'made', far from solving our problems, puts us back where we were.

And yet, on consideration, perhaps not quite.

The metaphysician started from Thought as a supra-experiential principle by participation in which the separate thoughts in private consciousnesses functioned in human communication.

The positivist, reducing these private thoughts to instances of verbal behaviour, shows that these function in human communication by participation in a fund or reservoir of common understandings: they are 'made' for this purpose.

What appears to have happened is that the positivist has replaced Thought, not by my verbal behaviour as such, but by my verbal behaviour as the manifestation of some governing principle of meaning or understanding.

Both the metaphysician and the positivist refer us to some governing principle, external to the individual and his activities. The former gives this principle a transcendental interpretation. The latter seems anxious to avoid giving it any interpretation.

But these considerations open up an aspect of modern thought that will repay more detailed examination.

20. *Sidelights on an ancient controversy*

A curious and disconcerting feature of contemporary positivistic philosophy is that, starting out as deliberate repudiation of all idealistic types of thought, with their emphasis on the act of knowing as (in some way or degree) determining the nature of the known, it has issued in a view of objects as functions of or constructions from sense-data, i.e. of objects as (in some way or degree) determined by the manner of their knowing.

And yet, despite this peculiar similarity in their philosophic idiom, there can be no question that the positivist does not *mean* to say the same thing that the idealist has been saying. But, acknowledging that there is a difference between the two modes of thought, the interesting question is, what *is* the difference?

The modern analytical movement, which was to give the lead in the emphasis on sense-data as the basis of knowledge, was, in its peculiarly English form, the expression of a revolt against the domination of that brilliant nineteenth-century exponent of idealist thought, F.H. Bradley. The developing thought of both Moore and Russell was the expression of a revolt against the seductive cosmic implications of the Bradleian world-picture. In particular it was a revolt against the doctrine that the only reality was a supra-experiential realm of Mind or Spirit – in Bradley's idiom, the Absolute; a doctrine which echoed, through successive modifications and accretions, Plato's realm of Pure Ideas, the legislative power of which gave meaning to the individual's otherwise incoherent experiential data.

Truth as Plato saw it dwelt above and outside experience. This was the realm of the Real, the world of sensory experience being mere deceptive appearance.

'In the first exuberance of liberation [from this idealistic repudiation of the world of sense],' says Russell in his *My Philosophical Development*, 'I became a naive realist and rejoiced in the thought that grass is really green, in spite of the adverse opinion of all philosophers from Locke onward.'

This repudiation of the idealist's repudiation of the world of sense, this urge to return to a belief in experience as the true mode of access to the real, was one aspect of a movement of thought that was finding various forms of expression at that time.

It is of interest then that Russell says, 'I have not been able to retain this pleasing faith in naive realism in its pristine vigour, but I have never again shut myself up in a subjective prison.'

Let us take a look at this 'subjective prison' as it had found expression in the idealism of Bradley:

'We perceive, on reflection, that to be real, or even barely to exist, must be to fall within sentience. Sentient experience, in short, is reality, and what is not this is not real.' And again, 'Find any piece of existence, take up anything that anyone could possibly call a fact, or could in any sense assert to have being, and then judge if it does not consist in sentient experience.' 'An unexperienced reality,' he insists, 'is a vicious abstraction whose existence is meaningless nonsense.'

It is of interest to compare this with the pronouncement of the anti-metaphysical positivist, repudiating the whole idealist tradition on the grounds that its claims were not only meaningless, but actually senseless, because 'they had no reference to any known experience.' But Bradley is claiming that all we know *is* experience. There is evidently something here that wants clarifying.

Taking an overall view of this situation, and not letting ourselves be put off by the idealist's rather overcharged mode of expression, we are struck by the interesting fact that both Bradley and those who are in revolt against his standpoint are insistent that experience is our only source of contact with reality.

Bradley expresses his view of knowledge which, in the Platonic tradition, sees the world of senses as 'mere appearance', in terms of 'sentient experience'. The 'realist', in revolt against this, expresses his view of knowledge in terms of 'sensory experience.'

Amplifying 'sentient experience', Bradley says, 'Feeling, thought and volition are all the material of existence, and there is no other material, actual or possible.'

But the dispute between the two modes of thought does not seem to be about the extension of 'sentient experience' to cover this wider range of human reactions, feeling, thought and volition. Those who speak of 'sensory experience' would probably not balk at this more hospitable use of the term. Then where does the difference lie, that could have yielded such an 'exuberance of liberation' in breaking free from the 'subjective prison' of the Bradleian world-view?

Actually the revolt of Moore and Russell centred around a technical question concerning a difference between 'internal' and 'external' relations. But we need not get ourselves involved in that. We want to stick to our overall view. And doing so, and taking a closer look at Bradley's standpoint, we see that, though he insisted on experience as the necessary basis of knowledge, he did not mean by 'experience' anything that we would normally call 'subjective'.

Here (to widen the ambience of our discussion) is another idealist thinker, A.E. Taylor, on this question:

> . . . to identify reality with experience does not mean identifying it with my own experience, just as it comes to me in actual life, still less with my own experience as I mentally reconstruct it in the light of some conscious or unconscious philosophical theory. My own experience, in fact, is very far from satisfying the conditions of completeness and harmony which we found in our last book to be essential to 'pure' or perfect experience. Reality [he adds] is a systematic Experience of which the components are likewise experiences.

Now if by 'subjective' we mean, as the dictionary assures us we do, 'pertaining to the subject', i.e., something which is peculiar to the experiencing individual, then the idealist was *not* confining Moore and Russell to a subjective 'prison'. The experience he was talking about was something he saw as 'Pure', or 'systematic', Experience, with a capital E to distinguish it from the mere momentary flux of the experience of some individual here and now.

But though it does not seem that the idealist's standpoint can properly be described as 'subjective', nevertheless it must have presented some of the elements of a 'prison', if escape from it gave such a sense of liberation.

At this point we may recall Russell's admission that he has not been able, in the subsequent development of his own standpoint, to retain his faith in the world of physical things and facts 'in its pristine vigour'.

He is not saying, of course, that the old idealistic 'prison' has closed around him again. Quite the contrary, he assures us that he has never again shut himself up in it. But as a matter of interest, let us take a look at the alternative view of knowledge in which he has come to place his faith.

'Thus,' he says, 'even in regard to what is distant in time and place, what we consider ourselves to know depends . . . upon sensations of our own. I think it can be said without any exception or qualification that every piece of empirical knowledge that a given person possesses he would not possess but for some sensation or sensations in his own life.'

This is a frankly subjective view of knowledge, of the kind that the idealist explicitly repudiated. And yet it has been arrived at on the basis of a repudiation of the 'subjective prison' of idealist thought. It is also a considerable remove, as Russell himself tells us, from the naive faith in the everyday world of physical things and facts, of grass that was really grass and really green, into which he was liberated when he escaped from the idealist's world of 'mere appearance'.

This is not intended as a criticism of Russell's standpoint. All we are interested in is the *fact* that the modern thinker, having repudiated the idealist standpoint that 'knowing determines the known' — and most of these thinkers have repudiated it with a much greater 'anti-metaphysical' emphasis than Russell — are found expressing their own view in a disconcertingly similar idiom to that of the idealists.

Both are in effect saying, knowledge is a function of

experience. The idealist is saying that it is a function of something he calls 'pure Experience', the constituents of which are 'individual experiences'. This has the sort of vagueness that the modern positivist will have nothing to do with. Knowledge, for him, means and can only mean something which is a function of the actual experiences of a real individual. And by 'actual experience' he means an individual's own sensory-data; and, as we have seen, he makes no distinction between 'natural' and 'verbal' data, he treats all the individual's data as natural data. He states his view – or did, until the 'retreat from philosophy' set in – in the explicit form that the knowledge any individual possesses is a construction from the data of his own experience.

Now this again strikes us as curious, because the idealist too, as we have seen, claims that the 'Pure Experience' he is talking about is a structure of 'individual experiences'. But his account of this structure is, to minds trained to the more precise idiom of modern thought, vague and unsatisfactory.

And yet it should be noted that the emphasis on experience, even in this vague form, was an advance on the earlier idealist conception of knowledge as a function, first of Spirit and then of Mind. The successive steps from Spirit (Plato) to Mind (Kant) can be seen as marking a gradual bringing down of the problem of knowledge from heaven to earth.

It may also be noted that this development has always been marked by the same conflict between the 'idealist' and the 'positivist' standpoints that we are now examining; and it has always been a clash of temperaments as much as of rational attitudes.

There are those who are so constituted that they like their truth to be presented to them with its full commitment of cosmical implications. To others these cosmical reverberations are merely a sort of philosophical flatulence; they are happier to feel the cobbles under their feet than to hear the winds of heaven around their ears.

In between these two extremes stands the majority of men,

who are less heard of because they are less philosophically articulate, and who are less articulate because they feel that each of the contending standpoints contains a certain virtue of truth, but not, as its advocates insist, the whole stock and funded capital thereof.

Our present business is not to take sides in this ancient dispute which seems somehow to have come to a crisis at the point in the development of thought where we modern men are doing our thinking. Our business rather is to refrain from taking sides and to discipline ourselves to discover, if we can, what if any is the reconciling point of mutual significance uniting two philosophical attitudes in which both parties, we might suspect, are looking at the same truth from opposite angles of insight.

The tendency of each, in response to the demands of temperament rather than of reason, is to tone down or deliberately evade the implications of its own standpoint which it finds inconvenient. And each standpoint, significantly enough, has a tendency to generate such unassimilable implications which, when followed up, threaten disconcertingly to carry the chosen viewpoint over to the position occupied by the enemy.

The result is that each tends to state his case in an idiom devised to emphasize its irreconcilability with the other. Our business is to take the opposite course, to break through these protective terminological outworks to the citadel within, where, perhaps, truth will be found waiting to be liberated.

21. *Variations on a common theme*

The first thing that we observe in connection with the claim of both the idealist and the positivist, that knowledge is a function of experience (by which each means, or purports to mean, something quite contrary to what is meant by the other) is that both 'knowledge' and 'experience' are terms that are characterized by a peculiar ambiguity.

107

Furthermore, our own inquiry has made clear that this is a systematic ambiguity: each of these terms with which we are now dealing has a dual significance. And in each case, the duality is of the same nature.

'Knowledge', for instance, may refer either to that body of common experience, our common world-picture (however this may have been arrived at) which, embodied in the system of concepts which finds expression in language, is passed on by one generation to the next by way of the unique kind of data we call *words*.

But 'knowledge' may also refer to the outcome, in the individual, of the procedure by which, bringing his momentary experiential data under the appropriate concept of the common world-picture, he is able to pronounce a judgment of the form (say) 'I see a dog'.

A similar, if not precisely the same, duality applies to the use of 'experience'. The term may be used to refer either to the established body of common experience, our common world-picture, or what in another sense we call knowledge, or reality, or truth (according to context and convenience); or, as above, it may refer to the individual experiencing in terms of the given body of common experience, i.e. bringing his momentary data, the movements in his private nervous system, under its concepts.

Now I think the fact that the dispute between the idealist and the positivist has centred around terms having this peculiar but precise ambiguity, goes some distance at the outset towards showing that they are both discussing the same thing, but discussing it from opposite angles of insight.

What is this common insight that they are both talking about? We might expect, I think, to find it more clearly expressed by the positivist than by the idealist, simply because he occupies a later phase in the development of thought than his rival. He may be assumed, in fact — though this would not at all be his intention — to be giving expression to an aspect of that insight which the idealist, for temperamental reasons, had played down or ignored.

We might even assume that modern analysis, with its urge to get to the ultimate units on which the structure of knowledge may be said to rest, has been carrying a necessary step further the insight adumbrated in general, and so less explicit, terms by the idealist.

But we want something more precise than this, and I think it is available to us.

Positivistic analysis (to repeat) has shown that the body of concepts or world-picture, which the individual uses for the interpretation of his moment-by-moment experience, is a construction from the data of individual experience.

The positivist, as we have seen, has shied away from this outcome of his own analysis; and I think we can now see the reason for this. Hag-ridden as he is by an anti-metaphysical phobia, any fact for which he could not produce an immediate rational explanation might — it just might — leave the way open for an incursion of metaphysics. It were better to deny the fact, and accept the consequences, than to leave his thought open to a rear attack from that quarter!

But we, ourselves, suffering from no such inhibitions, can accept the outcome of his analysis *as a fact still to be explained:* the fact that knowledge is a construction from the data of individual experience, though not, as his analysis has also shown, the immediate experience of any individual here and now. And we can also note the further fact that it is this construction from the data of individual experience to which the individual must refer his private data if these are to become communicable knowledge.

Bearing in mind the dual meaning of 'knowledge' and 'experience', one thing we may note is that the positivist is concerned with the individual factor as distinct from the common factor in the knowledge situation. In fact, as we have just seen, his temperamental leanings, together with the exigencies of philosophical disputation, have conspired to make him underplay and even deny the fact of knowledge disclosing this common facet. For the positivist, truth, to the extent that such a luxury is attainable by man, is something

109

that is immediate, demonstrable, and strictly pragmatic.

By way of contrast, let us take another look at the idealist's treatment of these matters.

'Truth,' says Harold Joachim in *The Nature of Truth*, 'in its essential nature is that systematic coherence which is the character of a significant whole.' This is the sort of pronouncement that the positivist would ban from philosophic discourse as not only meaningless, but senseless.

What does the idealist mean by a 'significant whole'? Joachim tells us: 'A "significant whole" is an organized individual experience, self-fulfilling and self-fulfilled . . . '

But what is an 'organized experience', leaving out of account for the moment one that is 'self-fulfilling and self-fulfilled'? Well, the body of common experience which, positivistic analysis shows, has been constructed from the data of individual experience, is an organized experience. And this body of common experience may be called the depository of truth in the sense that the individual must make his private experience coherent with it, if he is to achieve what we call knowledge.

But 'an organized *individual* experience' — what are we to make of this? I think it would be safe to say that what the idealist means is an *individual organized experience,* a single, internally-coherent body of experience. The same writer says later: 'A theory of truth as coherence . . . must be an intelligible account of the ultimate coherence in which the one significant whole' manifests itself.

It does not seem possible to say precisely what this means, except as an oblique, because unwitting (or perhaps unwilling) reference to the body of common experience which in fact we do possess, and which is in fact the depository of what we mean by truth. It doesn't seem possible to give it any other precise meaning, but it certainly makes sense when given *this* meaning.

And finally, an individual organized experience, or body of common experience, constructed from the data of individual experience 'self-fulfilling and self-fulfilled': what are we to make of this?

It certainly carries a rather strong overtone of the sort of metaphysics that is inclined to be self-defeating and self-defeated. It reminds us of Hegel's 'self-actualization of the absolute Idea'.

And yet, reminding ourselves that our body of common experience is a construction from the data of individual experience, a deposit of funded experience as we might say (lured into a rather too literary mode of expression in our endeavour to meet the idealist at some halfway point between the upper ether of Pure Truth and the rutted pathway of immediate experience), reminding ourselves of this, there seems to be a quite precise sense in which we can say that our common experience is self-fulfilling, i.e., that it creates, and so *is*, its own subject-matter.

And, if we accept this, there does not seem to be any great difficulty in 'self-fulfilled', when we consider that our common experience, derived *from* individual experience, is, as an organized whole, available to the individual as an instrument by means of which he may — indeed must — raise his subjective data to a level of meaning, and hence of power, that he alone could never have achieved.

But in any case, however strictly or liberally we may interpret the idealist's rather too impressionistic presentation of his chosen standpoint, there would seem to be no question that, in contrast to the positivist, he is taking his stand, in his account of knowledge, on the *common* as distinct from the *individual* element or factor in the knowledge-situation.

Consider again, for instance, Bradley's insistence that 'to be real, or even barely to exist, must be to fall within sentience. Sentient experience, in short, is reality, and what is not this is not real . . . An unexperienced reality is a vicious abstraction, whose existence is meaningless nonsense.'

We may assume that the idealist meant *something* by these grandiose modes of speech, that he was giving expression to an aspect of knowledge which he was sure existed, and which he was equally sure was important; was, in fact, *the* important aspect of knowledge. The only other assumption would be that he was regaling us with mere gratuitous verbiage having no equivalent in any thought that anyone had ever entertained; and we can hardly suspect a thinker of Bradley's status as practising such a deception on himself and us.

Well then, if the statement 'sentient experience is reality, and what is not this is not real' refers to something, what aspect of knowledge is there that it *could* refer to?

Strangely enough, when we put the matter in this way, we see that the answer, the aspect of knowledge that it must refer to, has been indicated by the positivist himself, though he himself has not seen it as the answer.

For the essence and the outcome of modern analysis is that it has shown that what had hitherto been regarded as Reality-as-such is in fact reality-as-experiential-construction. In other words, that the term 'reality' refers, not to a something which is independent of human experience, but to human experience, the sum or essence of human experience, itself.

There seems to be no escape from it. If we do the idealist the justice of assuming that he must be referring to *something*, then this is all he can be referring to; and in fact it is obviously what, without realizing it, he *is* referring to.

Modern analysis has the effect of revealing the core of significance in the idealist's otherwise elusive pronouncements. And when we have seen what the idealist was really saying, this in its turn helps us to grasp the significance of modern analysis.

Accepting that the idealist's 'Pure Experience' expresses a genuine insight (however vaguely grasped) and accepting that the outcome of the positivist's analysis is valid (despite the positivist's own failure to recognize such validity) then the idealist can only be formulating, in vague general terms, an insight which the positivist's analysis allows him to formulate in more explicit terms: that what we call reality is a construction from the data of individual experience.

And, of course, it is not a matter of chance that the

positivist's analysis should have arrived at a view of 'reality' which provides the idealist's idea of reality with the interpretation of it needed to make it intelligible to us. For the positivist, in his emphasis on the element of individual experience, was carrying a stage further the idealist's insight that knowledge was a function of experience, just as the idealist himself was carrying a stage further the earlier conception of knowledge as a function, first of 'Spirit' and then of 'Mind'. The positivist's more precise definition of 'pure Experience' was due to its being an analysis – a working out of the implications of that conception.

The one view is concerned with the fact of there being such a body of 'pure' experience – 'pure' in the sense of transcending the individual's immediate sensory data – and is content to state it boldly and without qualification. The other view, coming later and being more analytical, is concerned with the nature of the fact, and so states, as an essential part of the fact, the manner of its genesis.

In other words, the idealist finds his intellectual satisfaction in emphasizing knowledge as a systematic whole governing the organization of individual experience, while the positivist is more impressed by individual experience as providing the structural elements of that systematic whole.

22. *The nature of knowledge*

Summarizing our whole discussion, let us take another look at the cause of the positivist's failure. In the first place, having shown that the term 'world' necessarily means 'construction from the data of experience', he continued to treat it as meaning 'independently existing cause of experience', thus introducing a pervasive confusion into his thinking.

But further, even when 'world' was accepted as meaning 'experiential construction', the attempt to show how the individual constructed his world-picture by inference from the data of his sensory-experience, proved abortive. We have seen why this was so. It was because the individual was *not* constructing a world-picture by inference from his sensory data. He was using an already-established common world-picture for the *interpretation* of his data.

The positivist's failure, we can now see, was a complex one. The individual was not inferring from his sense-data to *Reality*. He was not, in any case, *inferring* from his sense-data. And finally, his sense-data were inadequate to account for the knowledge he possessed.

Of these three causes of failure, it was the latter one — the inadequacy of the individual's experience to account for the knowledge he possessed — that directly affected the development of philosophic thinking. For the conclusion to which it seemed to point — the conclusion to which everybody reacted without actually stating it — was that if *knowledge was not derived from the data of any individual's experience then it was not derived from experience*. But the whole positivistic movement of thought, with its repudiation of any extra-experiential source of knowledge, was based on the assumption that knowledge *was* derived from experience.

The positivist's sense of the collapse of this basic assumption created a dilemma which precipitated the 'crisis in philosophy', which in turn gave rise to the 'revolution in philosophy' in which the whole corpus of traditional problems was scrapped in favour of the philosophy of 'words in use'.

But when we look at the positivist's account of knowledge in relation to the idealist's account, it becomes clear that the collapse of the positivist's account had not shown that knowledge is *not* derived from experience. The positivist's tough-minded emphasis on sensory experience as the source of knowledge had had the effect of throwing his problem out of focus.

The idealist had been concerned with knowledge as *common* experience, governing the organization of individual experience. The positivist was concerned with *individual* experience — not

114

sensory experience as such, but sensory experience as peculiar and private to the individual – as providing the elements out of which common experience had been constructed.

The positivist had not shown that knowledge is not derived from experience. On the contrary, he had carried a stage further the insight, which the idealist had partially grasped and had then overstated and so falsified in the interests of his temperamental leanings: the insight that knowledge is a function of experience. What the positivist had shown was that, as common experience, *it had not been derived from the data of any one individual's experience.*

The positivist had tried to derive *common* experience directly from *an individual's* experience, although (a) the individual was not in fact so deriving it, and (b) as *common*, it could not have been so derived.

The interesting point is that the 'crisis in philosophy' was due to this misunderstanding and the subsequent 'revolution in philosophy', as a formula of escape from this 'crisis', rested upon the same mistake.

Seen in its historical context, a work such as *The Concept of Mind* can be recognized as a contribution – confused because misdirected – to the procedure which we referred to earlier as thought's elucidation of its own structure, a turning back of thought on itself and making itself the object of its own investigation. At first such a procedure is necessarily unconscious: this is what men are doing but they cannot yet realize that this is what they are doing. But gradually, in the nature of the case, in the nature of thought's inquiry into its own structure, the structure of thought begins to come up into consciousness. But men, still not realizing what they are doing – not realizing the nature of the procedure they are engaged in – now see themselves as *criticizing* ideas that previous generations had accepted without question. They see themselves as *criticizing,* not *inquiring into,* the structure of thought.

But to criticize means to judge from some given standpoint: in this case it necessarily means, to judge some area of thought from the given standpoint of some other area of thought. And this means to reject one area of thought while accepting another without question. At this point, the philosopher, in carrying on thought's investigation of its own structure, has 'set himself up' in judgment on thought, but in doing so has set aside an area of thought as his Archimedean point, which is assumed to be immune to criticism. But when, as with the failure of the Verification Principle, this area too begins to give way to critical scrutiny, the thinker who has set himself up as the judge of thought finds himself sawing through the limb he is sitting on.

Looked at from the point of view of one who has been using reason as a weapon with which he is cutting away what he regards as the non-functional parts of thought, this unexpected development looks like a threat to reason itself. The only way of escape, the only 'rational' procedure, seems to be to use the powers of reason to protect reason from bringing about its own collapse. The obvious tactic is to reassert the autonomy of reason by boldly using it to eliminate 'thought' as a factor in knowledge. It is just a 'dream of our language', a 'something' about which nothing can be said except by repeating the words used to express the thought, and 'a nothing would serve just as well as a something about which nothing can be said'.

Such a calculated attack on thought is in effect an assertion of the autonomy of reason, and an autonomous reason, of course, controls its own affairs in such a way as to safeguard itself against any recoil from the criticism which it is wielding as a weapon of destruction.

But providentially — or perhaps necessarily — such a sacrifice of reason in the interests of reason can't be made to work. Truth, like murder, will out. It turns out after all that something can and in fact must be said about thought. It becomes nothing but words in use, but this use of words turns out to be dependent on their having been 'made to be understood by anyone'. Thus, somewhat surreptitiously and obliquely, something very important has been said of thought:

it is only words in use, but words are found to have 'something' over and above their mere use, i.e. the fact of their being 'understood by anyone'.

The idealist, in his metaphysical enthusiasm, had treated my act of knowing as a mysterious transaction in which certain occult Essences or Forms had descended like a benediction upon my chaotic experience to give it such meaning as it was capable of. But when his insight is carried a rational step further, we can see thought as the expression of a common fund of meanings, a deposit of funded experience, by participation in which I am able to raise my private data to the status of communicable knowledge.

The idealist had tried to arrive, by a short-cut that by-passes rational inquiry, at the ultimate nature of knowledge: he tried to scotch inquiry by treating the problem of knowledge as already solved. The positivist, drawn on, first by his anti-metaphysical phobia, and then by the collapse of his own account of knowledge, tried to scotch the problem for all time by declaring that there was 'no such thing' as knowledge and so no problem, and so no need for any inquiry.

But what the positivist has in fact shown is that though thought is not a supra-experiential 'something' governing knowledge, it is not a 'nothing' either: thought is — or rather the term 'thought' refers to — something which, expressed in words, is a piece of common understanding. He has further shown — and this is the distinctive contribution of his procedure of analysis — that this common understanding, this body of common knowledge in terms of which the individual organizes his experience, is not a function of any one individual's experience.

This is what the positivist's analysis has shown. But, interpreting his analysis of knowledge as a *criticism* of knowledge, he naturally misinterprets the conclusion to which he has been brought.

Once sensations are admitted as the source of knowledge (it is argued) the sensible qualities of *things* in the *world* cease to be qualities of those things and become, instead, momentary states of our own minds and nervous systems: they will have the same status as stomach-aches and twinges of rheumatism.

But we can see what the trouble is here. It is an instance of thought caught halfway between the emergent view of things as constructions from experience (sensations) and the traditional view of them as the independently-existing cause of experience. What the argument proves — though unintentionally and unconsciously — is that sensations have not been combined into knowledge in the simple way the positivist had assumed. It is a confused reference to the fact, revealed by analysis, that the things of our common world are not constructions, here and now, from any one individual's sensations.

Another objection to a sensory basis for knowledge is even more interesting. We all know (it is said) how to use the concepts of seeing, hearing, smelling, but not the concept of sense-impression; we have to be introduced to this notion. So the concept of *perception* is on a more elementary or less technical level than that of *sense-impression*. We can know all that is a part of common knowledge about hearing and seeing, without knowing anything about sense-impressions. Thus (the argument concludes) the concept of sense-impression is not any part of the concept of perception.

This whole argument rests on the curious assumption that men had to have the concept *perception*, before they perceived. By analogy, we might say that they had to be familiar with the Newtonian Laws of Motion before they could walk.

It is only when knowledge is traced back to its pre-conceptual basis that we come upon sensations. It is then that we formulate the technical concept *sense-impression* as the name for the pre-conceptual, and so unconscious, elements out of which conceptual knowledge is constituted. Of course the concept of *perception* came before the concept of *sensation* — the latter only emerged at the end of a long and difficult analysis of knowledge; — difficult because it was the taking apart of our accepted structure of ideas and bringing up into consciousness the unconscious basis of our thought-processes. In our conscious thought-processes the concept of *perception* preceded that of sense-impression, but when *sense-impression* was finally arrived at, it was the concept of that which precedes perception.

The argument concludes that the concept of *sense-impression* is not any part of the concept of *perception*. It isn't easy to know precisely what this means. If it means that perception does not rest on sense-impressions, it conflicts with the procedure of analysis of which it is an expression. But if it means that men did not have the *concept* of sense-impression before they had the concept of perception, it is stating somewhat obliquely the outcome of the analysis of knowledge.

This whole confusion can be seen to have arisen from the failure of the attempt to account for common knowledge as a direct function of *an* individual's sensory data. The way out of this dilemma here adopted is the strange argument that because the *concept* of sense-impression only arose as the outcome of the analysis of knowledge, this analysis has not shown sense-impressions to be the (pre-conceptual) basis of knowledge.

What the positivist's contribution to the idealist's insight makes clear is that the problem of knowledge concerns the emergence of a fund of common experience out of the natural, i.e. pre-verbal, data of primitive individual experience.

Somehow man, alone among the animals, has transformed momentary and private natural data into permanent and common verbal data, in which is symbolized a common body of funded experience. *Somehow:* this is the problem toward which the thought of the present century — thought's inquiry into its own structure — has been moving.

Ryle closes *The Concept of Mind* with a characteristic sally:

Man need not be degraded to a machine by being denied to be a ghost in a machine. He might, after all, be a sort of animal, namely, a higher mammal. There has yet to be ventured the hazardous leap to the hypothesis that perhaps he is a man.

In the light of the foregoing discussion we might allow ourselves to revise this to: There has yet to be ventured the hazardous leap to the hypothesis that, as a higher mammal manifesting the peculiar characteristic we call intellect or reason, man's distinctive activities may be self-explanatory, if we can only discipline ourselves to look at the facts as we find them, and not let ourselves be tempted to manipulate the facts in favour of some temperamentally chosen formula.

Part Two

LANGUAGE

INTRODUCTION

It is a curious fact of the history of thought that philosophers have always been suspicious of language. Language never seemed able to do what the philosophers wanted it to do, i.e., express ideas unambiguously — the philosopher's ideas, that is. For this philosophers have been inclined to blame, not the ideas — why would they blame *them*? they were *their* ideas — but language.

Augustine said of time, If nobody asks me what time is, I know, but if I am asked, I know not. If we are asked what language is, the situation is even more frustrating, perhaps because of the more intimate relation between ourselves and language. Augustine's difficulty was, in fact, that of expressing in *words* his experience of *time*. The trouble was (so it would seem) that words were inadequate for the expression of experience.

But we should perhaps note that, in turning from the experiencing of time to saying what time *is*, Augustine had become a philosopher whether he meant to or not. And it was this peculiar philosophical demand that words seemed unable to fulfil. If you ask, 'What is the time?', no difficulty arises: you are *using* the word 'time'. But as soon as you ask: What is time? the ground seems to give way beneath your feet.

The reason for this is that you are now no longer simply using the word 'time', as an integral and natural part of the momentary flux of your experience; you are setting the word apart from your experience — or, more precisely, you are taking it out of the realm of experience into which it naturally fits, and setting it up, arbitrarily, in another realm, the realm of abstract thought, which is (or seems to be) alien to it.

Instead of using the word 'time', you are now critically examining it. You are demanding of it that it disclose to you what sort of thing it is, what function it performs and how it came to perform that function. That is to say, you are now trying to translate the *use of the word* into a *structure of ideas about the word*. And, to complicate the matter, you are trying to find the proper words, the mode of expression or kind of language, that will help you to formulate your ideas about words: you are using words to explicate the functioning of words.

We need not wonder then that, throughout the ages, philosophers have always shown an irritable dissatisfaction with language. Somehow it never seemed to be doing what they wanted it to do. And this they interpreted as showing its clumsiness, its inadequacy and, more specifically, its ambiguity and tendency toward contradiction.

At the very beginning of distinctively modern philosophy, we find Descartes complaining ' . . . words often impede me and I am almost deceived by the terms of ordinary language.' The Frenchman was a man of very different temper and outlook from an empiricist like Locke — didn't Locke set out by repudiating the very kind of intuitive ideas that Descartes accepted as the foundation and guarantee of his system? — but we find Locke speaking of ' . . . the imperfection that is naturally in language, and the obscurity and confusion that is so hard to be avoided in the use of words.'

Coming next to the good Bishop Berkeley, a gentle and kindly man, we find him complaining forthrightly ' . . . most parts of knowledge have been so strangely perplexed and darkened by the abuse of words, and general ways of speech in which they are delivered, that it may almost be made a question whether language has contributed more to the hindrance or advancement of the sciences.'

When we turn to David Hume, 'the best of men' as Jean-Jacques Rousseau asserted (though he was somewhat emotionally upset at the time), we find the same attitude manifested, but in an interestingly different way. 'If nature had so pleased,' says Hume, 'love might have had the same effect as hatred, and hatred as love.' This seems to be putting the blame squarely on nature. But, indirectly, it reflects on language. Because, in effect, he is saying that the sort of experience to which we refer by the word 'love' could have been the sort of experience we refer to by the word 'hatred'. But this is so curious a point of view that perhaps we should say that Hume's charge of ambiguity against language is itself too ambiguous for us to draw any precise conclusion from it.

But when we come to the contemporary scene in which philosophers — such is the direction that the development of thought has taken — are becoming increasingly concerned with language, the way it functions and the part it plays in their discussions, we find that there is no such ambiguity in the prevailing idea as to the ambiguity and general unsatisfactoriness of language as an instrument of philosophic discourse.

Expressing this prevailing attitude in a nutshell, we have the forthright pronouncement of F.W. Bridgman, ' . . . the language does not exist which is consistent with the structure of the world as analysis discloses it. Limited as we are to a language inherited from an uncritical past, we can talk together only by the exercise of mutual goodwill.' Which seems to be telling us that language *is*, while condemning it for *being*, a system based on mutual goodwill and common understanding; a view which another writer, Malinowski, expressed when he said, 'In its primitive uses, language functions as a link in concerted human activity.' Bridgman seems to see as a fault what Malinowski (an anthropologist) records as a fact essential to the nature of language.

A writer on 'Linguistic Behaviour', Skinner, speaks of the 'limitations which linguistic practices impose on human thought', which seems to see the instrument as hampering the function that it performs; as though, had I never had language imposed on me, I might have scaled intellectual heights from which I am now barred.

A philosopher and Greek scholar, F.M. Cornford, speaks of 'a whole apparatus of concepts and categories within which and by means of which all our individual thinking, however original and daring, is compelled to move. This common

125

inherited scheme of conceptions which is all around us and comes to us as naturally and unobjectionably as our native air, is none the less imposed on us and limits our intellectual movements in countless ways — all the more surely and irresistibly because, being inherent in the very language we must use to express our simplest meaning, it is adopted and assimilated before we can so much as begin to think for ourselves at all.'

And then, of course, finalizing and summarizing this contemporary expression of the historic attitude to language, is Wittgenstein. 'Philosophy,' he tells us, 'is a battle against the bewitchment of our intelligence by means of language.'

According to this view, the traditional problems of philosophy are due to this 'bewitchment' to which philosophers have succumbed. They have been exercising their minds over 'muddles mistaken for problems'. The corrective of this is the 'new way of philosophizing', the analysis of ordinary language to see how it actually works.

Ordinary language, we are told, is quite all right as it is. But in the outcome, the taking apart of everyday expressions to see how they actually work becomes another plaint in the familiar indictment of language. Linguistic analysis, as one of its exponents tells us, becomes 'an instrument of deflation'. The analyst becomes a professional debunker of other people's chosen ideas. It was perhaps too ambitious a programme, to show how language 'really works'. In any case, in practice it becomes an exercise in showing us how it doesn't work, how when we think we are saying something significant and perhaps important, we are really saying nothing at all.

And presently this attitude spills over into other fields of thought. A literary critic, Helen Gardner, tells us that 'The critic today . . . is disturbed by echoes of the dimly understood debates of the modern logicians, who have undermined the simple assumption that we all know what something *means* or indeed that we know what meaning itself is.'

A writer on the contemporary theatre tells us that for the avant-garde dramatist 'words are the end, not the beginning, so they are bogus, too far away from the first unmediated response, the gesture, retaining none of the process of responsiveness, frozen, clotted things.' The ideal drama (so it is suggested) would dispense with these treacherous tools, words. As a step toward this perhaps unattainable idea, the dramatist, if he can't do without words, can at least show us their meaninglessness, the futility and failure of communication. *Waiting for Godot* ends with Vladimir saying 'Well, shall we go?' Estragon replies, 'Yes, let's go.' And Beckett adds the stage direction, 'They do not move.'

For some peculiar reason, to talk about language, as distinct from simply and unconsciously using it, seems to be to condemn it. And I think we can see what the reason is. The philosopher starts out by asking questions such as, what *is* time? what *is* truth? what *is* nature? what *is* Reality? what *is* the World? More specifically, if his is an empirically-oriented type of mind, he may ask, not vaguely, What is the World?, but, How is the World constituted?

This seems to be a straightforward question to which, going about it in the right way and keeping strictly aloof from any sort of metaphysical moonshine, a sufficiently clear-cut answer should be possible. But, disconcertingly, this turns out to be far from the case. For the historical fact is that you set out to achieve an answer to a specific question — *How is the World, the objective World of determinate phenomena, constructed?* — and you finish up with the answer — *The world is a construction from the data of individual experience* — which does not answer the question you set out to answer.

Indeed, the answer you have arrived at directly negates the assumption on which your whole inquiry rested. You started by regarding the subject matter of your inquiry as being World as independently existing cause *of* experience; you have now shown it to be a construction *from* experience.

In the train of this confusion, all sorts of other frustrating confusions follow which, on any short-term view, can't be accounted for. And it is the short-term view that we are

committed to in contemporary thought. We have seen ourselves as solving, with our modern techniques of thought, all
the problems that earlier generations of thinkers had fruit-
lessly struggled with. But it then turned out that these problems had *not* been solved.

Instead of showing how the individual inferred his knowledge from the data of his experience, we have shown that his
experience was incompetent to account for the knowledge he
possessed. Instead of showing how the propositions in which
the individual expressed his 'inferences' from his experience
referred to Reality, we had shown that the 'reality' his
propositions referred to was itself an inference from individual experience but, contradictorily, not from *his* experience.
It seemed impossible even to get a clear view of these confusions, let alone to account for them.

And hovering in the background, as we have seen, was
the implication — too disturbing to be explicitly formulated,
but all the more disturbing for that — that if no individual's
experience would account for knowledge, then experience
was not, as the whole empiricist tradition had claimed, the
basis of knowledge.

In such a situation, which seemed to face us with the need
for a disturbing fact-facing and soul-searching, what was to be
done? Well, we know what *was* done. The verdict was that
we had been 'bewitched by words'. Language — and there
was a new bite to this modern indictment — was the cause of
all the trouble. All the long history of problems that never
issued in a solution — Augustine's problem (say) What is
Time? which, far from leading to a solution, led to time
being seen to have 'no counterpart in any known experience'
— all this long tradition of questions to which there seemed
to be no answers, was due (so it was now declared) to a
'failure to understand the logic of our language'.

'A traditionally conceived problem of knowledge', says a
modern philosopher, summing up the contemporary attitude,
'looked like sheer misunderstanding by the side of a sufficiently thorough study of the use of the verb "to know".'

But the problem of knowledge necessarily looked like sheer misunderstanding by the side of this new look at the verb 'to know', because this new look was itself the expression of a new approach to the problem of knowledge. And this new approach was itself the expression of the confusion we have just been examining. It was a formula of escape from that confusion in which the factors in the knowledge situation which seemed to be the cause of all the trouble were to be dismissed as philosophically irrelevant. Where a problem proved recalcitrant to our modern efforts at a solution, the formula said: There is no problem, it is merely that a picture has held us captive.

The new approach to the problem of knowledge, which was to expose the 'sheer misunderstanding' of the traditional question What is knowledge? or How do we know?, was alluringly straightforward and down to earth, designed to safeguard thought against further frustrations. The question, How is the world constituted? or What do we know? had seemed straightforward enough, but it had transformed itself, disconcertingly, into the question, How do we know? What is knowledge? This, in its turn, had seemed to be a question to which the empiricist could give an unambiguous answer — but it, too, had led to frustration and defeat just when it was thought that the final answer had been given. The question now to be asked was, not How do we know? but, How do we use the word 'knowledge'?

This way, it would seem, by a sufficiently acute and detailed examination of the uses of the verb 'to know', no mistakes could be made; we would disclose exactly what we were doing when we talked about knowing.

But of course, this question as to the uses of the word 'Knowledge', was to be asked *after* the attempt to solve the problem of knowledge had failed. Now, as a reaction to that failure, we were to ask ourselves what we *meant* when we used the word 'Knowledge', what, in our ordinary, everyday talking, we used the word to refer to. But clearly the time to have asked that question would have been before setting out

129

with our modern techniques to solve the problem of knowledge. It is a sound methodological principle, first to define
your problem as clearly as you can, before trying to solve it.

If the question, How do we use the word 'Knowledge'? had
been asked before, instead of after, the failure to solve the
problem, one important consideration would have emerged.
Knowledge is, the word 'knowledge' is used as referring to,
something that is *common* to all individuals (of the same
cultural level); what is not common and communicable − the
hermit's ecstatic vision, the inebriate's red rats and blue
centipedes − is not knowledge in any accepted use of the
term. But the attempt to solve the problem of knowledge
was being entered into on the assumption that each individual
inferred his own knowledge directly from his own experience.
The recognition that 'knowledge' is used as meaning 'common
knowledge' would have indicated that there was something
amiss about this approach to the problem of knowledge.

What had happened was that, neglecting to define the problem before setting out to solve it, we had failed to solve it.
And now, having failed to solve the problem, we proceeded
to define it in such a way as not only to explain away our
failure but to legislate for all future thinking, so that that
difficulty should never confront us again.

By the time the question came to be asked, How do we
use the word 'knowledge'?, it was precisely knowledge as
common knowledge that was dismissed from consideration
as 'sheer misunderstanding', and all that the philosopher was
to concern himself with was individual uses of the word
'knowledge', without reference to the common element, or
what we call meaning, which made the words the individual
used instruments of communication.

This opportune formula, by means of which problems
which we have failed to solve are to be 'dissolved', has the
effect of by-passing the very problem which the development
of thought has presented to the modern consciousness: *How
has common knowledge, our common world-picture, been
derived from individual experience?* To this question the

answer so far given by the procedure of analysis is the negative and so inconclusive one, *The common world-picture is not a construction from any one individual's experience.*

It is with this in mind that we must now take up the story at the point where the philosopher, faced with a failure which was inexplicable from the short-term view to which he was committed, so incontinently dropped it. We want to take our own look at the established body of common knowledge and the symbolic system — language, words and their meanings — by means of which each of us raises the data of our private experience to the level of communicable knowledge.

Chapter I

MODERN APPROACH TO THE WORD

23. *The cry of 'Fire!'*

In a hotel corridor at night somebody shouts 'Fire!' This noise, radiating outward from its point of origin — the mouth of, say, the night porter — impinges upon the auditory apparatus of everyone within a suitable range, and then becomes a series of neurological impulses in the nervous systems of the persons concerned; the noise becomes, that is, a number of independent and purely private sensory stimulations.

But then a remarkable thing happens. All the persons concerned *react in exactly the same way* to these various private stimuli. They all, independently and by their own private impulsion, grab their nearest valuable possessions — their false teeth or their diamond necklace, as the case may be — and head for the stairs with all possible speed.

If these people had a sound philosophical training they would know that they couldn't do this. But luckily this wouldn't prevent them from doing it.

The noise *fire* produces this remarkable result because it becomes a special kind of data we call 'word'. The peculiar property that radiates outward with this noise, giving it this power to affect all these different individuals in the same way, is what we call its *meaning*.

Here two possible mistakes lie in wait for us, against which we must guard ourselves. The first is to say that, having defined meaning as the power associated with a particular sound to affect all hearers in this way, we have now solved 'the problem of meaning'. The second is to say, 'Of course we haven't solved the problem of meaning by seeing it as such a power. We don't know any more what this 'power' is than we know what 'meaning' is. We can't explain one term any more than the other. The whole idea is inexplicable; being inexplicable it is meaningless; and so the whole problem is a pseudo-problem with which we need not concern ourselves.' The first is the traditional attitude which, in the modern climate of thought, is not — or should not be — any longer viable. The second is its contemporary equivalent.

The meaning of the word, then, is this peculiar and as yet inexplicable value that attaches to it, this power to cause individuals who, by virtue of their individuality, are separate and isolated physical and psychic units, to act as though they were one individual.

But if (say) a New Guinea primitive had been among the hotel guests, this remarkable power of the word would have had no effect upon him. The noise *fire* would not have come to him as a special kind of data, having the unique value, *meaning*; it would come to him simply as a (perhaps rather peculiar) piece of natural data.

This draws our attention to the fact that the other guests, who grabbed their valuables and ran, stood in a special relation to this particular noise, and it was only by virtue of this special relation that it was able to exercise its peculiar power over them. Unless they all had been preconditioned to respond to the sound in a special way, and unless they had all been preconditioned to respond in the same way, the fire might have been disastrous.

Though each of the individuals concerned received the sound, the word 'Fire!', as purely *private* data, they all responded to its *common* meaning. This was because they had all been preconditioned to do so; they had all been trained from infancy onward to respond in a predetermined way to this specific sound.

But the question now arises, How had they been so predetermined, how so trained? The obvious answer is, by having these word-meanings impressed upon them by their elders, by repetition and example. They were taught the word 'fire' by having the sound *fire* made to them in the presence of an actual fire, and so learning that this sound had this particular meaning, that it was the symbol for that specific thing.

But this straightforward account of the matter gives rise to all sorts of peculiar difficulties, only one of which concerns us at the moment. The difficulty is this: In the above account, the word 'fire' is used to introduce the beginner to the word 'fire': words are being used to inculcate words; to inculcate, that is, these *common* meanings which are symbolized by their specific sounds. But where did the words come from in the first place?

For 'in the first place' words cannot have been used to inculcate words – actually to initiate and set going this strange apparatus of words. It is not just a matter of making sounds and allotting them meanings. Before the sound can acquire its meaning, the meaning itself – this *common* element that causes all the hotel guests to act in the same way – must be arrived at. This meaning, this power to make all who hear the sound act in the same way, must (to repeat) be something that is common to all parties concerned; not some capricious and personal piece of interpretation, but something that is equally valid, has the same authority, for all of them. This power, this meaning, before it can become operative, must be arrived at, and that means, it must be *agreed upon*, and agreement means *common* agreement.

But how, without the use of words, are men to arrive at the agreement which is to constitute meaning? How are they to set up a system of words, a language, without first having language with which to arrive at the necessary agreement?

24. *Who gave words their meaning?*

Our own look at the problem of knowledge and its symbolic system, language, has brought us face to face with the *word* as the pivot on which our whole structure of common understanding turns. The word is the point of contact between the discontinuities and indeterminacies of elementary individual experience and the body of common experience we call the world or reality.

In our progression toward this recognition of the vital role of the word as (to vary the metaphor) the keystone of the arch of knowledge, we saw that the first naive and natural statement of the problem of knowledge took the form: How comes it that the human individual, whose contacts with the world are brief and personal and limited to his own private data, is nevertheless able to know as much as he does know?

But this formulation, resting as it did upon the assumption that each individual created his own world-picture from his own experience, brought us up against the fact, which seemed to contradict the above assumption, that the individual *learns* his world-picture from his elders; and this, further, seemed to contradict the assumption that the individual's world-picture resulted from a direct confrontation of the *world*.

But this, again, brought us up against the fact that each individual, as an individual, is inescapably confined to his own experiential data, so that even the instruction of his elders reaches him as data which are private to him.

But this in turn brought us up against the fact that what the individual finally arrives at, no matter what view we take of his experiential data, is, not his own private world-picture, but his own replica of the common world-picture.

This, however, though an obvious fact, seemed to present an insoluble problem: How could the individual build up a *common* world-picture on the basis of his *private* data?

But this seemingly insoluble problem arose, we finally saw, from the assumption — until isolated for objective inspection it didn't seem like an assumption at all, it seemed like an obvious fact — that all the individual's experiential data were of the same order or value.

This we saw to be mistaken. Data are of two kinds, 'natural' and 'verbal', the latter being peculiar to the human individual. And once we had realized this, once we understood the role of these verbal data in the inculcation in the individual of the common world-picture, it became clear that the whole complex problem of knowledge was incapsulated in the question of the word and its meanings.

Once we had put on one side the obstructions and pro-hibitions of the 'revolution in philosophy', this was the course our inquiry naturally took. It led us to language, to the word and its meaning, as the core of the problem of know-ledge.

It is of interest then that those who, following the 'revolu-tion in philosophy', have repudiated the problem of knowledge as a pseudo-problem with which the philosopher need not concern himself, have set up in its place the examination of the working of language as the true business of philosophy. Instead of a generalized inquiry into the 'nature' or 'essence' of language and meaning, on the assumption that there is one characteristic function that language performs, one way in which words mean, there is to be a detailed and rigorous inquiry into the actual functioning of words in use. We are not to *think* about language but to *look* directly at it and see what sort of thing it really is, how it really works.

Earlier philosophers, said Wittgenstein, had got themselves into a muddle through a failure to understand the workings of language. What they thought of as a problem which they must solve was 'a muddle felt as a problem'; by taking a harder and closer look at language as it is actually used, we will avoid this muddle, and so will resolve — more precisely 'dissolve' — the ancient and troublesome problem.

Approaching the problem of meaning in this way, Witt-genstein says, 'A word has the meaning somebody has given it.' Such a view, it will be seen, effects a tremendous sim-plification of the problem of meaning. Meaning had been thought of traditionally as a sort of aura surrounding a word, a mysterious property or power by cashing-in on which (so to speak) we can use the word for our purposes of com-munication. But the question then arises, what is the *nature* of this aura of meaning accompanying the word? How do we cash-in on it? The problem seemed insoluble. Wittgenstein thought that he had finally solved it in the *Tractatus*, and then found that he hadn't. Must we then fall back again on 'some power independent of us' as the source and guarantor of meaning?

Wittgenstein's post-*Tractatus* treatment of meaning disposes – or let us be cautious and say, seems to dispose – of all these difficulties at a stroke: 'A word has the meaning somebody has given it.' The idea undoubtedly has a certain plausibility that appeals to us, over and above the relief we feel at not having to fall back uneasily on some supra-human power for the solution of our problem. Every word, it would seem, must have been used, on some specific occasion, for the first time. It must have been used *ab initio* by some individual, who thereby *gave the word its meaning*.

This of course does not mean simply its meaning *for him*. If the word is to have what we call meaning, it would be essential, not only that the individual in question *gave* the word a meaning, but that the meaning he gave it should be *accepted* by his fellows. It would be a necessary condition of the word's coming to have meaning, that the meaning he gave it should appeal to his fellows, so that they henceforth accepted the word as having that meaning.

Indeed, on consideration, it is precisely *this* that 'meaning' means; it is precisely this that (adopting Wittgenstein's approach to these matters) the word 'meaning' is used to mean. A word means what it is generally accepted as meaning. Failing such general acceptance – if, for instance, the word remained peculiar and private to the individual who invented it – it would not be said to have a meaning in the ordinary sense. It is (in a sense) its general acceptance that constitutes its meaning.

If the word our individual adopted as having a certain meaning failed to suggest that meaning to those about him, if it proved inadequate for the purpose he had devised it for, it would not have gone into general circulation and so would not have become what we call a word.

But thinking further about the matter, we can see that we

have just unwittingly uncovered a peculiar problem. Our original and apparently simple and straightforward statement of the matter was that somebody 'gave the word its meaning'. Consider for instance the word 'joy' – any word at all will do, we merely want to get down to cases. We are picturing (in accordance with Wittgenstein's suggestion) the occasion when somebody gave the word 'joy' its meaning. We are assuming, that is, that until then the word 'joy' had no meaning, it was standing round, so to speak, unused because no meaning had so far been allotted to it. Then this individual – somebody with what we might call a genius for language – said, 'Let the word "joy" mean "joy".' Or perhaps he merely used the word to mean *joy,* and at once everybody's reaction was, Why, 'joy' is precisely the word to express *joy.*

But now see what a peculiar assumption we find ourselves making: we have assumed that everybody had the feeling *joy,* for which hitherto there had been no name; and that, on the other hand, they had had the word 'joy', for which there had been no meaning; and that when this man with a sense of language, used the word 'joy' as the name for the feeling, *joy,* they at once recognized the word as expressing the feeling, and accordingly adopted it for that purpose.

But see what has happened. We started out by assuming that our individual gave the word its meaning; that the word 'joy' was standing round waiting for the meaning *joy* to be given to it; but in that case, 'joy' was not a word; until the meaning *joy* was given to it it was only a sound.

As a preliminary to any study of how words are actually used, the first thing to do is to see how the word 'word' is used – this is the same methodological principle that we saw applied to the word 'knowledge'. And the word 'word' is used as referring to a sound plus a meaning. Some arbitrary sound that I may choose to make – I myself, for instance, have a private way of referring to a certain kind of weather as 'Glumph' – is not a word, it is only a sound. A word is a sound plus a meaning, and a meaning is – the word 'meaning' means – a *common* meaning.

139

So the original situation did not consist of a *word* being given a meaning, of men possessing a purely functionless word, to which they one day allotted a function. It consisted of a *sound* being given a meaning. Or, more precisely — and we are trying to be precise in order to see how language really works, the sort of thing it really is — it consisted of a sound being used to symbolize a meaning. In fact we might go further and say that, as a basic principle of language, a sound was *specially devised* to symbolize that meaning. But that is a point that will come up for consideration later.

In the meantime another and highly significant consideration presents itself. On the one hand we have difficulty in accepting the idea of the functionless sound 'joy' having been in use before any meaning was found for it. On the other hand we now find it necessary, in giving an account of the transformation of the *sound* into a *word* by being given a *meaning,* to assume that the meaning, the *experience,* must have already existed, waiting (so to speak) for a sound to express it.

So that what happened is that, in trying to work out the idea of a word having been given a meaning, we have been forced to recognize (a) that (in keeping with the way we use the word 'word') 'joy' was not a word until it was given a meaning, it was only a sound, and (b) that it was not that the sound was given a meaning on the occasion of its first use as a word, but that an already existing meaning, an experience common to all men, was given (as we might say) a sound.

But this is a complete reversal of the assumption we started with. We accepted, as the straightforward and down-to-earth solution of the ancient and elusive problem of meaning, the proposition that 'every word had the meaning that somebody had given it'. It now seems that this only appealed to us as a solution of our problem because we had not given the matter proper thought. As soon as we begin to think about it, we see that the problem of meaning is not to be disposed of in this quick and easy way.

But of course, this wasn't our solution. It was simply that, not having given the matter any thought, we too readily accepted the solution offered to us by Wittgenstein. It was *his* solution – or resolution, or dissolution –of the problem of knowledge. And the interesting point is that, whereas we accepted it as the solution because we had not then given the matter any thought, it was for Wittgenstein the outcome of long and profound thought. This is an interesting fact that we must look further into. In the meantime, we feel impelled to ask, But surely Wittgenstein himself gave some more detailed account of *how* words – or let us now, in pursuit of precision, say *sounds* – got their meanings? And he in fact did do so, though, as so often with him, his statement is brief and rather cryptic.

> I want you to remember that words have those meanings which we have given to them; *and we give their meanings by explanations.*

I have italicized the key words here. As they stand, they hardly tell us what we want to know. But Wittgenstein goes on:

> I may have given a definition of a word and used the word accordingly, or those who taught me the use of the word may have given me the explanation . . .

This, however, is still not very helpful. The procedure he is now talking about is not, except in some very imprecise and unphilosophical sense, 'giving meanings to words'. It does not refer to somebody, for the first time, giving a meaning to a word (sound). In fact, it does not refer to the *giving* of a meaning at all except in the loose and ambiguous sense of 'Give me the meaning of "joy" ', which as a request for a definition, assumes that there is a word 'joy' with an accepted meaning. It is only the confusion between two senses of the word 'give' – two ways in which the word 'give' is used – that gives the impression that the problem of meaning has been further explicated. In the actual outcome, the problem has been further obscured, by confusing the learning (or teaching) of words and their meanings with their origin, the original devising of a specific sound to symbolize a given meaning.

We see the same procedure at work in another statement of Wittgenstein's concerning learning and language. 'One thinks,' he says, 'that learning a language consists of giving names to objects.' We must be careful, here; we are being shot at with a double-barrelled gun. We are having attributed to us not only a view of the nature of learning, but a view of the nature of language. We are being told that we think language is a system of names given to objects. For the sake of discussion let us accept this not-very-plausible doctrine. We say, 'Language consists of names which have been given to objects.' But having said that, would we say, 'Learning a language consists of giving names to objects'? Of course we wouldn't — not unless we had no idea of what the word 'learning' meant. Knowing what it means — knowing how it is actually and ordinarily used — we would say 'Learning a language consists of familiarizing ourselves with the names that have already been given to objects.'

Learning is not giving names *to* objects — it is learning the names *of* objects. Here the confusion is between some original 'giving of meanings to words', and someone who has been taught the word's meanings, now being able, when asked, to 'give the meaning of the word'.

We are reminded of Wittgenstein's comment that earlier philosophers had got themselves into a muddle, and had then mistaken the muddle for a problem. The situation now seems to be that we have been involved in another muddle as a way of escape from the problem. The difference is — and it is a significant difference — that, whereas earlier philosophers had been unaware of being in a muddle, the present situation is that the muddle is to be deliberately adopted as a way of thought. We are being offered the alternative: If you accept this way of looking at language and meaning, you can escape from the problem they present; if you don't accept it, you must fall back on the original muddle. The implication is that there is nothing in between.

25. *The shopkeeper and the shopping list: paradigm or parody?*

The examples we have just glanced at of Wittgenstein's approach to the emergent problem of words and meanings disclose a peculiar confusion, or, to use Wittgenstein's word in reference to earlier thinkers, muddle. This muddle we spoke of as deliberate, as opposed to the earlier unconscious muddle. But this, though correct, is not quite fair to Wittgenstein. The word 'deliberate' suggests 'deliberate dishonesty'. But Wittgenstein was above all a passionately honest man.

This is a situation that requires some explanation. In his Preface to his *Philosophical Investigations,* he says:

> The thoughts which I publish in what follows are the precipitate of philosophical investigations which have occupied me for the last sixteen years [since the collapse of the standpoint of the *Tractatus*]. They concern many subjects: the concepts of meaning, of understanding, of a proposition, of logic, of the foundations of mathematics, states of consciousness, and other things. I have written down all these thoughts as remarks, short paragraphs, of which there is sometimes a fairly long chain about the same subject, while I sometimes make a sudden change, jumping from one topic to another. — It was my intention at first to bring all this together in a book whose form I pictured differently at different times. But the essential thing was that the thoughts should proceed from one subject to another in a natural order without breaks. — After several unsuccessful attempts to weld my results together into such a whole, I realized I should never succeed. The best that I could write would never be more than philosophical remarks; my thoughts were soon crippled if I tried to force them on in a single direction against their natural inclination.

This is probably one of the most revealing documents in the whole history of thought: 'My thoughts were soon crippled if I tried to force them on in a single direction against their natural inclination.' In the preceding section we

L

143

have been doing what Wittgenstein here confesses that he found himself unable to do: we have been following his thoughts, his 'remarks', through to the point where their full implications begin to emerge. And we did this quite easily; it required no logical skill or philosophical insight.

Then why did Wittgenstein, a thinker of the first order, have such difficulty? Because, he says, he seemed to be forcing his thoughts against their 'natural inclination'. But it was when we, ourselves, followed the 'natural inclination' of his thought, that its logical implications, which we had not at first been aware of, became obvious to us. It required no more than an application of the doctrine of 'words in use', of seeing what the words, in which the thought was expressed, were actually used as meaning.

But in fact, we know what the source of Wittgenstein's difficulty was. It was that when he tried to elaborate his thought into a systematic pattern, *its* 'natural inclination' was to point back to just that problem of meaning which it was *his* natural inclination, since the collapse of the *Tractatus,* to exclude from philosophic discussion.

When, for instance, he says, 'A word has the meaning that somebody has given it', the immediate effect is to put the whole question of meaning on such a footing that the 'problem of meaning' is disposed of. But if he were to try to develop this 'remark' in any systematic way, his thought — his requirement that the problem of meaning is not to be discussed — would soon be 'crippled'.

Wittgenstein's fundamental difficulty is this: the failure of the *Tractatus* standpoint has convinced him that the problems he had been trying to solve were insoluble; and they were insoluble because they were pseudo-problems; and as pseudo-problems they were 'diseases of thought' which, as such, required to be purged from the human mind. This could be achieved if, (for instance) instead of asking 'What is the meaning of this word?' we were to ask 'How is this word used?' As Wittgenstein himself expressed it, in a 'remark' that has come to have the status of a philosophical principle,

'Don't ask for the meaning, ask for the use.'

But as we have found, and as Wittgenstein, as his Preface shows, also found, if, having placed a limitation on thought by asking for the 'use' instead of the 'meaning', you do conscientiously ask for the use, you find yourself brought back to the problem of meaning. If then you feel that it is urgently necessary to purge thought of this 'disease' — and Wittgenstein plainly did urgently and sincerely feel this — there is nothing for it but to place a further limitation on thought. Though you are to ask for the use instead of the meaning, you are to restrict yourself to only such reference to use as will not involve any reference to meaning.

It is obvious that to achieve this there can be no systematic and detailed argument. Nothing must be explicit, there must be suggestion and insinuation, rather than plain statement; questions raised and left unanswered, or answered by a still further question; subjects taken up, followed a certain distance, then dropped, to be taken up later with new accretions of significance which seem, somehow, to have carried the whole discussion an important stage further — and here 'an important stage further' means further away from the intrusive problem of meaning.

Wittgenstein is a master of this new way of philosophizing, which to the initiated presents an almost hypnotic fascination, and to the uninitiated, almost insuperable difficulties of understanding and consequent frustration and irritation. Anybody casually picking up the *Philosophical Investigations* will find it almost impossible to discover what it is 'all about'. This is because what it is all about is never explicitly stated. And it is never explicitly stated because, in the nature of the case, it cannot be so stated; the 'diseases of thought' are to be got rid of by a process of 'brainwashing', and such a process consists in setting up barriers to any reference to the forbidden thoughts.

But it will be of interest to glance briefly at the way in which Wittgenstein sets up his new subject of inquiry, 'words in use', in such a way as to exclude any reference to meaning.

145

At the outset of the *Philosophical Investigations,* he says:

> Now think of the following use of language: I send someone shopping, I give him a slip marked 'five red apples'. He takes the slip to the shopkeeper who opens the drawer marked 'apples'; then he looks up the word 'red' in a table and finds a colour sample opposite it; then he says the series of cardinal numbers — I assume that he knows them by heart — up to the word 'five' and for each number he takes an apple of the same colour as the sample out of the drawer. — It is in this and similar ways that one operates with words. — 'But how does he know where and how he is to look up the word "red" and what he is to do with the word "five"?' — Well, I assume that he *acts* as I have described. Explanations come to an end somewhere. 'But what is the meaning of the word "five"?' — No such thing in question here, only how the word 'five' is used.

Knowing Wittgenstein's peculiar requirements for a philosophy of language, we can recognize this as a move to get the inquiry of the *Philosophical Investigations* started on a basis that will exclude any reference to meaning. If we feel the same urgency to shake ourselves clear of this pervasive problem, we will applaud his account of the shopkeeper and the shopping list as an ingenious and (to the extent that we accept it) successful basis for a new approach. But if we are not driven on by the same necessity and sense of urgency we will feel impelled to ask, But is it in this and similar ways that one operates with words?

And even before we attempt to answer this question we are struck by the use of the word 'one' here. It may have no significance, but — knowing our Wittgenstein — it could be that we are being committed to the view that the functioning of words is a phenomenon that is peculiar and private to an individual. Wittgenstein doesn't *say* that this is so, and in fact argues elsewhere against the idea of a 'private language'. But by speaking of 'one' operating with words he conveys, or at least commits us to the view, that what we are here

dealing with can be understood without any reference to anyone but the individual operating with the words in question.
Indeed, the use of 'operating' gives the discussion another
nudge in the desired direction: words, it is suggested, don't
function, as we just now expressed it, they are operated with.

It is too soon for us to attempt to say how words *do*
function, but even as far as we have gone we can say that
they do *not* function – 'one' does not 'operate' with them –
in the manner described. In the first place words – whatever
their nature and however they work – are the small change
of communication. I wrote my list to convey to the shopkeeper that I wanted apples, on the assumption that any
normal shopkeeper would know what my words meant, i.e.
what they were intended to convey, what I was using them
for.

But, having sent my list by a messenger, my intention, the
purpose for which I wrote my words, plays (according to
Wittgenstein) no part in the transaction. In fact, from then
on it is not, as he describes it, a transaction. It isn't even an
instance of how we operate with words, for the shopkeeper
is not concerned with what I have written *as* words but
simply as marks on paper. He simply compares the mark I
have made, 'apples', with a mark on one of the drawers. He
looks at my mark, looks along the drawers till he sees one
with a similar mark on it, and produces what I want without
any idea that my mark 'apples' *meant* apples: this was the
whole purpose of this curious piece of shopkeeping lore.

But two difficulties at once present themselves. What a
lucky chance it was that the mark on the drawer was exactly
the same as mine. Normally the mark on the drawer would be
'APPLES', not as I wrote it, 'apples'. It was lucky, too, that
the mark on the drawer was 'apples', in script, just as mine
was. Indeed it must have been in a script *exactly* like mine
for the shopkeeper to be able to make the comparison. In
fact, as individual handwritings differ so much, the mark on
the drawer must have been either in *my* handwriting or an
exact copy of it, otherwise the difference between my mark

LANGUAGE

on the shopping list and the mark on the drawer would have completely defeated the shopkeeper.

The fact is that if I got my apples it was either by a series of extraordinary lucky chances or else — the second and more important point — the shopkeeper did after all know that what I had written was not just a mark but was the specific kind of mark we call a word, and that it *meant* the kind of thing that was in the drawer in which were kept, as the mark 'APPLES' indicated, the apples.

Wittgenstein himself obviously realized that if his story of the shopkeeper is followed out in detail it will lead back to words and their meanings — that, in other words, it is not in this or in any such way that we operate with words — when he finally says, 'I assume he *acts* as I have described. Explanations come to an end somewhere. No such thing as [meaning] is in question here, only how words are used [by the shopkeeper alone in his shop].'

If we are prepared to accept all these lucky chances, supported by these assumptions and reservations, then the problem of meaning need trouble us no more.

'If we look at this example,' says Wittgenstein, 'we may perhaps get an inkling how much this general notion of the meaning of a word surrounds the working of language with a haze that makes clear vision impossible. It disperses the fog to study the phenomena of language in primitive kinds of application in which one can command a clear view of the aim and functioning of words.'

Wittgenstein seems to be suggesting that the shopkeeper comparing the marks on the paper with the marks on the drawer provides a paradigm of the working of language, before meanings intruded to make things difficult — difficult for the philosopher, that is, though of course infinitely more fruitful for mere communicating men.

But if we are interested in — not overawed and defeated by — the problem of meaning, we will leave the shopkeeper alone in his shop to carry on (or fail to carry on) his own affairs in his own queer way, and consider instead an instance

148

such as that of the cry of 'Fire!' in the hotel corridor. Here we have a paradigmatic situation that brings out the real workings of language as, not a private act, but a transaction. For it illustrates for us the *common* element in the spoken word, and it is this common element that we refer to when we use the word 'meaning'.

But even if we accept Wittgenstein's chosen example we can, by sticking honestly to the facts, give an account of the shopkeeper's procedure which is *really* rigorous while still being independent of the idea of his activities as involving any reference to meaning as a mystical haze obscuring the working of words.

And in fact there is one respect, at least, in which we can straightaway put the above account on a sounder footing. There is no need to evade, as Wittgenstein does, the question of how the shopkeeper knows what to do when confronted with my list, because we know how he knows this: he has been taught what to do. As far as his actions are concerned there is no mystery to make us uneasy, and Wittgenstein himself later makes this point when he points out that the use of language is governed by rules which must be learned.

We know that from infancy onward the shopkeeper (otherwise he wouldn't be a shopkeeper) has been inducted into a system of symbols — spoken sounds and marks on paper. — That is to say, he has been conditioned to respond in certain specified ways to certain sounds or marks, in much the same way that Pavlov's dogs were conditioned to respond to the sound of a buzzer. There is, however, a significant difference between the two procedures of conditioning. Pavlov's dogs were trained to produce a natural response, salivation, to a stimulus they normally would not have responded to in this way. But our future storekeeper was trained to produce a non-natural response, reaching for apples in this instance, to a non-natural stimulus, a specially devised sound or mark — devised, that is, for the special purpose of serving a predetermined end.

So our shopkeeper has been conditioned to respond in a

certain way to certain symbols. We know, roughly, how this conditioning has been achieved. The general principle is that when he was a child his elders patted him on the head and said, 'That's the little man,' and their approval – often more indirect than this, of course – reinforced his use of the given symbol, at the same time familiarizing him with the uses to which it can be put.

Meantime – an important point not so far referred to – his future customers have been submitted to a similar conditioning; they have been trained in a similar pattern of responses to the same system of symbols. So that when, finally, the shopkeeper looks at my shopping list – that is to say, when he experiences certain visual sensory-data, certain stimulations of his optic nerves – he is able to respond to such purely private data – the movements in his nervous system – in the way that I, who wrote the list, intended that he should.

By this time – remember, this process of training has been going on since infancy, so that the system of symbols and responses has been *built into* his developing consciousness – by this time his acts of producing the appropriate response to the given symbol have become so habitual, so much a part of his nature, as we might say, that he is quite unconscious of them, and it is only at the level of philosophical inquiry that we can be aware what is actually taking place. And even then, as we see, if we have other philosophical fish to fry, it is quite easy to ignore this subliminal transaction between a given stimulus and predetermined response.

So, in our account of the shopkeeper's dealings with my shopping list, there is no more reference to meaning than there was in the other account. But our account is fuller and more rigorous than the other; we haven't had to assume the very thing that needed accounting for – the shopkeeper's ability to respond appropriately to my list – or brush aside the questions that naturally arose.

At the same time, it must be admitted that our account, though preferable, and just as rigorous as Wittgenstein's, in that no reference is made to meaning as a mysterious, extra-human explanatory principle justifying the shopkeeper's behaviour, is intolerably prolix. But this prolixity was due to the fact that we were *describing* the procedure, not *using* it. If we are simply using the symbol-response procedure, as we normally and unthinkingly do, our account of the shopkeeper's doings can be reduced to much simpler terms, without any loss of rigour. We can say, 'The storekeeper, knowing the meaning of the words I had written down, knew I wanted apples.'

This simpler version, of course, brings us back to 'words' and 'meanings'. But we see now – and this must be reckoned a significant gain – that there is nothing mysterious involved in the use of these terms in describing the shopkeeper's behaviour when confronted with my list. They are simply abbreviations, compact and convenient ways of saying what we have just been saying at greater and more informative, though rather boring, length. It saves time, trouble and patience to use an abbreviation like 'meaning' in describing what the shopkeeper did, and we can do so without any qualms, because we know how he came to be able to respond appropriately to the symbols I had written down.

If he happened to be that exceptional thing, a shopkeeper who had never been initiated into the established symbolic system, he might have to compare the mark 'apple' on my paper with a mark on the drawer where the apples are, in order to produce what I want, though it is doubtful if, on those terms, he would last long in business, or would even have been in business in the first place. But this would not be a paradigm case of how one operates with words. And if I had written 'Two pounds of apples', he would certainly have been put to it to find the drawer containing the 'of's.

Well, then, our account of the shopkeeper's response to the shopping list being (let us claim without any mock modesty) a better one than Wittgenstein's – more informative as to what actually happened, and more rigorous – would Wittgenstein have been willing to accept it in place of his account? The answer, on all the evidence, is, No. This is so because, though our account makes no more reference to meaning than his did — it merely speaks of predetermined responses to given symbols, and so tells us all and more than he told us — it points directly to the question: How did these non-natural symbols come to be associated with these predetermined, non-natural responses? And *that* is the traditional problem of meaning.

But having said this, we now become aware of a further advantage that accrues from our more detailed account of the shopkeeper's behaviour. For it helps us to break the spell of the traditional formulation of the problem, which, as we know, seemed to make the problem insoluble, thus causing Wittgenstein to repudiate it as a 'muddle seen as a problem', a 'pseudo-problem', a 'disease of thought'.

Traditionally, the question asked was: What *is* Meaning?, the 'is' and the capital M having the effect of attributing to meaning the sort of supra-experiential status that, in fact, put it beyond rational explication. When philosophers revolted against this frustrating transcendental approach to the problem, they next said — too precipitately and overconfidently, we now know — 'Why, meaning is simply something man himself has created out of his own experience of the world about him.'

But, the question then arose, *how* did he create meaning out of his experience of the world? And the simple answer was: Each individual is equipped with a sensory system; on the basis of the impressions produced in his sensory system by the things around him, he builds up his knowledge, and the necessary language — words and their meanings — with which to express it.

But this simple and plausible account of the matter, which was tossed up rather too brashly as 'one in the eye' for the transcendentalists, wouldn't work any better than the transcendental account had done. If the philosopher had stopped to think, he almost certainly would have seen why it wouldn't work. But he didn't stop to think. His nerve failed him and he ran for cover. He took refuge from the problem of meaning, which he couldn't accept as a mysterious aura and couldn't account for as a function of human experience, by setting up as a paradigm of our use of words what was in fact a parody of that use.

And this parody had the disastrous effect of further confusing an already confused issue, by shuffling out of sight the fact that what the shopkeeper is doing is not something that is private and peculiar to him, an isolated and self-sufficient piece of behaviour on his part — which is, we can see, the original unworkable individual-experience view of meaning creeping up on us again in disguise. What he is doing, i.e., responding appropriately to the symbols he sees on the paper before him, is something that gains its significance and proves functional and fruitful, and effective in a general pattern of human intercourse, by the fact that the symbols to which he responds, and the responses he makes, are part of an already established, commonly-held communication system. And this — as our fuller account makes clear, and as, in any case, logical analysis has shown — is something which, to the extent that it is a function of human experience, is not a function of the experience of the individual who in any given case is responding appropriately to the presented symbols.

Any plausibility that Wittgenstein's account has is due to the fact that the shopkeeper isn't doing what we are told he is doing. The account only works because it 'cashes in' on the common body of meanings which it claims to eliminate. If I get my apples it is because the shopkeeper, on seeing my list, interprets his private visual data in terms of the established system of common concepts.

And this is not a procedure in any way analogous to the comparing of marks, it is a procedure of an entirely different kind; and it is this difference of kind that makes language the unique thing it is; and it is this uniqueness, this peculiar difference from any other activity practised by living creatures, that seems to call for explanation, and to be, by its very nature, capable of explanation.

And — a further challenging consideration — it would seem that an explanation of this unique human achievement would itself constitute not only a new, but a *new kind* of knowledge; for it would be the elucidation of thought by thought, which, otherwise expressed, would be thought's self-elucidation.

What does this mean? As of now, we can't say. But perhaps if we don't run away from the facts, we may find out. But for those who are nervous in the dark there is always the comforting bed-time story of the illiterate shopkeeper and the five red apples.

26. *'Primary' and 'secondary' meaning*

But surely, it might be said, Wittgenstein could not have devoted sixteen years of concentrated thought to these matters without somewhere stumbling on the fact that, after all, what he was talking about was something that functioned as it did, that was the sort of thing it was, just because it was *common* to all men; the fact, more precisely, that his account of the shopkeeper and shopping list only served his purpose of disposing of the question of meaning, because it was an instance of an individual interpreting his immediate sensory data, on seeing the symbols on the paper, in terms of an already established system of common meaning. Surely this fact must have forced itself upon his notice somewhere in all his minute discussion of the working of language.

And, indeed, it did force itself upon him, more than once.

'Here,' he says, 'one might speak of a "primary" and "secondary" sense (meaning) of a word. It is only if the word has the primary sense for you that you can use it in the secondary sense.' This is clearly a reference to the store-keeper's producing his response to the *common* symbols, giving the meaning 'apple' to his immediate sensory data, by bringing these under the appropriate common concept 'Apple'.

And again, ' . . . we cannot be dealing with the same

concept of experience here. It is a different though related concept.' Here the suggestion of two *different* but related kinds of experience is evidently a reference to *common* experience — our system of common concepts, our common world-picture — as distinct from subjective individual experience which becomes communicable as knowledge by being brought under — interpreted in terms of — the common concepts.

Again, more obliquely and yet more to the point, he says, 'Interpretations by themselves do not determine meaning.' The shopkeeper, for instance, didn't determine the meaning of the symbol 'apple' which I had written down — except in the same, ambiguous, sense of 'determine' that we saw used of 'give' in an earlier example. It is clear from the fact that I had written down the symbol in full confidence that the shopkeeper would know what I wanted that there was no question of the meaning of the symbol being dependent on the shopkeeper's interpretation. The meaning — the common meaning — clearly predated the shopkeeper's interpretation.

Again: ' . . . the form of expression we use seems to have been designed for (by?) a god, who knows what we (I?) cannot know . . . ' (We are reminded here of a comment of Bertrand Russell's: 'Our words seem to know more than we know.') The reference here is obviously to the fact that the established body of common experience transcends the experience of any of the individuals who participate in it.

This hidden theme, in fact, pervades in an obscure way a facet of Wittgenstein's thinking to which he attributed great importance. We have already looked at his statement that 'one thinks that learning a language consists in giving names to objects'. As we then noted, if one gives the matter a moment's thought one does *not* think this; the meaning of the word 'learning' — its accepted use — prevents us from doing so: to *learn* names is not to *give* names. But the statement is a double-barrelled one, and we now want to look at the other half, the suggestion that one thinks that language is a system of names given to objects.

This thesis, that words meant by naming what they referred to, that this was the essence of language, the *one* thing that it did, was the assumption underlying the doctrine of Logical Atomism, which Wittgenstein took over from Bertrand Russell and elaborated in the *Tractatus* in his own characteristic way, and finally abandoned.

We needn't concern ourselves with the rights or wrongs of the thesis itself, whose peculiar features were not at once obvious to its exponents because of the highly technical nature of the considerations that had led up to it. All we are interested in is the fact that, having abandoned the idea of *meaning* being *naming*, Wittgenstein, as we have seen, didn't say, 'That being so, what *does* meaning essentially consist in?' He said, instead, 'That being so, there is no such thing as meaning.'

But that being accepted, the question arises, What is it that gives sense and significance to the words we use? The answer Wittgenstein gave to this was, 'The way we use them. A word means what it is used to mean.' (We have already looked at one implication of this, 'a word has the meaning that somebody gave it on some occasion of its use' — and the difficulties that this gives rise to.)

What now concerns us, though, is that, once the idea of words as meaning by naming what they refer to has been abandoned, the idea that there is *one* function that words perform also goes by the board. Instead, 'There are *countless* different kinds of use of what we call "symbols", "words", "sentences".'

If we think of the countless number of words that there are, and the countless uses to which each word can be put, how can we possibly hope to 'explain' all this complexity and diversity? The best we can hope to do is to 'describe' it. 'Explanation,' Wittgenstein tells us, 'must give place to description.' The detailed description of how words are actually used — as in the case of the shopkeeper responding to the shopping list — is to be the sole business of the philosopher.

There arises here, perhaps, the thought that, after all, it has not been shown, with the abandonment of meaning as naming, that there is no *one* thing that words do. It might be suggested that, on the contrary, it has been shown by the very fact of this complexity and diversity of uses to which words are put, that the essential and characteristic function that they perform is to serve the multifarious and complex demands of human communication; that this is the one thing that words do.

But Wittgenstein didn't want words to have one kind of use, he wanted them to have 'countless' uses, all different, for in this way there was no temptation to try to 'explain' that one function, as he himself had been tempted into doing in the *Tractatus*. So, having rejected the idea that naming was the one thing that words did, he 'taught us' to give up all idea of there being any single characteristic job that words did.

'It is important to note,' he said, 'that the word "meaning" is being used illicitly if it is used to signify the [thing] that "corresponds" to the word. That is to confound the meaning of a name with the bearer of a name.'

What Wittgenstein is in effect saying is that when I use the word, say, 'man', as in 'I see a man', the word 'man' as I here use it does not *mean* the man to whom I am referring. A moment's reflection will show us that this is correct, and that it is quite a significant point. Because a moment later, seeing another man, I can again say 'I see a man', and now the word 'man', as I use it, *refers to* a different man to the one referred to in the first sentence. So the word 'man' cannot *mean* what in each of the two different statements it *refers to,* for in that case it would have two quite different meanings.

Now this brief discussion of Wittgenstein's reason – and a perfectly good reason it is – for rejecting the idea of words meaning by naming, draws our attention to two interesting points. The first is that Wittgenstein here shows us – though this was certainly not his intention – that a word cannot correctly be said to 'mean what it is used to mean'. If this were correct, then when I said, 'I see a man', the word 'man' would mean the man I was referring to on that occasion of the use of the word, and Wittgenstein has just shown us – and we have agreed – that this would be a mistake. And the situation would become further complicated when I used the word a second time to refer to another man, for then it would now 'mean' (falsely) that man.

The other point raised by Wittgenstein's rejection of *meaning* as *naming* is even more interesting. For it leaves us with the word 'man' as having two senses of meanings, or, say, functions. When I say 'I see a man', I am certainly using the word meaningfully, though the word does not here *mean* the man I am referring to. What is the explanation of this peculiar situation?

Wittgenstein himself has already given us the clue to it. This is an illustration of what he speaks of as the 'primary' and 'secondary' sense of a word. It is only if the word has the primary sense for me, he says, that I can use it in the secondary sense. When I say 'I see a man', what I am doing is, giving my secondary sense interpretation to the primary or general term, man. Or, as we expressed it, in reference to the shopkeeper and the shopping list, I am giving the meaning 'man' to my immediate sensory data – my 'seeing' of the man – by bringing these data under the appropriate common concept, *man*.

So what Wittgenstein has here done – in addition to incidentally pointing to a peculiar ambiguity lurking in 'words in use' – is to illustrate the fact – which it was his purpose to deny – that the sort of thing we mean by 'meaning', the sort of thing we use the word 'meaning' to refer to, the sort of thing that he has aptly called primary meaning, is not a function of the experience of the individual using the term (say) 'man'.

In other words, to talk of the meaning residing in the use is to talk of 'secondary' sense determining 'primary' sense, though Wittgenstein has said that it was only because the word has 'primary' sense that it can be used in the 'secondary' sense.

We have met this peculiar characteristic of contemporary thought before, this vacillation of thought between the two senses of knowledge and meaning common to 'primary' knowledge, the knowledge which is common to all the members of the group, and individual or 'secondary' knowledge, the knowledge achieved by the individual in the act of bringing his private data under the system of common concepts. At the outset of our inquiry we saw the physiologist, taking up the task of accounting for knowledge, telling us first that 'The brain of each one of us does literally create our own world', then that 'Our ways of observing and speaking are not our own but are inherited and learned', and finally, returning to the original standpoint, 'Each individual forms his own way of life, his own order and rules.'

Chapter II

SIDELIGHTS ON LINGUISTIC PHILOSOPHY

27. *The 'Fido' fallacy: connotation and denotation*

Wittgenstein, as usual, doesn't give us any systematic exposition of what was meant by 'use' in the phrase: Don't ask for the meaning, ask for the use. He is content to point out that the concept of meaning has been accepted as implying that there is just *one* function that words perform, whereas, he is now saying — now, after the failure of the *Tractatus* account of meaning — there are *countless uses* to which words are put.

Here, to adapt a phrase of Wittgenstein's, we have a whole revolution in philosophy condensed into a drop of language. But the condensation is so drastic that the uninitiated reader, approaching for the first time the *Philosophical Investigations*, is likely to find himself completely at a loss as to 'what it is all about'.

And what makes it all the more puzzling is that, whereas in the *Tractatus* Wittgenstein had been concerned with an approach so highly technical to so technical a problem — the logic of symbolic reference — that the outsider wasn't even tempted to try to understand it, now, in the *Philosophical Investigations* he seems to be asking the most disarmingly naive questions, and going about answering them in a straightforward, common-sense way. But very soon this proves to be delusive. Simple as the questions asked seem to be, the uninitiated reader can't make out what they are 'getting at', what it is that Wittgenstein is trying to establish.

At this point what is wanted is a drop of philosophical history to provide the background to the revolution in philosophy that the innocent reader has found himself

161

plunged into. Professor Ryle has sketched in such a background for us in a paper on 'The Theory of Meaning', and we can conveniently use his account of the matter as our point of departure.

Outlining the steps by which philosophy was progressively deprived of its subject-matter, first by the advances of the empirical sciences, and then by the break-away movement of psychology as a science in its own right, Professor Ryle shows how philosophy, from being a superior science of mind, became a simple — but not so simple as it turned out — inquiry into concepts and propositions and what they meant.

> Thus, by the first decade of the century it was dawning upon philosophers and logicians that their business . . . (had) to do with a special domain which was not bespoken by any other discipline, namely, the so-called third realm of logical objects or meanings.

It was here that Wittgenstein, coming to Cambridge as a student of philosophy under Russell from an earlier devotion to engineering, plunged with an eagerness and intensity that was to characterize his whole philosophical career, into the complex problems that were arising as a result of a new method of inquiry, symbolic logic, into a new set of questions, those of the relation of language to Reality. Out of this early phase emerged the *Tractatus* in which, Wittgenstein claimed, the problems dealt with had been 'definitely solved'.

And now the first shadow of the forthcoming 'revolution in philosophy' was cast across the busy scene.

'At this point,' says Ryle, 'the collapse of the denotationist theory of meaning began to influence the theory of philosophy . . . '

At this point we had better stop and see precisely what this means. What was the denotationist 'theory of meaning', why did it collapse, and how did its collapse influence the theory of philosophy, the idea, that is, of what philosophy was about?

'For our purpose,' says Ryle, 'it is near enough true to say that the first influential discussion of the notion of meaning given by a modern logician was that with which John Stuart Mill opens his *System of Logic* (1843).'

Mill took over from Hobbes, though with some important modifications, the idea of words as *meaning* by *naming* thoughts. But Mill at once asks, 'Are names more properly said to be the names of things or of our ideas of things?' And answering his own question, he says, 'when I say "the sun is the cause of day", I do not mean that my idea of the sun causes or excites in me the idea of day, I mean that a certain physical fact, which is called the sun's presence (*and which, in the ultimate analysis, resolves itself into sensations, not ideas*) causes another physical fact, which is called day.'

The parenthetical statement which I have italicized is of peculiar interest. It is an early reference to an idea which recurs repeatedly throughout Mill's discussion of meaning. The idea finds explicit expression in the statement 'that *all we know* of objects, is the sensations which they give us and the order of the occurrence of those sensations', or, as he puts it in a famous phrase, 'matter is the permanent possibility of sensation'.

The interest of this is that it reminds us of Russell's claim, 'I do not see physical objects; I see effects which they produce in the region where my brain is . . . What is really known is a correlation of muscular and other bodily sensations with changes of visual sensations.' It is of interest to note that where Russell attributes his idea of things to his own sensations, Mill speaks of 'sensations of our own, and of other sentient beings', and even of 'all the distinctions which have been recognized, not only by a single inquirer, but by all inquirers taken together.'

This latter idea is not further developed by Mill and is even later on contradicted. But it is of interest because, while affirming that words are names, not of our ideas of things, but of the things themselves, he is at the same time saying that what we call things are complexes of sensations, and even complexes of or constructions from all men's sensations. He sees words as names of things which are complexes of sensations. So he is saying (a) that words are names of things-themselves and (b) that they are names of sensory complexes.

Though Mill doesn't stop to work out these two seemingly contradictory notions of meaning (which we note simply as a fact; not as a criticism; even as formulated some seventy years later by Russell, the difficulty persists that we are said not to know *things* but only the sensations *they* cause in us) — these two notions of meaning crop up in another form in Mill's thought; in his famous distinction between words as both *connoting* and *denoting*.

The distinction arose in the first place when Mill, elaborating his doctrine of words as meaning by being the names of things-themselves, not of our idea of things, pointed out that words did not name things in the same way that proper names name things. As Ryle, discussing Mill's treatment, puts it: 'A dog may be called "Fido", but the word "Fido" conveys no information or misinformation about the dog's qualities, career, whereabouts, etc. . . . Dictionaries do not tell us what proper names mean — for the simple reason that they do not mean anything. The word "Fido" names or denotes a particular dog, since it is what he is called. But there is no room for anyone who hears the word "Fido" to understand or misunderstand it or fail to understand it.'

What this amounts to, in fact, is that 'Fido' is not a *word* in any proper sense of the term. Mill saw this when he compared a proper name such as 'Fido' to the mark which the robber in the Arabian Nights made in the house which was to be plundered. 'The mark has a purpose,' says Mill, 'but it has not properly any meaning . . . when we propose a proper name, we perform an operation in some degree analogous to what the robber intended in chalking the house.'

Ryle makes the same point when he goes on, 'Proper names are arbitrary bestowals, and convey nothing true and nothing false, for they convey nothing at all . . . calling a star by a certain name is not saying anything about it, and saying something true or false about a star is not naming it.' And he adds, 'Saying is not naming and naming is not saying.'

Now the interest of all this is that, in a round-about way that we needn't go into, the doctrine — the dual doctrine actually — that words named things, and that for every word there was a thing which was the meaning of the word, became the basis of that Logical Atomism which, enunciated by Russell, was worked out by Wittgenstein in the *Tractatus* to the point where it proved to be unworkable; the point, as Ryle puts it, where 'the collapse of the denotationist theory of meaning began to influence the theory of philosophy'.

'Mill,' says Ryle, 'got a further important point right about these genuine proper names ("Fido", "London", etc.); he said that while most words and descriptive phrases both denote or name and connote, proper names only denote and do not connote.'

What precisely is this distinction between *denotation* and *connotation?* Simply stated it is this: Proper names merely name or denote a specific individual object, such as my dog Fido; real words both connote or mean a certain *class* of things and denote (or name) an *individual instance* of that class. 'Tree', in the dictionary sense, connotes or means a certain class of things and is used by me to denote (name) an individual instance of the class 'tree'. The word 'tree', as it appears in the dictionary, does not denote (name) any individual tree, it connotes or means all things of the kind 'tree'. I, being familiar with its connotation, can use the word 'tree' to denote (name) the particular tree I am interested in at the moment.

This is obviously the same distinction between the two senses of meaning referred to by Wittgenstein as 'primary' and 'secondary' sense. 'It is only if the word has the primary sense for you [its dictionary meaning or connotation] that you use it in the secondary one [its denotation or use-meaning].'

This distinction between the two aspects of meaning crops up in various technical forms. A noted logician, Rudolph

Carnap, remarks in his *Meaning and Necessity*, referring to Frege's use of 'nomenatum' (denotation) and 'sense' (connotation), 'It seems to me that we find in the historical development *two* pairs of correlated concepts, appearing in various forms.' In Frege's use of 'nomenatum' we can recognize the view of meaning as naming; there is on one hand the 'sense' or connotation or dictionary meaning, and on the other hand the 'nomenatum' (nomen = name) or thing named or denoted by the use of the word. Carnap, pointing out various difficulties arising from the use of the 'name relation' for the explanation of meaning, prefers to substitute for nomenatum and sense the terms extension and intension, and supports his standpoint with a skilful technical argument.

28. *From naming to denotation*

The interest of the foregoing is that it shows us the extent to which the *denotation* of words — my use of the word to indicate or denote my present experience of the sort of thing *connotated* by the word — has become associated with the idea of *naming,* as though words, in their denotative use, named things in the same way that 'Fido' names my dog Fido.

But when I say, pointing to Fido, 'that is a dog', I have not *named* the dog in the way that 'Fido' names him. I have said, in effect (as Mill himself implied, without working out the implication of this standpoint), 'The sensations I am now experiencing belong under the common concept *dog*.' I know that this is so because I have been taught that sensations of that kind come under that concept. The concept defines a class of things, or say experiences, and I say that my present experience belongs to that (common) class.

So, in the same way that naming a thing — 'Fido', 'London', 'Bill Smith' — is not, as Ryle has pointed out, saying anything about that thing, so saying 'That is a dog', is not naming the dog in question. Ryle himself expresses this succinctly,

'Saying is not naming and naming is not saying.' 'That is,' Ryle says, 'Mill virtually reaches the correct conclusions that the meaning of an expression is never the thing or person referred to by means of it;' — when I say 'That is a tree,' the tree I refer to is not the meaning of 'tree' — 'and that descriptive phrases, and, with one exception, single words are never names, in the sense of 'proper names'. The exception is just those few words which really are proper names, i.e. words like 'Fido', and 'London', the words which 'do not appear in dictionaries' — which are not, in fact, words at all in the proper sense.

Naming, Ryle makes clear, has nothing to do with meaning, either with the connotative or the denotative sense of meaning.

This brings us back to the point we set out to explicate, ' . . . the collapse of the denotationist theory of meaning' — marked by Wittgenstein's repudiation of the *Tractatus* — 'began to influence the theory of philosophy' — began the development which led to the 'revolution in philosophy' and found its complete expression in *Philosophical Investigations*. 'In the *Tractatus* . . . ,' says Ryle, 'Wittgenstein still had one foot in the denotationist camp . . . It was only later still that he deliberately withdrew his remaining foot from the denotationist camp', when he said 'Don't ask for the meaning, ask for the use.'

At this point we become aware of something amiss. Connotation is the *meaning*, in the dictionary sense, the 'primary sense', of the word. Denotation is the individual's *use* of the word to indicate an instance of that meaning. But now we are told that Wittgenstein instituted the 'revolution in philosophy' by taking both feet out of the denotationist camp and treating meaning as use. But, denotation *being* use — my *use* of the word to *denote* an instance of the class *connoted* by the word — it would seem that what Wittgenstein has actually done by adopting the use-aspect of meaning, is to place both feet deliberately *in* the denotationist camp. Well, not deliberately, in that case, because this is obviously not what he thought of himself as doing, any more than it is what Professor Ryle thinks.

What has happened to cause this confusion in the accepted account of the 'revolution in philosophy'? Wittgenstein, as we see, has adopted *denotation* in place of *connotation*, the 'secondary' or use sense as against the 'primary' sense of meaning. But it is said that, in doing so, he has taken his foot out of the camp he had previously belonged to, in the *Tractatus*. What camp did he belong to in the *Tractatus*? What was he trying to do?

As we know, his purpose in the *Tractatus* was to show the relation between language and Reality. How did he approach this task? Let us get at this by noting a comment of Ryle's, 'I want to make you at least suspect that this initially congenial equation of words and descriptive phrases with names is from the outset a monstrous howler. . . . It was, as he himself says in his new book [*Philosophical Investigations*], a fetter round the ankles of Wittgenstein in the *Tractatus* . . .' This is what Wittgenstein was referring to, in his peculiar oblique way, when he said, in a passage we have already examined, 'One thinks [i.e. he himself had once thought] that learning a language means giving names to objects.' The point is further clarified by Ryle's reference to 'the denotationist assumption that almost all words, all phrases and even all sentences are alike in having the one role of naming.'

So the camp that Wittgenstein belonged to, the doctrine that he sponsored, was that words were names of things, that they *meant* by naming, or, as it was said, by *naming* or *denoting*.

This assimilation of meaning to naming was, as Ryle puts it, a 'monstrous howler'. But now, I think, we can see what happened to cause the confusion we are examining. The *Tractatus* was based on the assumption that meaning was naming, and that naming was denoting.

When it was said that, after the collapse of the denotational theory of meaning, Wittgenstein took both feet out of the *denotationist* camp, what is really meant is that, after the collapse of the theory that meaning was naming, Wittgenstein took both feet out of the *naming* camp. Accepting meaning now as *use,* he adopted, whether this was what he regarded himself as doing or not, a denotationist theory of meaning as against a connotationist theory.

Mill had said that real words, as distinct from proper names which had no *meaning,* both connoted (their 'primary' sense), and denoted (their 'secondary' or use-sense). Wittgenstein is laying the foundations of the new way of philosophizing by placing the emphasis on denotation and leaving connotative meaning out of consideration.

He once thought that naming was the one function that words performed; he now thinks that they have, not one function, but *countless uses.* By-passing connotation, he has moved from naming to denoting as the job that words do; leaving the 'primary' sense out of account, he has concentrated on the 'secondary' sense as giving the essence of meaning, though he has himself said that the use of the word in its secondary sense is dependent upon its primary (connotative) sense.

In the light of this we can understand why it is that, when Ryle turns to an elucidation of 'use' in 'Don't ask for the meaning, ask for the use ', his account presents peculiar difficulties.

'The use of an expression, or the concept it expresses, is the role it is employed to perform, not any thing or person or event for which it might be supposed to stand.' The latter part of this statement is simply telling us, what we have already seen to be the case, that the meaning of a word is not some thing that it is said to name or stand for.

What interests us is the statement that 'The use of an expression is the role it is employed to perform.' The defining phrase here is 'employed to perform'. To perform means simply, to do. To employ, is to make use of. 'Role' is somewhat ambiguous here, but, with 'employed to perform', it seems to mean 'what the word is used for'. So 'the use of an expression is the role it is employed to perform' seems to tell us no more than that the use of a word is what it is used for.

This account of 'use' may seem satisfactory to anyone who has already accepted the dictum that meaning is use. But to anyone trying to understand what this precisely means, the above account will hardly prove helpful.

Again Ryle says, 'To know what an expression means involves . . . knowing a set of bans, fiats and obligations, or, in a word, it is to know the rules of the employment of that expression.' It is these rules for the employment of the commonly held system of concepts that we are inducted into from infancy onwards, and are thus enabled to use these concepts for the organization of our private experiential data. Knowing the *rules* we are able to *use* the concepts. But this means that the meaning resides in the rules of employment, the connotation or primary or dictionary sense of the word, not in its denotation or use.

'Considering the meaning (or Mill's "connotation") of an expression is considering what can be said with it, i.e. said truly or falsely, as well as asked, commanded, advised or any other sort of saying. In this, which is the normal sense of "meaning", the meaning of a sub-expression like a word or phrase, is a functional factor of a range of possible assertions, questions, commands and the rest.'

This, we can see, is intended to show the meaning of a word as dependent upon its possible uses; 'a word means what it is used to mean.' But do the possible uses determine its meaning, or does the meaning determine the possible uses? The purpose of this formulation, of course, is to deny the latter and assert the former. But if you must know the rules for the word's use in order to be able to use it — and this certainly is the case — then it is the meaning that determines the use, and not the other way around.

The meaning of a word, Ryle goes on, 'is a distinguishable common locus of a range of possible tellings, askings, advisings, etc . . . ' This seems to make clear that it is the meaning, the 'distinguishable common locus' or dictionary sense, that determines the possible uses.

170

The confusion we have found in the account of Wittgenstein's transition from his *Tractatus* to his *Philosophical Investigations* standpoint, carries over, as we might have expected, to the attempt to clarify the sense of 'use' in, 'Don't ask for the meaning, ask for the use'. And this, of course, affects our interpretation of the 'revolution in philosophy' which has followed from this change of standpoints. For, in saying that Wittgenstein in his later phase abandoned denotation, we cut ourselves off from seeing that what he actually did was to abandon the connotative aspect of meaning and claim the denotative or use aspect as being the whole of meaning.

We can see why 'it is not as easy as is sometimes supposed to trace the sources of this captivating, and, up to a point, brilliantly successful movement.' We can even see why, in the final showdown, there is some undefined doubt as to the success which, in its heyday, was attributed to it with such undiscriminating enthusiasm.

29. *The experience of meaning*

The linguistic philosopher cannot ask himself the simple question, 'What is the meaning of the word "meaning"?' And yet to this question there is a perfectly straightforward answer.

The word 'meaning' means, i.e. is used as referring to, the power that belongs to certain sounds, to produce in those who have been appropriately preconditioned, a disposition to experience or act in a certain way.

At this point, of course, an exponent of the 'new philosophy' would at once confront us with a few hard-headed questions: 'What is this mysterious "*power*" you speak of so glibly?' 'What do you mean by "preconditioned"?' 'What do you mean by "appropriately" preconditioned – how do you know when the conditioning is appropriate or inappropriate?'

It might seem hard-headed and down-to-earth to insist that, because we cannot here and now give any account of this peculiar property that words possess of causing us all to respond in the same way, we cannot talk about it, we cannot have anything to do with such 'mysterious' properties. But what we are talking about is not, in the sense in which we are talking about it, mysterious. It is simply the observed fact that words do affect people in that way.

The word 'power' as we have used it is a convenient short-cut word, just as 'meaning' itself is. If we wanted to be more precise, we could say that 'meaning' (we are here referring to the primary or dictionary sense of the word) records the observed fact that — as happened in the hotel corridor — a sound of the special kind we call 'word' produces in *different* individuals the *same* (rather, a similar) response.

And we are not here referring, glibly or otherwise, to anything 'mysterious'. We know why all these individuals react in this common way to the sound in question: it is because they have been trained from infancy to do so. And we know whether or not any individual's reaction is the appropriate one, by the fact that his reaction is of the kind intended by the person uttering the sound in question.

The general charge laid by Wittgenstein against a word such as 'meaning' is that we have been deceived by the fact of possessing the word into thinking that there is necessarily something that it stands for, some one property which is common to all the uses to which words are put, meaning being this thing or essence that all words manifest in common. This, it is argued, is a delusion; there is no one way in which words function, they function in countless ways. 'I am saying', Wittgenstein tells us, 'that these phenomena have no one thing in common which makes us use the same word for all.'

This, once again, is only satisfactory if we share Wittgenstein's peculiar prepossessions. But if we don't, we will feel unconvinced by what he is saying, and this without any desire to rush to the defence of some metaphysical Essence of Meaning. We might even feel that, on his own statement of the case, he has missed the real point at issue.

He says that 'these phenomena' (of words used in everyday

SIDELIGHTS ON LINGUISTIC PHILOSOPHY

communication) 'have no one thing in common which makes us use the same word (meaning) for all.' Wittgenstein, that is, is noting the fact that we do use this word, 'meaning', for all cases of the (successful) use of words; but he asserts that these cases have nothing in common that *makes* us use the word 'meaning' for all such cases.

But, if we agree that words, in their various uses, have nothing in common that makes us use the word 'meaning' in relation to them, then what does make (or has made) us use this word in this connection? For, as Wittgenstein points out, we do use the word in this way. It isn't sufficient to say that this is a mistake, that there is nothing, no common element or factor or property, for 'meaning' to refer to. This doesn't dispose of the fact that we do use the word as though there *were* such a common property attaching to all words.

The question now is, how did this universal idea come to take possession of men's minds? We are not now asking, What is meaning? — we are asking the much more down-to-earth question, How did men come into possession of the idea they express by the word 'meaning'?

To say, as Wittgenstein appears to be saying (though, as usual, he has not said anything very explicit, and in any case has almost certainly expressed the contrary view elsewhere) that there is nothing, no property or factor, to which the word 'meaning' refers, is to face us with the peculiar problem of man's possession of a word which has no correlate in his experience. Never having experienced anything of this kind, men nevertheless felt impelled to devise a word for it.

This is all very mysterious. If we didn't know about Wittgenstein's anti-metaphysical prepossessions, we might suspect that he was here trying to involve us in some 'Promethean Fire' account of language. What has happened to his argument to give this peculiar impression? It seems to be due to the uncompromising stance he has got himself caught in, *metaphysics or nothing*. This bedevils his whole approach to words and meanings. Everything must be set before us in a sort of metaphysical motley which, because of its absurdity, we can't accept, but which, when it is stripped away, leaves — nothing.

'Suppose,' says Wittgenstein, 'someone said: every familiar word, in a book for example, actually carries an atmosphere with it in our minds, a "corona" of lightly indicated uses. — Just as if each figure in a painting were surrounded by delicate shadowy drawings of scenes, as it were in another dimension, and in them we saw the figures in different contexts.'

Nobody, of course, would think of meanings in connection with figures in a picture, and nobody ever feels or thinks of a word carrying its meaning about with it like a vague atmosphere or halo. You *could* think of words and meanings in this way, but nobody actually does. If they did, communication would soon break down; the essential fact about the use of words is that their use is built in to our growing faculties from infancy onward, so that it is normally unconscious.

But, having set up his aunt-sally account of meaning, Wittgenstein proceeds to dispose of it:

> . . . if it is like this, if the possible uses of a word do float before us in half-shades as we say or hear it — this simply goes for *us*. But we communicate with other people, without knowing if they have this experience too.

If I do have this curious experience of meaning, Wittgenstein seems to be arguing, this only holds for me, it has no common validity; but words do have common validity, men do communicate, as he himself says. Strangely enough, this rather confused argument seems to be the answer to Wittgenstein's earlier difficulty. Men do communicate by the use of words. At first (historically speaking, that is) they must have simply *communicated;* then, in time (evolutionary time) they become aware of this fact of communication of which words were the instruments: this was what words did — they brought about communication — this was their peculiar property or power. So men, not only using words as instruments of communication, but *experiencing*, now, this fact of words being capable of being so used, came to the concept of meaning.

Failing to account, at once, for this peculiar property of words — and this was, in fact, to prove to be a long and difficult task — men thought of meaning as some thing, or essence, belonging to the word. This was their first essay at an account of meaning. It was little more than a preliminary isolating of the concept as being capable of explanation — a considerable intellectual feat in itself.

But meaning proves elusive to explication. In time, philosophers are sure that they have solved the problem — only to reach the frustrating conclusion that their 'solution' was a mistake. We know what happened then. It was declared, not that the attempted solution was a mistake, but that the concept of meaning itself was a mistake; men had been deluded by their possession of the word 'meaning' into thinking that there was some mysterious entity or essence, some elusive atmosphere or corona accompanying a word, some ghost-like presence waiting round to give significance to any use of the word.

The modern thinker very easily disposes of all this mysterious, metaphysical paraphernalia trailing round after words. And having convicted this idea of absurdity, it follows — it is assumed to follow — that there is nothing else, that men have never had any experience to justify their use of the word 'meaning', and so there is 'no such thing' and so nothing to be accounted for: nothing but 'words in use'.

> Our problem is analogous to the following: says Wittgenstein, If I give someone the order 'fetch me a red flower from the meadow', how is he to know what sort of flower to bring, as I have only given him a word?

And a word, he is suggesting, 'simply goes for *us*,' i.e. for the person using it. Well, if this were so, it wouldn't be what we call a word . . .

But whatever difficulty there may be here does not simply concern the word 'red'. If there is a difficulty about 'red', there is a similar difficulty about 'flower'. But then, of course, there is the same difficulty about 'meadow', and then about 'fetch' and 'me' and 'a' and 'the' and 'from'. The difficulty, if there is one, is about human communication, about language. But Wittgenstein isn't intending to bring human communication into question — else he wouldn't be writing a book to tell us about it. Well, then, what is he doing?

He is suggesting that when I try to communicate with you, all I can do is use words. (A certain Sweeney noted this fact some years ago.) I can only give you words, and this involves an act of interpretation on your part; you must *understand* what I mean. But what is this queer business called 'understanding'? But we know the answer: There is 'no such thing as understanding', only 'words in use'. It was in the course of this particular discussion that Wittgenstein first introduced his shopkeeper interpreting a shopping list.

The simple fact is that by the time he has got the above transaction into a shape that will allow him to dispense with the concepts of meaning and understanding, he has produced a travesty of language. The job of language is to ensure some sort of reliability and order in our mutual communications. On Wittgenstein's account it was the purest fluke that I got my apples. And in any case, his account of the matter from the grocer's end doesn't explain why I should have said or written, 'I want six apples', on the assumption that this would mean what I intended it to mean, or in fact anything at all, to somebody else. In fact, how did I even come by the capacity to make these complex sounds and marks?

If human communication had been the sort of thing Wittgenstein describes it as being, it would never (so to speak) have arisen in the first place.

Wittgenstein has set out to give us an example of what he calls 'operating with signs'. And this is what he has given us. But words are not signs; they don't operate in the same way that signs do. Banked-up clouds are a 'sign' of rain, but they don't *mean* rain in the way that the word 'rain' does. If we feel that meaning is mysterious and inexplicable, and so to be avoided, we can do as Wittgenstein does: treat words as 'nothing but' signs, and so escape our difficulties. But if we are going to be honest with ourselves, we will have to admit that in some way that we don't yet understand, words perform the function which men, experiencing it, have called meaning.

30. *The dismemberment of language*

Meaning is — the word 'meaning' refers to — a kind of essence of common experience which men have (somehow) abstracted out of the primitive flux of individual experience. What we call meaning is a newer and higher kind of experience than anything the individual, alone, could have achieved. It is only as a *whole,* as the thing it essentially is, that meaning has meaning. Wittgenstein's procedure in *Philosophical Investigations* was to lay out this finely-textured whole on the philosophical dissecting table and to take it methodically apart — well, no, not methodically but with infinite patience and persistence — to see how it worked, to see the 'actual workings of language'. Why was it, then, that the overall effect of his investigations was (as a literary critic already referred to has expressed it) 'to undermine the simple assumption that we all know what something *means,* or indeed that we know what meaning itself is'?

The explanation of this, of course, is that Wittgenstein set about his investigation of the 'actual working of language', after the failure of the *Tractatus,* on the assumption that the idea of meaning was just a 'haze' that made the understanding of language difficult. Those who accepted this starting-point regarded the new way of philosophizing 'with a kind of awe as well as an intense satisfaction'. Awe at the simplicity and boldness of Wittgenstein's approach, satisfaction at the fact that at a stroke problems were disposed of which, just when they had seemed on the point of solution, had degenerated into frustrating 'perplexities'.

What had brought Wittgenstein to the adoption of this

revolutionary linguistic approach to these intractable problems? It had been said that 'It is by no means as easy as is sometimes supposed to trace the sources of this movement.' However, Professor Ryle has indicated how such a question is to be approached:

'Consequently, to understand the work of an original philosopher' — such as Wittgenstein and, we might add, Professor Ryle himself, whose *Concept of Mind* carried forward the new movement with such widely acclaimed success — 'it is necessary to see — and not merely to see but to feel — the logical *impasse* by which he was held up. We should always be asking the question, Just what was the conceptual fix that he was in? What dilemma was pinching him? Nor is it always easy to identify or describe the *impasse*, since he himself would seldom, if ever, be able to diagnose his trouble.'

This latter comment is, as we have seen, peculiarly applicable to the dilemma the modern philosopher found himself caught in. He had set out to show on the one hand how the individual inferred his world-picture from his sensory data, and on the other hand, how the propositions in which he expressed these inferences were related to Reality. It was the failure of both these enterprises that precipitated his dilemma. It was his inability to recognize the cause of this failure, to 'diagnose his trouble' as Professor Ryle puts it, that was responsible for the 'crisis in philosophy' and for the 'awe and intense satisfaction' with which he embraced the Wittgenstenian way of escape from this crisis.

As Professor Ryle says, it is only if we understand the nature of the philosopher's dilemma that we can understand the manner of his reaction to it. In this case, as we have seen, the cause of the failure to show (1) how the individual inferred his knowledge from his data and (2) how the propositions in which he stated his inferences were related to Reality was that (1) the individual was not *inferring* knowledge from data, he was *interpreting* data in terms of an inherited system of knowledge; and (2) this system of knowledge *was* his reality and it was to this reality and not to

178

some Reality-as-such that his propositions were related.

Briefly, the philosopher's failure was due to the fact that the individual was not doing what the question asked had assumed him to be doing; it was a failure to show him as doing what in fact he was not doing. In other words, the problem of knowledge had been incorrectly stated.

What the philosopher was now faced with was, a re-examination and restatement of the problem of knowledge. The course that was in fact followed, under Wittgenstein's guidance, was to reduce the problem of knowledge to the question, How do we use the term, 'Knowledge'?, in such a way that no reference was to be made to the fact of knowledge being essentially *common* knowledge. It wasn't *denied* that 'Knowledge' meant common knowledge – this would have been too obviously absurd – but it was to be treated *as though* its common factor was irrelevant to any understanding of it, as though, in fact, it was an actual hindrance to understanding.

So a large part of the procedure was devoted to showing not only how language 'actually worked' but that the ideas of knowledge and meaning, and indeed of language itself, and all allied terms, were, when analysed, 'essentially meaningless'.

The revolutionary nature of Wittgenstein's reaction to the *impasse* with which philosophy was faced can only be realized when it is understood that not only were traditional problems to be looked at in a new way, through the study of language, but language itself was to be looked at in the new way.

The procedure was, as we have seen, to place the offending terms, such as Meaning, Language, Knowledge, on the dissecting table and take them apart to see how they worked. As might be expected, this treatment of what we might call a living tissue of understandings like language has the effect of showing that it doesn't work.

'You say the word "March" to yourself', says Wittgenstein, 'and mean it at one time as an imperative, at another as the name of a month.' But of course, these are not the same *word,* they are the same *sound* used to symbolize two different meanings. This sort of thing won't do as an analysis of how words 'really work'.

'And now,' says Wittgenstein, 'say "March!" — and then "march *no further*!" — Does the *same* experience accompany the word both times — are you sure?' And of course, you're not sure, because the use of words is so habitual to you — hasn't the art been handed down from one generation to another, and instilled into you personally since infancy? — that you have no consciousness of any such experience, much less two different experiences.

For page after page of *Philosophical Investigations,* with examples of the utmost ingenuity — the ones we have just glanced at are conveniently simple — Wittgenstein dismantles the intricate and delicate fabric of mutual understanding that men have (somehow) fashioned out of the raw material of individual experience. And why does he put language, 'a form of life', as he himself calls it, to this prolonged torture? Because, in the *Tractatus,* through a failure to understand the logic of language, the way it works as an instrument of communication, he had asked the wrong question and so arrived at an answer that contradicted the facts.

This technique of what we might call pejorative analysis is used to good effect by Professor Ryle in *The Concept of Mind.* Putting the long-suffering John Doe into the witness box, he asks: 'How many cognitive acts did he perform before breakfast, and what did it feel like to do them? Were they tiring? Did he enjoy his passage from his premises to his conclusion, and did he make it cautiously or recklessly? Did the breakfast bell make him stop halfway between his premises and his conclusion? Just when did he last make a judgement? . . . '

This is all very amusing, but, one might be tempted to ask, Is it philosophy? — except, of course, that this would merely show that one was not 'with it'. However, Professor Ryle himself has answered this question for us in another context (*Dilemmas*).

What sort of questions should an enquirer put to persons to test their claim to have 'seen' something (say, a rabbit coming out of a conjuror's hat)? He will not ask them to describe in retrospect what experiences they had had, for instance what feelings they had felt, what ideas had crossed their minds, or what after-images, if any, interfered with their subsequent vision; and of course he will not ask them intricate questions of physiological or psychological sorts, to which they are in no position to give any answers.

So the answer is that the sort of thing Ryle is doing in *The Concept of Mind* may be all good clean fun but it isn't philosophy. And we can see the sense — the important sense — in which it is not philosophy.

Since the time of Plato, the concept of Mind, with its distinguishing capital M, has recorded the fact that the patterns of behaviour under which the individual subsumes his experience to give it communicable form, have not been drawn from the individual's own experience. Somehow these patterns transcend the individual's experience. The traditional explanation of this has been that 'Mind' refers to some extra-experiential Essence or Power.

Now to 'debunk' Mind and show that it is 'nothing but' these patterns of behaviour has the effect of obscuring the point at issue. What Ryle's 'logical geography' of the concept Mind shows is, not that mind is 'nothing but' these behavioural patterns, but that these patterns are not to be accounted for in terms of an extra-experiential Essence or Power, but as (somehow) drawn from experience, though *not,* as logical analysis has shown, from any one individual's experience.

What Ryle is in fact doing is, making his contribution toward the clarification of the problem of knowledge. But *The Concept of Mind* is so devoted to the debunking, by wit, ridicule or any other means, of the idea of mind, that its positive contribution toward the twentieth-century tracing back of our body of knowledge to its basis in experience is completely lost sight of.

But 'lost sight of' is not quite correct. The whole purpose of Ryle's witty debunking of mind is to carry out the Wittgensteinian programme of juggling out of sight the real problem that arises when Mind, as a transcendental Essence governing our behaviour as rational beings, is replaced by these *common* patterns of behaviour themselves. It is not easy to discuss with philosophical objectivity a question which, if pursued too far, tends to bring to light a problem which it is your whole purpose to avoid. Wittgenstein set the task; other writers have found their own individual means for carrying it out.

31. *The Whorf-Sapir hypothesis*

A philosopher who inherited a beautiful Persian carpet was so intrigued by its pattern — its subtle structure of colours and forms — that he was impelled to unravel it to see how the pattern was constituted, what it consisted in, what, in short, the pattern — the pattern-as-such, the essence of the pattern — actually *was*. When last heard of he was writing a paper for a philosophical journal, announcing his discovery that there was no such *thing* as the pattern, there was nothing but a lot of distinct and separate coloured threads. Indeed, his final conclusion was that, on further investigation, it would be found that there were no such things as these threads either.

Meantime, across the Atlantic, a fire insurance company was giving one of its inspectors the job of examining a large number of fire reports to see if any clue could be found to a general cause of fires.

What the insurance people were interested in, of course, was the physical conditions leading to fires. But the inspector, named Benjamin Lee Whorf, turned out to be a man with a curious and inquiring cast of mind. Leafing through the company's accumulated fire reports, he became aware of certain psychological factors, over and above the purely physical circumstances contributing to the outbreak of fires.

Employees, he found, reacted not only to the actual meaning of notices warning of fire risks, but also to a meaning suggested by the *form* of the notices. For instance, they were careful in the presence of a notice reading 'DANGER: Gasolene Drums Stored Here', but were careless in the presence of a notice reading 'DANGER: Empty Gasolene Drums Stored Here'. The word 'empty' had the effect of counteracting the idea of 'danger', although the empty gasolene drums, being full of explosive vapour, were actually the more dangerous: 'empty' suggested 'null, void, negative, inert'.

From these down-to-earth beginnings stemmed a new and revolutionary view of language, which came to be known as the Whorf-Sapir hypothesis, Edward Sapir being a professor of anthropology, and specialist in linguistics, at Yale, under whom Whorf later studied.

The 'hypothesis' opened up an entirely new line of thought for those who were interested in language and its relation to culture and human behaviour generally. In 1953 discussion of the new principle was brought to a focus in a Conference of anthropologists, linguists and philosophers at Chicago University. The outcome of much debate, for and against, was perhaps not very exciting. It was agreed that what was required was a further programme of research into various detailed aspects of language and its functioning in relation to culture before any definite conclusion could be arrived at regarding the Whorf-Sapir view of language.

But it was recognized that such research faced a fundamental difficulty. As one participant expressed it, 'One of these difficulties has been in evidence from the very beginning of our conference: the fact that we must talk about questions involving language in a particular language. If it is true that a language pre-determines for its speakers certain modes of observation and interpretation, we require as a first step to seek some means of breaking through the barrier.'

Stating this peculiar difficulty, the speaker stated, briefly, the Whorf-Sapir hypothesis itself, the central idea of which is that language functions, not simply as a device for reporting experience, as we naively assume, but more significantly, as a way of defining experience for its speakers. Language doesn't *express* the sort of experience we have, it *determines* the sort of experience we have.

The hypothesis has been expressed in various ways. Sapir, for instance, spoke of 'human beings being very much at the mercy of the particular language which has become the medium of expression for their society.' Whorf speaks of the various uses of language as 'introducing confusions of thought, of which for the most part we are unaware'.

It will be evident from the foregoing that the Whorf-Sapir hypothesis expresses an important insight into the nature and working of language. But it is a strange fact, that where the philosopher gains a new *insight into* the nature of language, he at once translates this into *judgment on* language.

A contributor to the Conference remarks ' . . . to the extent that language forces experience into rubrics, it is a screen between reality and the human being.' In similar vein another remarks that 'the next great task would be to devise new forms of speech to bring us even closer to reality.' To Whorf, as we just saw, our inherited categories were 'a source of confusion' in our thinking, and Sapir saw us as being 'at their mercy'.

This seems to be the prevailing reaction to the new insight: Language has been so to speak 'caught out', we have at last 'seen through it', seen how it deceives us. This general attitude of sitting in judgment on language finds final expression in what is called the 'relativistic' view of language.

Looked at from the new standpoint, the categories of our language system are seen, not as reflecting 'absolute' features of Nature as these would necessarily present themselves to any observer in any cultural setting, but as being relative to the culture in which the categories happen to occur. A tree (on this view) is not an objective something that presents itself as the thing it is to all observers, to be reported by them by the term 'tree'. On the contrary, the tree (or any other so-called natural phenomenon) that the individual sees is not the *cause* of his using the category 'tree', but is a function or expression of his possessing, as part of his cultural heritage, the category 'tree'. Briefly, it is not a tree which he experiences that determines the category 'tree', but the category 'tree', which is part of his inherited language system, which predetermines him to have the experience he calls 'tree'.

This relativistic view of language has been interpreted as completely reversing some of our most cherished traditional views. For instance, Kant and those who have followed in his footsteps have thought of Time and Space as being basic to all knowledge, because they were necessary forms of experience, in terms of which, by the very nature of our minds, we interpreted the flux of our experience.

This view of Kant's was itself, in its day, very revolutionary. Previously Time and Space had been, not properties of our minds, in terms of which we must experience, but objective properties of 'absolute' nature, which forced themselves upon our experience.

Kant took Time and Space out of Nature and centred them in the human mind. They were now absolutes, not of Nature, but of our inborn ways of experiencing. The Whorf-Sapir hypothesis has carried this revolution a revolutionary step further. Time and Space and all the categories of our thinking are now no longer absolutes, either of Nature or of the constitution of the human mind, but are relative to the language-system we happen to subscribe to. Living in another culture (for instance Hopi, which Whorf studied extensively) we would have quite a different conception of (say) Time.

Men had once thought of language – the particular language they had been brought up to – as bringing them in direct contact with an objective Reality. But the relativist standpoint seems to make it clear that if they had been brought up to another language-system, they would have found themselves making contact with a quite different 'reality', which, however, would have seemed equally objective and real.

Using this new principle of linguistics, the relativist has

been able to play havoc with some of our chosen ideas about ourselves and our knowledge and our relation to what has been naively called Reality, with a capital R to indicate its objectivity, its aloofness from us and our experience. To have got to know this aloof Reality so thoroughly has seemed like a mighty feat of the human intellect, of which man could be justly proud. But now, by another, and it would seem even greater, feat of the intellect, the relativist has been able to show us that this was all a delusion. We were not making contact with an aloof Reality. We were having the sort of experience that our language habits predisposed us to have. The 'reality' we were making contact with was a function — almost, it would seem, a fiction — of our accepted system of categories.

As in the case of the linguistic philosopher's destructive analysis of the concept of meaning, the disturbing effect of which, we saw, had spread far beyond the confines of the philosopher's study, here too the Whorf-Sapir hypothesis has had reverberations in other fields of thought. We find a noted sociologist warning us that 'The first rule for understanding the human condition is that men live in a second-hand world . . . None of us stands alone confronting a world of solid fact: no such world is available: the closest we come to it is when we are infants or when we become insane . . . Communications not only limit experience; often, they expropriate the chances to have experience that can rightly be called "our own". For our standards of credibility and of reality itself, as well as our judgements and discernments, are determined much less by any pristine experience we may have than by our own exposure to the output of the cultural apparatus.'

Carried to its logical limits, the new view of language was seen as implying that 'What we see depends on our apperception, our line of interest, which, in turn, is determined by training, that is, by linguistic symbols by which we represent and summarise reality.' And this, it is argued — with that boldness in following their thought wherever it may lead, on which those of a 'relativistic' turn of mind tend to pride themselves — forces us to acknowledge that human knowledge 'is in no way singular as compared with that of the sea-urchin, the fly or the dog.' This we can recognize as yet another chapter in the by now familiar indictment of language.

32. *From Whorf to Wittgenstein*

Stated as a thesis emerging out of the specialized study of linguistics, the Whorf-Sapir hypothesis sounds like, and was presented as being, a revolutionary and challenging view of language; and, treated in this way at the Conference referred to, it was seen as giving rise to all sorts of problems that required further, more detailed and more specialized investigation, which in their turn would become the subject of later conferences.

Luckily, it is not necessary for us to become involved in the programme of technical problems in comparative linguistics which the contributors to the Conference seemed to see stretching before them. For the purposes of our own inquiry, we may take a more naive and unspecialized view of the Whorf-Sapir hypothesis. And, indeed, our inquiry has itself provided us with the means for doing so.

For, regarded not as a specialized hypothesis but as a part of the developing pattern of modern thought, the hypothesis can be recognized as a statement of the fact, which we have seen to be emergent in contemporary thought, that what we call 'the world' is not an independent something 'out there', which is the *cause* of experience, but is a *construction from* experience.

We have seen this emergent fact giving rise to the problem Wittgenstein tackled in the *Tractatus*. It presented itself to him in the purely logical form, How does language refer to Reality? (His spelling of 'reality' with a lower-case 'r' does not alter the fact that it was Reality-as-such that he had in mind.) Brought down to cases, the question resolved itself into, When I give expression to my experience of an atomic fact, how does my expression, a structure of symbols (spoken or written) fit the fact?

The problem defeated Wittgenstein. We now know why this was so. It was because the manner in which he approached the problem assumed that what he was called upon to explicate was a relation between (a) an individual and (b) Reality-as-such. While, later, he was developing a new way of philosophizing as a retreat from this problem that had defeated him, the phenomenalists were giving the whole problem a new twist by showing that reality was (the word 'reality' referred to) an experiential construction, not to Reality-as-such. This, as we can now see, threw the problem Wittgenstein had been struggling with into an entirely new light, and explained why he had been unable to solve it.

But then the phenomenalist, too, ran into difficulties. When he turned to any actual individual and tried to show how he constructed reality as an experiential construction from his own experiential data, he failed to do so. And we know why he failed. It was because the individual to whom he turned was not constructing his world from his own experiential data; he was interpreting his immediate experiential data in terms of an already constructed world-picture. (This was a matter of observable, and in other contexts recognized, fact, not a matter of theory.)

It was this fact, that the individual did not build up his own world-picture from his own experience, but experienced in terms of the world-picture which was embedded in the language of his culture, that found expression in the Whorf-Sapir hypothesis.

Sapir says, 'The fact of the matter is that the "real world" is to a large extent unconsciously built on the language habits of the group . . . We see and hear and otherwise experience very largely as we do because the language habits of our community predispose certain choices of interpretation . . . Language is a self-contained, creative, symbolic organization, which . . . refers to experience largely acquired without its help.'

And Whorf: 'We dissect nature along lines laid down by our native language. The categories and types that we isolate from the world of phenomena we do not find there because they stare every observer in the face; on the contrary, the world presented is a kaleidoscopic flux of impressions which has to be organized by our minds — and this means largely by the linguistic system in our minds.'

If you approach this fact by way of a specialized interest in linguistics, the aspect of it that strikes you as significant is its denial of the accepted view of language as a means by which the individual records his direct experiences of the absolute facts of Nature or Reality. You see him instead as predetermined to experience, to 'dissect nature', in the way his inherited language-system dictates. And in this change of emphasis you see the claims of language to give a true picture of nature or reality, as having been 'debunked'. It is a short step from this to the claim that language, instead of putting us in contact with reality, cuts us off from reality, is a 'screen between us and reality'.

But that last step, though a short one, introduces a confusion into the Whorf-Sapir hypothesis that is fatal to any understanding of it. It sees me as deceived by an inherited conceptual system, which cuts me off from reality; what I think is reality is only what I see in terms of these inherited concepts. But there are two difficulties here. The term 'reality' itself, on this view, must be part of this inherited conceptual system, otherwise how did we come by it?: or does it, in the whole of our language, have some absolute transcendental status? But in that case, in seeing things in terms of the accepted system of concepts, I am not cutting myself off from what we mean by reality, I am bringing myself into contact with what we mean by reality.

What the Whorf-Sapir hypothesis is actually telling us is — not that language cuts us off from reality (for if it did, what meaning could 'reality' have except this 'cut-off' view to which we are confined?) — but that (a) 'reality' is a concept, and as such a part of an inherited conceptual system which is common to all the members of our cultural group, and (b) each one of us, as individuals, gives coherence and meaning to our private perceptual experience by bringing it under the forms of this common conceptual system — (a complex procedure which, it may be remarked, distinguishes man from the fly, the dog, the sea-urchin, the spider and the migrating bird).

Once we have got the Whorf-Sapir hypothesis into focus in this way, we can see that, in an interesting way, it parallels and complements Wittgenstein's picture of the shopkeeper interpreting the shopping list. Wittgenstein's purpose there, as we saw, was to suppress any reference to meaning, with its attendant idea of a factor of common understanding which, not being immediately explicable, might open the way to a resurgence of metaphysics. To this end, Wittgenstein pictured his shopkeeper as isolated in his own private world, simply 'acting as described'.

But, though Wittgenstein persuaded himself that there was no reference to meaning here, only to 'words in use', he was in fact, as we saw, 'cashing in' on an established common conceptual system. What his lone shopkeeper was actually doing — as would have been clear if the shopper had been pictured as speaking his requirements, not conveying them in written symbols — was, interpreting his immediate sensory data (his seeing of the symbols) in terms of the common conceptual system which was part of his cultural heritage.

What Wittgenstein was doing, for his own special purposes, was, emphasizing the individual's contribution to a performance which involved an interaction between an individual's momentary experience and an established body of common experience. Wittgenstein's emphasis, to repeat, was on the individual element in the transaction.

Looking again at the Whorf-Sapir hypothesis, we see that it too refers to this typical transaction between individual and common experience. But, approached from the specialized standpoint of linguistics, its emphasis rests, not on the individual element, as with Wittgenstein, but on the common element. Where Wittgenstein shows us the individual interpreting his private data in terms of the common conceptual system, the Whorf-Sapir hypothesis shows us the common conceptual system determining the individual's interpretation of his data. It shows us language as the means by which the individual makes contact with a reality having the authority — which his own data lack — of common acceptance.

The individual is not 'at the mercy' of language, or 'cut off from reality' by it. Without language and the entry it gives him into the common world-picture, he would be confined within the limits of his own indeterminate private flux — (which, we should perhaps add, to forestall an objection, would not be indeterminate *for him,* but would simply be all that he had; a most meagre 'all' compared with the range of experience that the abstracted forms of common experience open up to him). It is worth noting that Whorf himself emphasized that the individual's private data presented no more than a 'kaleidoscopic flux of impressions' until they were organized under the rubrics of the common conceptual system.

If we have set ourselves up as sitting in judgment on language, we may see the individual as cut off from real knowledge, as living in a 'second-hand world'. But when we take the wider philosophical view, we realize that the alternative 'first-hand world' would be that indeterminate flux of the individual's moment-by-moment experience out of which, by the instrumentality of language, of words and meanings, we have, somehow, lifted ourselves.

The two accounts of the knowledge situation, that of Wittgenstein and that of the Whorf-Sapir hypothesis, are complementary. But there is one advantage that the Whorf-Sapir hypothesis has over Wittgenstein's account. By its emphasis on the common factor in the knowledge situation, it points to a question which the other account obscures — is, in fact, devised to obscure. The question is this: If the categories embodied in language dictate the sort of experience we have, what has dictated the sort of categories we have?

In a remark of Sapir's already quoted there seems to be some kind of oblique reference to this problem. 'Language,' he says, 'refers to experience largely acquired without its help.' This might seem to contradict the claim, which is the basis of the Whorf-Sapir hypothesis, that language determines experience. But perhaps this seeming contradiction is to be explained by the point noted by Wittgenstein, that 'we cannot be dealing with the same concept of experience here;' that 'experience' has two meanings, a 'primary' and a 'secondary' meaning.

At any rate, we know that, in our ordinary practice, 'experience' *is* used in two allied, though distinct, senses, as referring either to common experience or to the individual's bringing his private data under the categories of common experience. As we have seen, these two senses are frequently confused. (We ourselves have used 'experience' – perhaps inadvisedly – in a third sense, as referring to the individual's undetermined private data, the momentary movements in his nervous system.)

What Sapir seems to be referring to in saying that 'language refers to experience largely acquired without its use' – which, in any case, is the fact – is that language refers to a kind of experience, common experience, which antecedes the individual's use of language, his use of the common *forms* of experience for the interpretation of his momentary data. It would hardly be possible to think systematically about language and experience without becoming aware, however vaguely, of these two complementary aspects which they display.

In tracing the various strands in the complex texture of modern thought, we have found that there is one question to which they all lead: *What is the nature and origin of the system of symbols we call language and the common world-picture which it embodies?*

This is the problem which the historical development of thought has brought to the forefront of the modern philosophic consciousness. And it is the problem which, as we have seen, characteristically 'modern' philosophy is especially designed to evade, after a preliminary bold, and finally unsuccessful, approach to it — over-bold in the first place, and correspondingly timid in the outcome.

Our business now is to take up this problem at the point where the modern philosopher tried to seal it off behind a barricade of taboos.

Chapter III

THE EXPERIENTIAL BASIS OF KNOWLEDGE

33. *What the individual knows*

This is a suitable point at which to re-emphasize that the purpose of our lengthy and perhaps too detailed examination of the underlying confusions of the 'new philosophy' has not been to 'knock' that philosophy in the interests of a return to metaphysics. It has been part of the tactics of the advocates of the linguistic approach to traditional problems to suggest that anyone who didn't agree with the 'new way of philosophizing' simply 'couldn't take it', that he shrank from the 'new clarity' and hankered back to the old and comfortable confusions.

But it has not been our purpose, in so persistently exposing the 'new confusions', to reject them in favour of something more familiar and consoling; nor even to expose the current confusions as a job worth doing for its own sake. The whole purpose of the foregoing lengthy discussions of the Wittgenstenian way of thought has been to bring to light the fact that *the modern philosopher, in his efforts to show that the traditional problems of philosophy were insoluble pseudo-problems, was unwittingly pointing to the solution of those problems.*

What we now want to do is, to gather together all the strands of our inquiry and take a look at the problem of knowledge on our own account. To get the situation sorted out, we will have to put up with a certain amount of repetition. What we are actually doing is, at last pushing our way out of the confusions which have gathered around the problem with the accumulation of efforts to solve it. To shake ourselves free of these confusions, we will have to be quite sure, at each

195

point, precisely what we are saying; otherwise we will find ourselves slipping back into the ways of thought which, as we have seen, have led philosophy into frustration and finally futility. Our business is truth, and, as Einstein once said, 'we must leave elegance to the tailor.'

Let us first take another brief look at the problem as it presented itself to the philosopher in the first decades of the present century.

As stated by Bertrand Russell, the problem was this: 'all knowledge which is based on what we have experienced is based upon a belief which experience itself can neither confirm nor refute, and yet which seems to be as firmly rooted as any of the facts of experience.'

What Russell was concerned with here was the *grounds* on which we infer knowledge from experience. And the further this question was pursued the more doubtful these grounds appeared. The question persistently presented itself: How did I get from my sensations, regarded as the necessary basis of knowledge, to the knowledge I possessed? I say, 'I see a tree', but all I in fact have is certain sensations. How do I make the leap from the sensations to the tree?

It is at this point that the philosopher's difficulties began to pile up. For the sensations that I experience are subjective and discontinuous, whereas the physical objects I 'see', the trees, men, mountains etc., are objective and continuous.

Strangely enough, though it seemed impossible to get from subjective sensations to the objective things of the external world, it seemed to be logically demonstrable that these objective things were, in some peculiar sense, conjunctions of sense data.

The immediate difficulty, and the one that precipitated the philosophical crisis, was that though the philosopher was able to show that the knowledge the individual possessed was a construction from the data of sense, the actual knowledge possessed by any individual to whom the philosopher turned was found to transcend his own experiential data. Or, conversely, no individual's experiential data was competent to account for the knowledge he possessed. It was found that the individual was not arriving at knowledge by direct inference from his sense-data. Every individual act of knowing seemed to be based on 'a belief which experience could neither confirm nor refute and yet which seemed to be as firmly rooted as any fact of experience itself.'

Briefly: the individual's knowledge seemed to rest upon principles which could not have been drawn from his own experience. But this seemed to be in direct conflict with the view that knowledge was derived from experience; it seemed to involve reference to some extra-experiential source of these validating principles of knowledge, to 'some power outside ourselves'. And the whole aim and confident claim of the empirical philosophers, as against the metaphysicians, was that knowledge was to be explained without any such 'occult' principles being invoked.

In the closing pages of his *Human Knowledge: Its Scope and Limits,* Russell summed up the problem in these terms:

> The principles are 'known' in a different sense from that in which particular facts are known. They are known in the sense that we generalize in accordance with them when we use experience to persuade us of universal propositions, such as 'dogs bark' . . . But although our postulates can, in this way, be fitted into a framework which has what we call an empiricist 'flavour', it remains undeniable that our knowledge of them, in so far as we do know them, cannot be based upon experience, though all their verifiable consequences are such as experience will confirm. In this sense, it must be admitted, empiricism as a theory of knowledge has proved inadequate, though less so than any other previous theory of knowledge.

More briefly, he says, 'And whatever these principles of inference may be, they certainly cannot be logically deduced from facts of experience. Either, therefore, we know something independently of experience; or science is moonshine.' This is Russell's final answer to the question which he posed to himself in the Preface to *Human Knowledge:* 'How comes it that human beings, whose contacts with the world are brief and personal and limited, are nevertheless able to know as much as they do know?'

This was the problem – the problem of how the individual builds up his world-picture from the data of his experience – that other philosophers, under the guidance of Wittgenstein, were to 'solve' by declaring that it didn't exist. And the curious and paradoxical fact is that, in this, the Wittgenstenians were right. That is to say, they were right in what they said, but wrong – fatally wrong – in what they meant by it.

34. *How the individual knows*

How comes it that the individual, whose contacts with the world are 'brief, personal and limited', knows as much as he does know? We now know the answer to that question, and the strange fact is that it has always been known, even to those who found this question unanswerable. We know, too, why it seemed to be unanswerable; why, in fact, in the form in which it was asked, it *was* unanswerable.

The reason for the philosopher's failure to confirm his thesis that knowledge was a construction from the data of experience was that he interpreted this as meaning that each individual inferred his own knowledge from his own experience – this is the import of Russell's question. But, in fact, the individual to whom he turned to test his theory was *not* inferring knowledge from his experiential data; he was *interpreting* his experiential data in terms of an already constructed body of knowledge, an established body of common concepts.

There was no mystery about this. All the relevant facts were open to observation and were perfectly well known. The individual was inducted into the established body of knowledge, the accepted categories, by his elders, and he then was able to use these categories as a means for raising his own private experiential flux to the level of communicable knowledge.

There is nothing esoteric or occult here. The individual is taught a certain way of looking at the world or reality — more precisely, he is taught a certain 'world' or 'reality' — and this becomes the mode of organization of his own subjective and indeterminate experiential data.

But, simple and obvious as this fact is, two difficulties seem to stand in the way of its proper evaluation in relation to the problem of knowledge. As soon as it is stated that the 'reality' each one of us experiences is dictated by the world-picture we have been brought up under, thinkers of a certain temperament immediately hail this as proving that human knowledge 'is in no way singular compared with that of a sea-urchin, a fly or a dog'. The effect of this on thinkers of the opposite temperament is to make them want to deny that our established world-picture has any effect on our way of experiencing.

The outcome is that each party to this clash of temperaments takes it for granted that, once I am inducted into the thought-ways of my cultural group, the knowledge I thenceforth achieve is relativistic and hence spurious, not true knowledge but mere self-delusion. One type of thinker takes a 'tough' line and welcomes this conclusion (there seems to be some sort of intellectual satisfaction in depreciating the intellect — perhaps one has thereby shown that one's own intellect rises superior to the general degradation). The other type of thinker can see no escape from this conclusion except by denying the fact on which it rests.

But it *is* a fact that we all experience in terms of the thought-ways of our society; we could not make ourselves intelligible otherwise, we could not raise the private flux of our experience to communicable level. At the same time, of course, using these thought-ways, we adapt them to our individual needs: we are not their helpless captives, they are our instruments ready to hand to be used by us and further developed in the act of being used. They, the established thought-ways, enlarge our individual capacities for experience; we, as individuals with our own unique experiential equipment, enlarge and enrich their content in the act of experiencing in terms of them.

And it is not a fact that the knowledge that I achieve through the instrumentality of the common world-picture is at no higher level than that of a dog or a fly or a sea-urchin. This sort of thing only goes unquestioned because it sounds tough and rather daring.

What the relativity of my knowledge to the common world-picture shows is that knowledge is not a simple function of the individual's own experience. It doesn't show that there is no such thing as knowledge. What it shows is that knowledge is not the sort of thing we have assumed it to be, that it does not derive from experience in the way our formulation of the problem of knowledge has assumed.

But even when these difficulties are examined and disposed of, a further difficulty presents itself. The fact that each of us is taught the world-picture we come to possess, that we do not infer it directly from our own experience, and that we henceforth interpret our momentary experience in terms of this common world-picture — these facts are so directly under our noses that we don't have to look to see them. They are so simple and obvious that, although they are beyond dispute, they do not seem to be of any philosophic importance. Everybody, even the most simple-minded of us, knows that we go to school and are there taught to formulate our ideas according to certain accepted rules and principles. But if we are trying to formulate a theory of knowledge, a fact such as this does not seem dignified or important enough for our purpose.

But the trouble is that, if we overlook these obvious facts, the question that seems naturally to present itself, once we start thinking about the problem of knowledge, is: How does the individual build up the knowledge he possesses from the data of his own experience? and to this question there is

200

no possible answer, because the individual is not doing what the question assumes that he is doing.

It is at this point, of course, that the 'last ditch' argument crops up, that the individual *does* build up his own world-picture from his own data, because even the words with which his elders instruct him must reach him as sensory data which are private and personal to him. We have already noted that this argument, which treats a word as having no other value than the sound of a dog barking or a wave breaking on the shore, rests on a fallacy which obscures the essential nature of the word, the way it is *used*, the way it *works;* the fallacy that finds expression in Wittgenstein's remark that you cannot understand me because I have 'only given you a word', and that my words only 'go' for me.

It is a chastening thought that it was the failure to solve this pseudo-problem of how the individual did what in fact he was not doing, that precipitated the 'revolution in philosophy' in which, ironically, the problem is declared to be an insoluble pseudo-problem.

So, as a preliminary to any approach to the problem of knowledge, we must reject the question as to how the individual builds up his world-picture from his own data, because what the individual is in fact doing — this was the essence of the Whorf-Sapir hypothesis — is, interpreting his data in terms of an already established world-picture into which he has been inducted as part of his cultural heritage.

But this at once draws our attention to another aspect of knowledge which must be taken into account as a preliminary to formulating our problem.

When we ask, how does the individual build up the knowledge he possesses from his own experiential data? we have by implication involved our question in a still further assumption that conflicts with the known facts. For the form of our question implies that the body of knowledge to be accounted for is something that is private and peculiar to the individual. It is not explicitly stated that this is so, but it is what the form of our question implies.

But, of course, the individual's knowledge is not something that is peculiar and private to him. It is something that he shares with the other members of his cultural group. It is because what he arrives at is so shareable, because it is communicable in terms of the common categories of thought, that it is what we call knowledge. It is only by virtue of the fact that what he arrives at is *common,* that we use the word 'knowledge' to refer to it.

If we ask how the individual builds up his knowledge from his own experiential data, we are asking how he builds up, from his *subjective discontinuous* experiences, a picture of a world which is to be *objective and continuous*: objective in the sense that it is valid for all individuals, and continuous in the sense that it is accepted as existing even when that particular individual is not experiencing it.

The essence of knowledge — or, in Wittgenstenian terms, the sort of thing that the word 'knowledge' is used to refer to — is that it is common to all individuals. If it is not common, if it is private and peculiar to the experiencing individual, like the D.T. sufferer's pink rats, then it is not knowledge, it is not what we mean by knowledge.

So, in addition to the observed fact that the individual is *not* constructing a world-picture from his momentary experiential data, but is 'cashing-in' on an already constructed world-picture, there is the further difficulty of supposing that any world-picture that the individual *might* construct (supposing that this was what he was doing) would have to be valid for, in fact compulsive for, all the other individuals of his group. We would have to picture one individual as dictating the concepts and values for the whole cultural group.

35. *The genetic approach*

So far we have done no more than clear away the more obvious obstructions to a rational approach to the problem of knowledge. But once we have taken into consideration the fact that the individual is not constructing his world-picture from his own immediate data, but is interpreting his data in terms of an already constructed world-picture which he has learned from his elders, we are brought face to face with the real nature of our problem. For this consideration at once alters the whole time-scale of the problem in knowledge.

When Wittgenstein said that language is just a part of our natural history he distorted the problem of language and knowledge in a way that cut off inquiry at the tap-root. For what he was in effect saying was that, without any effort on our part, knowledge starts afresh with each one of us, like the song of the bird or the pattern of the spider's web. But the fact is, of course, that unless knowledge were transmitted (by way of language) from one generation to the next, it would die out. Knowledge, for the individual, begins with his induction into the common world-picture, but the common world-picture does not begin with the individual.

And the significance of this fact, that knowledge has continued by being passed on from generation to generation, is that the problem of knowledge does not lie in the present, it lies in the past. To pose the problem of knowledge in the form 'How do I as an individual come into possession of the knowledge I possess?' is to confuse the beginnings of knowledge *for me* with the beginnings of knowledge *as such*. The knowledge I possess is my replica of the established body of common knowledge, the common world-picture. I did not create it, I entered into it as my cultural heritage.

So the problem of knowledge is not something to be solved here and now. Knowledge, as something which is transmitted from generation to generation, is an historical growth, having its roots in man's pre-cultural past. The problem of knowledge is the problem of the emergence of knowledge out of experience. It is the problem of the emergence of knowledge out of a state of pre-cultural nescience.

But now, having noted this fact, that the beginning of knowledge means its beginnings in our pre-cultural past, a further significant consideration emerges. To ask, 'How do I build up my conception of things in time and space?' is not only to falsify the problem by making an assumption which is contrary to the fact, for that is not what I am doing; but it is to make the further assumption that knowledge, as it emerged out of experience, was knowledge of a determinate world of things in time and space. It pictures a pre-cultural individual as looking about him and seeing, say, a tree.

At first, being not yet fully emerged from his original state of nescience, he is puzzled, but gradually he recognizes the thing he is looking at as the thing it actually is, a tree, a determinate object there in space, and now in time. But, as modern analysis has shown, he doesn't 'see' the 'tree'. What happens is that he experiences certain sensations, and it is out of such sensations that the tree, the familiar object of our common experience, is to be constructed.

The problem of knowledge, *the problem of the emergence of knowledge out of experience,* is precisely the problem of the emergence of this picture of a determinate, objective common world out of the data of experience. Our proto-cultural forebears, to whom we must turn for a solution of our problem, are not to be conceived of as confronting the world of things and events in time and space which is familiar to us. *That* is to assume the point at issue.

The problem of knowledge is the problem of how this picture of a *determinate, continuous, objective world* was constructed out of the *indeterminate, discontinuous subjective data of primitive individual experience.*

But at this point we run up against two further objections which apply specifically to this genetic approach to the problem of knowledge. It will be said, in the first place, that to push the problem of knowledge back into man's distant past in this way, does not solve the problem. It only deludes us into thinking we have solved it, whereas we have merely involved ourselves in that philosophical nightmare, an infinite regress. The problem, it will be said, is no more solvable in the past than in the present.

The answer to this objection is of peculiar interest because it draws our attention to a significant aspect of the problem of knowledge. In the first place, we *have* knowledge. That is to say, the problem *has* been solved. And it is clear that, as something which has been transmitted from one generation to another, something which is an historical growth, it is in the past that it has been solved; it is in man's distant past that knowledge had its beginnings in experience.

But now, bearing this in mind, if we picture to ourselves (however vaguely at this point) those elementary beginnings of knowledge, we do not see our pre-cultural forebears struggling with a 'problem' which they must somehow solve'. That would be to picture them as being, like ourselves, faced with an already established and highly complex structure of ideas constituting a common world-picture, and puzzled as to how this structure has emerged out of experience.

That is the *problem* of knowledge, the problem as it presents itself to *us*: the problem of accounting for an already constructed body of knowledge. But our pre-cultural fore-bears were not trying to account for a body of knowledge which was already constructed. What they were doing was, setting about *constructing* the body of knowledge which we, later, are to try to account for.

And in doing this they, our primitive forebears, were not setting out to 'solve' a 'problem'. To put the matter in that way is to picture them as saying to themselves, 'How can we create knowledge, a common picture of an objective world of things in time and space, out of the data of experience?' And to put the thing in those terms is to see how absurd the idea is.

No, the beginnings of knowledge out of experience did not present a problem to be solved. By pushing the question, as to how knowledge emerged out of experience, into the past we will be solving *our* problem of knowledge, but this will not be a pseudo-solution, resting on an infinite regress, an endless succession of causes each guaranteed by a preceding cause. It will be a purely empirical account of how men, without any deliberate intention on their part, brought the indeterminate and discontinuous elements of individual experience together to constitute a common, objective world-picture, a system of categories abstracted from experience and available for the interpretation *of* experience.

But, this being said, we come up against the second objection to the genetic approach to knowledge. It will be said that, even if tracing our body of knowledge back to its beginnings in man's primitive past does not involve us in an infinite regress, such an approach can still tell us nothing about those beginnings, and so nothing about the experiential basis of knowledge. This is so, it will be said, because we can have no empirical, factual knowledge of those pre-historic, in fact pre-cultural beginnings. In the nature of the case, men could not have left any record of what they were doing, so that anything we might say about their first groping steps towards knowledge, language and culture generally would be no more than idle speculation, on which no conclusions could be based.

The answer to this objection brings us to the heart of our problem – *our* problem – of how the picture of a common objective world has been derived from subjective individual experience.

36   The 'Egocentric Predicament'

The philosophical objection that we can know nothing about the conditions which governed the emergence of knowledge out of man's proto-cultural past is an interesting example of an argument which, without anybody's intention, is quite naturally used to prove two conflicting standpoints.

When mention is made of knowledge as a body of common experience, the retort is at once made, as we have seen, that there can be no such thing as common experience because each individual, by the very fact of his individuality, is the prisoner of his own sensory system. This, which we have already examined as the 'last ditch' argument, is known in philosophy under the title 'the Egocentric Predicament', which is defined as, 'The epistemological predicament of a knowing mind which, confined to the circle of its own ideas, finds it difficult, if not impossible, to escape to a knowledge of an external world.'

That is to say, the knowledge I possess must have been derived by me, by way of construction or inference, from my own private data. Or simply, I can experience my data, you yours, and never the twain shall meet.

The strange feature of the so-called Egocentric Predicament is that, if it existed, we would not be able to say that it did, for it is the essence of the predicament of our confinement, as individuals, each to the narrow circle of our own private data, that there can be no communication between us. But to *state* the predicament is to *communicate* — it is for me to tell you that I can't communicate with you or you with me. But in telling you this I am communicating with you, and in so doing, disproving my claim as to the existence of the Egocentric Predicament.

What could be more frustrating than a philosophical viewpoint, which one feels to be urgently and necessarily true, but which one can't speak about without thereby proving that it is neither urgent nor necessary nor true?

So, clearly, the 'predicament', the confinement of the individual within the meagre limits of his own experiential resources, the agitations in his private nervous system, does not apply to *cultural* man.

But we must note that it is only by virtue of the Word, that (still not yet understood) depository of common meaning, that we, as individuals, stand emancipated from our private prisons. If we did not have the liberating talisman, the Word, we would still be the captives of our own limited experiential resources.

It is necessary to emphasise this point, because it is here that the real significance of the Egocentric Predicament begins to emerge, and it seems to be just this significance that we tend to miss.

P

We are so overawed by the fact of the Egocentric Predicament that we fail to see, (a) that it does *not* apply to cultural man, the possessor of the Word, but (b) by the same token it did apply to *pre-cultural man, groping his way toward the Word which he did not yet possess.*

In other words, the Egocentric Predicament is a statement of the necessary condition that governed the emergence of common knowledge out of individual experience.

It is a statement of the fact that the elements out of which common knowledge has been constructed are experiential data which are private and peculiar to the experiencing individual. This may seem to be obvious, once stated. But, until stated, it is not so obvious as to prevent us from insisting, when reference is made to common knowledge, on the Egocentric Predicament; and then, when reference is made to the beginnings of knowledge out of pre-cultural experience, insisting that we can know nothing of the conditions governing such beginnings.

Perhaps we may still not be clear as to the significance, in relation to the problem of knowledge, of the fact that knowledge, our established body of common experience, necessarily rests upon the discontinuous and indeterminate data of primitive individual experience. But we now at least have a clear view that, by virtue of the Egocentric Predicament, this is so.

Amidst all the confusions that beset the problem of knowledge, to have isolated this fact is itself an important achievement. How important, and in what way it is important, will emerge as we proceed.

37. *The fable of the lonely man*

'And yet', says a contemporary philosopher rather plaintively, 'how, if not by the use of our senses, could we come to know anything about our environment?' The difficulty is that, inescapably true as this appears to be, it does not seem possible to establish any such relation.

It is the intractability of this problem that has led to the view, expressed by the same thinker, 'Perhaps it is time to consider the possibility that nothing more can be achieved [by trying to trace this relationship between sense-data and knowledge] and to undertake instead the proper investigation of the immensely complex vocabulary of perception in ordinary language' — the study of 'words in use'.

The question we now want to consider is, would this problem, which, the above writer tells us, has been unceasingly discussed since the time of Locke and Berkeley, be any more capable of a solution a hundred thousand years ago, than it is today? Then, even more than now, men had only their senses from which to start 'building knowledge'. And further, the only data available to them were *natural* data. The Word, with its unique common *verbal* data, was just what men had to achieve on the basis of their private and incommunicable natural data.

In the previous section we saw that when we transferred the problem of knowledge from the present into the past we tended to picture a pre-cultural individual confronting a determinate world of things in time and space which he was somehow to get to know on the basis of his own experience. We saw that this was to misconceive the problem. For it was precisely this world that was to be created from the data of experience. The primitive individual didn't 'see' a 'tree'; he had certain sensations of a kind from which the tree was, in time, to be constructed.

So we must not assume, as the starting-point of knowledge, the determinate space-time world which we want to account for. We must take as our starting-point the discontinuous and indeterminate, subjective data of individual experience, private and peculiar to the individual, as yet not mediated by the word and its common meaning. The basis of knowledge is to be the individual's *natural* data. He has no access yet to verbal data. It is out of the natural data that the verbal data are (somehow) to be constituted.

209

There is a famous remark of John Stuart Mill, to the effect that 'if there were but one rational individual in the universe, that being might be a perfect logician; and the science and art of logic would be the same for that one person as for the whole human race.'

I think we may take this as implying that the essential nature of the complex structure of ideas we call knowledge is such that it may be regarded as being a construction from the experience of a solitary individual confined as above to his own subjective data.

This presents the problem of knowledge to us in its starkest form. How is the individual — we are thinking here of a primitive, pre-cultural individual — to be conceived as generating concepts, which shall be functional and valid, not only for his own experience, but for the experience of all other individuals, out of the transient flux of his own sensory data?

We have spoken of such an individual as confined within the limits of his own experiential data. But this is to see the matter from *our* point of view. For him there is no such sense of confinement; the interesting fact is that where the 'Egocentric Predicament' *does* apply it is not a predicament. Our primitive individual simply *has* his experiences. Or better, perhaps, he simply has his being, and his experience is just part of his being. He experiences what he is capable of experiencing; his capacity for experience marks the limits of his consciousness; and his consciousness is no more than a succession of moment-by-moment adjustments to the various tensions and releases recorded in his nervous system.

Some of these tensions, as we know, are due to internal causes, hunger, sex etc., others to external causes. But we must not imagine our solitary individual making the distinctions between these that we make. All his experiential data, whatever their source, are characterised by the fact that they are *his*. He is a self-contained experiential unit, meeting each occasion as it arises. What he 'learns' from experience takes the form of a direct physical reaction.

Having accidentally burnt himself at the fire, our solitary

individual 'learns' to avoid that experience in the future. But he does not learn 'I must avoid that experience in the future.' That is to say, he does not *conceptualize* his experience.

And indeed, why should he? His experience is immediate, personal, direct; it is *his* uniquely and privately. He has no need to conceptualize it. Why would he feel the need to say 'I must avoid that experience in the future' – or even any elementary version of this? That piece of wisdom has been recorded directly in his nervous system. He has no need of a concept, because he has that much more direct and reliable form of wisdom, a conditioned reflex.

For him this form of unmediated knowledge is sufficient. It meets all his needs because his needs are adapted to the limits of his purely personal knowledge. The power of this form of knowledge lies in its simplicity and immediacy. Why should our solitary individual put himself to the trouble of translating his simple immediate experience into the form of a complex conceptual system? There is nothing to *make* him do so, nothing to make him want to do so.

I think we can dismiss Mill's claim as mistaken. The complex conceptual scheme we call knowledge cannot have arisen on the basis of the experience of a solitary individual as pictured by him. But then, how did this conceptual system arise?

But as soon as we ask that question, we see that Mill's picture of a solitary individual generating knowledge out of his own experience involves another mistake. For it is the characteristic of the human individual that he is not a solitary individual. Man is one of the social creatures. To picture a solitary individual dependent for his knowledge on his own experience is to set up a purely artificial situation, and one out of which knowledge could not, and in any case did not, arise.

Still, it might be said, the fact remains that our individual is solitary in the sense and degree, already agreed upon, that he is confined within the limits of his own experience. Without the mediation of the Word – and it is that mediation that we are trying to account for – he is, if not physically, then psychically, a solitary, with only his own experience to build on.

But here the important point emerges that part of his experience is social experience, it reflects his contacts with the other individuals of his group. And, recognizing this fact, I think we can go further and say that this is the most important part of his experience; it is the most obtrusive, the most insistent, the most demanding, the most rewarding and the most frustrating.

It is with the other individuals of his group that he sleeps, eats, hunts, quarrels, has sexual relations. It is a corollary of his social state that he is dependent on them. It is equally the case that they are dependent on him. He and they are mutually dependent; they continually act and react on one another; they continually *experience* one another.

And here we have arrived at a further fact in answer to the objection that we can know nothing about our pre-cultural forbears that is relevant to the problem of knowledge, the problem of the generation of a common objective determinate world-picture out of the discontinuities and indeterminacies of subjective, individual experience.

The problem, in its modern form, has been how to get from individual experience to objective world, or reality. But in the first place modern analysis has shown that 'world' or 'reality' is a construction from individual experience. And now, referring the problem back to its beginnings in man's condition as a social being, we see that this was not, in the nature of the case, a simple, direct construction by a solitary individual from the data of his own experience.

We have seen that a solitary individual, as pictured by Mill and in fact tacitly assumed in the modern formulation of the problem of knowledge, would have neither the need nor the impulse to create his own conceptualized world-picture out of the data of his experience; his own experience, as it comes to him, is good enough for him.

Nevertheless, we finally find him in possession of a conceptualized world-picture, a highly complex picture, which

(a) his own experiential data is found to be incompetent to account for, and (b) which he holds in common with the other individuals of his group.

It is obvious, then, that what we call knowledge, as it has emerged out of the primitive data of experience (a) is not and could not be a simple product of the experiential data of one individual, and (b) is, and could only be, a social product, a product of the existence of men as social beings.

In other words — as the outcome of modern analysis has already suggested to us — *knowledge is a function of individual experience, but not of the experience of any one individual.*

Knowledge, we know, is common knowledge. We now see that it is common in the precise sense that it is a complex function of the experience of individuals who are social beings.

38. *The implications of the obvious*

When we remind ourselves that the confusions of the 'modern revolution of thought', through which we have been groping our way, are due to the failure of the attempt to show how an individual derives the knowledge he possesses directly from his own experiential data — when we recall this basic aspect of the modern thought-situation, we can see that we have now got the problem of knowledge into a drastically new form.

For, once we have traced the body of knowledge we actually possess, back to its pre-cultural beginnings, we see that its essential nature is, not that it is a product of a solitary individual's experience, but that it is a social product, a product (somehow) of all men's experience.

The modern philosopher was caught in the dilemma that, though it could be shown that knowledge was a construction from the data of individual experience, no individual's experience was competent to account for the knowledge he actually possessed. This seemed to present an impossible and paradoxical situation, and in the long run, the philosopher escaped from his dilemma by giving up the insight, which his logic guaranteed, that knowledge was an experiential construction.

But as soon as we take into account the essentially social nature of knowledge, there is no paradox, no difficulty. Knowledge is a construction from the data of individual experience, but not — this was the philosopher's gratuitous and fatal assumption — from the experiential data of any one individual.

The attempt to show knowledge as deriving directly from an individual's own experience failed, not only because the individual was not deriving knowledge, in the manner assumed, from his experiential data, he was interpreting his data in terms of a given body of knowledge; but also because, in any case, the given body of knowledge which he was using for the interpretation of his experience, had not been derived directly from an individual's experience as assumed. The attempt to solve the problem of knowledge failed because it rested upon a misconception of the nature of knowledge. It did not take into account the essential *social* nature of knowledge.

But the curious fact is that in recognizing the social nature of the conceptual system, our common world-picture, we are still not out of the woods. For it now transpires that there is a yet further and most obstructive objection standing across the path of our philosophic adventure.

This is an objection which, though it pervades contemporary thought, is not easy to put a finger on; it is not an objection that would be explicitly raised in reply to an assertion of the essential social nature of knowledge. It is an attitude of mind rather than a deliberately formulated thesis. Where reference is made to it, the reference will be incidental, almost accidental, by way of a chance aside. But the objection is all the more potent just because it is a pervasive attitude of mind.

A contemporary philosopher, referring to an aspect of the problem of knowledge, discussed by a fellow philosopher, says:

214

The point he is making is not the one often made in the past by philosophers, namely that we are essentially social creatures and could not, as a matter of fact, have the sort of awareness of ourselves which we have as human beings, or indeed be at all the sort of persons we are, were it not for the very intimate relations we have with one another. No one would seriously dispute this point, and it is not anything so trivial that (he) is affirming; he is concerned with a much more subtle logical difficulty . . .

So we must now face the fact that, though it has cost us so much effort to elicit the fact that knowledge, as an experiential construction, has been drawn from the experience of all men as social beings — that this is the essential nature of knowledge, the recognition of which resolves at one stroke the 'problem of knowledge', the failure to solve which precipitated, first, the crisis in philosophy and then the 'revolution in philosophy' — we must now face the fact that, to the philosopher, this will not seem like a conclusion of any significance whatever.

Difficult as it has been to arrive at, on account of the obstructions that stood in the way of getting it started, it now appears that our labours have been misdirected. We thought that to point out the solution of the problem that had been the cause of all the philosopher's troubles would be recognized as a major philosophical achievement. But this, it now seems, was a mistake. We expected the philosopher to exclaim excitedly, 'Why, of course; the fact that knowledge is a social product is the solution of the problem that caused all our difficulties.' But instead, the philosopher remarks indifferently, 'Well, of course knowledge is a social product. But what of it?' We have laboured to bring to light a fact which is obvious, readily acknowledged, and finally trivial.

And yet the problem of knowledge has been taken as meaning, 'How does the individual derive his knowledge from his own experience?' — and, as we have seen, the philosopher's failure to answer this question was due to the

215

fact that the individual was not doing what the question assumed. We now further see that this failure was also due to the fact that knowledge, as a product of man's social existence, is not a structure of the kind assumed. The problem was, as the philosopher declared, an insoluble pseudo-problem, though not for the reasons put forward to him.

How is it, then, that the philosopher would not regard the essential social basis of knowledge as having any relevance for the problem of knowledge? Why should it seem to him that a fact which accounts for his failure to solve the problem of knowledge is 'trivial' and so not to be taken into consideration?

The explanation of this is that the philosopher is concerned with what is called *epistemology,* or the *theory of knowledge.* Having dismissed the metaphysical or transcendental account of knowledge as resting on principles that stand outside and above man and his experience, on a 'power independent of us', he has set himself the task of giving a theoretical account of knowledge, an account dependent on us in the sense that the philosopher himself has reasoned it out. He is interested in a 'theoretical construction' or 'a rational reconstruction', not in an empirical account of the emergence of knowledge out of experience.

The metaphysician had tried to give a *speculative account.* In opposition to this the modern philosopher sought to give a *theoretical account.* Repudiating speculation, which assumed principles of inference transcending the experience of the individual, he set himself the task of accounting for the knowledge the individual was found to possess in terms of the individual's own experience. Instead of a speculative account he wanted a formal or theoretical account. This was his approach to epistemology or theory of knowledge.

Now it is clear, I think, that in the same way that a speculative or transcendental approach does not meet the empirical philosopher's formal or theoretical requirement, so too an account of knowledge based on the simple and obvious fact that man is a social being, will appear just as unsatisfactory

216

for a formal or theoretical point of view. When the full powers of the intellect, aided by all the resources of modern logical techniques, have been brought to bear on the question of how knowledge is derived from experience, the suggestion that the fact of man's being a social creature gives the answer, will hardly seem significant, or even relevant.

But in any case, so simple and obvious an explanation will not seem *intellectually satisfying* to one who is seeking a theoretical explanation. If you have been looking for a subtle, logical relationship between individual sense-data and reality; or if you have been considering knowledge as the expression of a 'truth-functional calculus' of 'atomic propositions'; or if you are developing the thesis that 'to be is to be the value of a variable' – if, having devoted yourself to such tasks, you are presented with the proposition that we are essentially social creatures and could not, as a matter of fact, possess the complex body of knowledge we do possess, were it not for the very intimate relations we have with one another, you would not dispute the assertion – no one would seriously attempt to do so – but you would hardly even pause to listen to it before going on with your more urgent and interesting philosophical business.

And the fact is, the proposition, *Man is essentially a social being and his knowledge is consequently a social product,* does *not* answer the sort of questions the philosopher finds himself involved in. But this is because these questions are a by-product of the failure to take account in the first place of the empirical facts concerning the nature of knowledge.

The further the philosopher gets away from the facts, the more subtle and complex his thought becomes, until finally he comes to value subtlety and complexity for their own sakes. At that point in the evolution of his thought-processes, a simple and straightforward solution of his problems will seem, by contrast, to be trivial and irrelevant, a solace, perhaps, for philosophical incompetents, but of no value or interest to those who are grappling with the more profound questions that modern techniques of inquiry have brought to light.

In the final outcome, when such an inbreeding of complexity on complexity finds the philosopher no nearer to a solution of his problems, he comes to accept the comforting thesis that it is not the business of philosophy to seek solutions, but only to ask questions, without any concern for what the answers may be. From then on, *no* solution of his problems, least of all a simple and obvious one such as we have been led to, is of any interest to him. Faced with such a suggestion, he merely knits his brows a little harder and murmurs to himself, 'But to be *is* to be the value of a variable.'

It is a generally accepted methodological principle that, where more than one explanation of a given phenomenon is available, the most simple explanation shall be the one chosen. This is a modern variation of Occam's famous razor: don't introduce more entities, don't complicate your explanation more, than is necessary. (The same idea turns up in Russell's famous dictum, 'Wherever possible logical constructions are to be substituted for inferred entities', which is to say, the things of our everyday experience are to be treated as logical constructions from sense-data.)

But the doctrine of simplicity is not as simple in application as it may sound. A theory may seem simple just because we are familiar with it, though in fact it may be highly complex. By contrast a much simpler theory, with which we are not familiar, and the acceptance of which involves a fundamental revision of our normal thought processes, seems highly complex, and sets up all sorts of resistances. Indeed, the difficulties of applying the doctrine of simplicity have proved so great as to lead to a Theory of Simplicity, which, however, is itself so complex that it had better be relegated to the foot of the page, where the reader may make what he can of it.[1]

[1] 'Our understanding of the theory of simplicity, when applied to sets of extra-logical bases, depends initially on our taking into account a number of crucial refinements of logical structure.
'One such refinement concerns the distinction between a 'sequence of predicate P' and 'a place-sequence of predicate P'. For let P be an n-place predicate. Then a sequence of P is any ordered n-ad of elements,

So the accepted methodological rule, that the simpler explanation shall prevail over the more complex, does not mean that the social account of knowledge will make an immediate appeal to the philosopher as disposing of the complexities − or, as we have seen them, confusions − that dominate contemporary thought. The social account will not be seen as having the virtue of simplicity, it will rather seem to have the stigma of triviality.

Our purpose in elucidating the above objection to taking seriously the necessary social basis of knowledge, has been to face up to the fact, that has dogged our footsteps from the very beginning of our inquiry, that what we are doing is not *philosophy*. Whatever else it may be, it is not what is today regarded as philosophizing. It is as well to be clear about this, so that, as we proceed to follow out the implications of the social view of knowledge − and of course we still don't know *how* men proceeded to derive common knowledge from subjective experience − we will not tend to lose our nerve as we find ourselves coming up with the solutions of problems which are at present consigned to the limbo of insoluble pseudo-problems. The philosopher's nerve failed him when he couldn't solve these problems. We must guard against ours failing, when we find that we can.

Fundamentally, the difference between our procedure in following out the implications of the social view of knowledge, and that of the theoretical or formal approach, is that, whereas the modern philosopher has wanted to place his own interpretation on the facts, we will be simply examining the facts to see what interpretation is implicit in them.

The rule we will be following will be, 'Don't think: look'. As against this the rule the philosopher, faced with the social

---

a, b, . . ., n, such that Pa, b . . ., n is true. Conversely, P has just one place-sequence, consisting of a sequence of distinct variables, $p1$, $p2$, . . . pn, such that $p1$ represents the i th place of P. This distinction must be carefully observed in the construction of proofs.

'Other refinements of logical structure are provided by definitions, which now follow . . .'

nature of knowledge, and the effect of this on his 'revolution in philosophy', prefers is, 'Don't look: think.'

But in this approach, though we will be in conflict with the present mood of philosophy, we will not be running counter to what we may call the logical development of thought. We will simply be following the course that thought would have followed if the philosopher had not lost contact with the business of tracing knowledge, truth, reality, our common world-picture (whichever way of expressing it may be best suited to a given context) back to its basis in the data of individual experience.

For we can see that a dictum such as that of Bertrand Russell, that philosophy is concerned with logical constructions from sense-data rather than with the things of our every-day experience, is an expression, however oblique and obscured by technical considerations, of this progressive analysis of our common experience into its basic elements and constituent principles.

Let us, then, accept the fact that, by current standards, we are not philosophizing. We are merely working out the implications of the obvious.

Chapter IV

THE WORD

39. *The paradox of language*

'Language,' says Susan Langer in her *Philosophy in a New Key*, 'is, without a doubt, the most momentous and at the same time the most mysterious product of the human mind . . . If we find no prototype of speech in the highest animals, and man will not say even the first word by instinct, then how did all his tribes acquire their various languages? Who began the art which, now, we all have to learn?'

That is the 'paradox of language', that to possess it we must be *taught* it by our predecessors, but this is not how it could have *begun;* it seems to be necessary first to possess language before it can be possessed.

'And why is it not restricted to the cultured races,' Langer goes on, 'but is possessed by every primitive family, from darkest Africa to the loneliness of the polar ice? Even the simplest of practical arts, such as clothing, cooking, or pottery, is found wanting in one human group or another, or at least found to be very rudimentary. Language is neither absent nor archaic in any of them.' To which she adds, resignedly, 'the problem is so baffling that it is no longer considered respectable.'

'It is best,' adds another authority, Edward Sapir (we have already met him in connection with the Whorf-Sapir Hypothesis), 'to admit that language is primarily a vocal actualization of the tendency to see reality symbolically, that it is precisely this quality which renders it a fit instrument for communication, and that it is in the actual give and take of social intercourse that it has been complicated and refined into the form in which it is known today.'

221

These comments on this ancient and intractable problem suggest some interesting considerations. 'Who began the art,' asks Langer, 'which now we all have to learn?' But this raises the question, Can we think of language, a social product, a product of men living together as social beings, having been started by *an* individual? The conception becomes all the more difficult when we take into account that, as emphasised by Langer, all the races of men, no matter where they may be, however far removed from one another they may be, possess a fully developed language. There would seem to be no answer to the question, Who began these many, widely separated and diverse languages?

Sapir, on the other hand, emphasizing the social nature of language, its origin 'in the actual give and take of social intercourse', sees it as 'primarily the vocal actualization of the tendency to see reality symbolically'. But as we have seen, and as both logical analysis and the Whorf-Sapir Hypothesis make clear, what we call reality is itself a social product, a construction from experience. So there would seem to be a difficulty in treating language as resulting from our seeing reality symbolically, for 'reality' is in this sense a symbol; 'reality' does not refer to an independent 'something' that causes our experience, it refers to a conjunction of complex experiences: 'reality' is itself a symbol for this experiential complex. The word 'reality' is part of the symbolic system we call language, and so language cannot be said to originate from a tendency to 'see reality symbolically'.

But the fact is, as Langer points out, that men everywhere, no matter how primitive and backward they may otherwise be, have language; and furthermore, each group has its own language, so that this peculiar instrument of communication must have been achieved again and again, independently, by groups of men each with their own way of life, their own way of experiencing.

'Language,' says Sapir, 'is a purely human and non-instinctive method of communicating ideas, emotions and desires by means of a system of voluntarily produced symbols.'

Other creatures, of course, communicate with one another; when, at night, one dog starts to bark, other dogs join in; fowls cluck at one another and hens have warning sounds which their chicks respond to when there is a hawk overhead; and any farmer can tell you that all his animals have their own peculiar 'modes of expression', by which he can tell whether they are contented or not. But none of these is in any way comparable to human language (despite many brave efforts to study the 'speech' of animals).

Only man achieves language and speech, and man, as we see, has so strong an urge toward this peculiar achievement that he produces it in all circumstances and in the face of all impediments. And the greatest of these impediments is (quoting Sapir again) that 'there are, properly speaking, no organs of speech; there are only organs that are incidentally useful in the production of speech sounds.'

This is a very curious fact. 'The lungs, the larynx, the palate, the nose, the tongue, the teeth, and the lips, are all so utilized, but they are no more to be thought of as primarily organs of speech than are the fingers to be considered as organs of piano-playing, or the knees as organs of prayer.'

Despite all these natural impediments, men everywhere have perfected the art of speech. And we know how considerable these impediments are when we try to learn a foreign language. How difficult it is to make those various organs, with which we articulate our native tongue, cope with the articulations of a tongue not our own! the pronunciation and accent defeat us. Well then, consider the difficulty, in the beginnings of speech, of disciplining these various organs to a task they were not intended for. There must have been a unique urge behind this unique achievement.

But we are not here concerned with speech, which after all is only the outer dress of language. Nor, in fact, are we concerned with language itself, language *as such*. We are only concerned with it as the outer dress of knowledge and thought. It is knowledge that we are interested in, as a system of commonly held concepts or ideas, constituting a common world-picture, which (somehow) social men have derived – and as we have seen, derived again and again to suit their own peculiar needs – from the raw material of experience.

Though language is only the garment of knowledge or thought, the peculiar fact is that thought itself has no being, no physical existence (so to speak) until it is embodied in language. Men must have possessed the concept, say *tree*, they must have carried on their affairs in terms of the concept, before they had the word 'tree' to express it. The situation was certainly not as Wittgenstein, for his own peculiar reasons, suggested, that they had the word 'tree' and then one day somebody said 'Why not use the word "tree" to mean *tree*?' and everybody said, 'Yes, let's.'

Concepts, as abstractions from experience, preceded language and made language necessary. And yet, unquestionably, until the concept was embodied in the word, it must have led a wraith-like, a vague and indeterminate existence. Language must have had the same determinative effect on concepts, giving them permanent form and defining (placing a mark around) their meanings, as writing had on spoken language, and as, in turn, printing had on written language.

So, though it is the concept that is the soul and vital spark of the arbitrary word-sound that symbolizes it, and it is the concept as an abstraction from experience that we are interested in, it is more convenient to talk about language than about the concept itself.

And indeed, on consideration, it might seem that language must remain mysterious and inexplicable while it is studied as a thing-in-itself. Perhaps it can be understood only when it is seen as an instrument devised for a specific function, the function of expressing a given content, the commonly-held system of concepts which social man has abstracted from the discontinuous and indeterminate flux of individual experience.

40. *The evolutionary approach*

The peculiar question raised by language – and so, of course, by knowledge and thought generally – is: *How did that BEGIN which now can be achieved only by being LEARNED?*

In Pierre Teilhard de Chardin's *The Phenomenon of Man,* an attempt is made to trace an evolutionary development from 'primary matter' to modern cultural man. It is a bold and challenging undertaking – sufficiently so to have brought Teilhard, who was a Jesuit monk as well as a noted paleontologist, into conflict with his superiors. It is of interest for our present inquiry because, in Part Three of his story, he deals with 'The Birth of Thought'.

'When for the first time in a living creature,' he says, 'instinct perceived itself in its own mirror, the whole world took a pace forward.' Thought, he is saying, is the evolutionary offspring of instinct. This is, in effect, his answer to the question as to the *beginning* of that which now must be *learned.*

Traditionally, a quite different answer has been given to this question: thought and knowledge had descended upon us from some upper ether of Pure Ideas. But when we postulate a realm of Pure Ideas, what we are in effect doing is, making an abstract picture of our actual processes of thought, having no reference to any immediate experiential content, and then using this picture, abstracted from workaday thought, to explain workaday thought.

In the light of what we now know about the distinction between the established body of *common* concepts, and the *individual* here and now experiencing in terms of these concepts, we can recognize the transcendentalist as accounting for this two-term thought-situation in terms of its *common* element. When he claims his Pure Ideas as independent of *all* experience he is recording the fact that the given body of common experience transcends the experience of any of the individuals who interpret their immediate data in terms of it.

And this is simply another aspect of the fact, which modern analysis has revealed, that this body of common experience has not been drawn from the data of the individual who is found in possession of it.

But if the transcendental view of the origin of knowledge won't work, or rather works only because it assumes the point at issue, what of the empiricist or experiential view? This, on examination, is seen to be, not the contrary and refutation of the transcendental view, but the obverse side of the same picture. Where the transcendentalist emphasised the element of *common* experience in the two-term thought situation, the empiricist concentrates on the element of *individual* experience. But this, though, like the transcendentalist view, it gives a useful working account of knowledge, does not account *for* knowledge. This is so for three reasons. In the first place, the individual is not *inferring* his knowledge from his experience; in the second place, the experience of *an* individual is not competent to account for *common* knowledge; and finally, the beginning of knowledge in the individual, as he is inducted into the established body of common concepts by his elders, is not the beginning of knowledge.

When we turn to the attempt to derive thought and knowledge from instinct, we are confronted directly with the problem of the beginning of thought and knowledge.

The difficulty about a transcendental view of thought and knowledge is that, picturing these as an incursion into life from some supra-mundane realm of Pure Ideas, it sees thought as discontinuous with life, as something imposed on life from without. Teilhard de Chardin is arguing that thought should be explicable as part of life, as continuous with the evolutionary process to which life belongs.

This does not (so one like Teilhard would argue) violate our sense of the dignity and uniqueness of thought, nor does it conflict with the demands of a scientific outlook. Here we might remark that, from an evolutionary standpoint — evolutionary in the broadest sense of 'unfolding' or 'development', of 'descent with modification' — the scientific outlook is itself a part of life, as too, is the religious outlook: awe, from which religion springs, leads to wonder, from which science, the desire to understand, arises. If thought, knowledge, rational understanding, can be shown to be, not something imposed upon life, but continuous with life, an integral development from, and expression of, life, then we can begin to see human culture to be, as we would expect it to be, a *unity*, not a chance system of standpoints which are irreconcilable, though each represents a necessary facet of human nature.

That would appear to be the manner of thinking which inspires the attempt to treat thought as continuous with life, emerging out of living processes as the necessary expression of their meaning and purpose. Thought is to be accepted as the thing it demonstrably is, a unique phenomenon which sets man apart from all other creatures, but which is at the same time continuous with his evolutionary past.

Emphasizing in this way the continuity of thought with other life processes, it seems natural to see thought as developing from instinct, as transforming and transcending instinct. On this view, instinct, at its highest point of development, would be seen as burgeoning into thought. But in fact instinct, as we find it in its most developed and specialized form in the highly organized social insects, does not seem to *presage* thought; rather it seems to *preclude* thought.

Teilhard is fully aware of this. '. . . this perfection (of instinct),' he says, 'is conditioned by the extreme rapidity with which their psychology becomes mechanized and hardened . . . its acts seem to become charged with habit soon transformed into reflexes'; and we find them, (in his picturesque phrase), 'pathetically struggling in a blind alley.'

If then, thought is to derive by a continuous development from instinct, it must be at a lower, less specialized level.

We recall here Teilhard's phrase, 'When for the first time in a living creature instinct perceived itself in its own mirror...' This gives us a picture of thought emerging out of instinct.

Elaborating this picture, he says: 'By this individualization of himself in the depths of himself, the living element, which heretofore had been spread out and divided over a diffuse circle of perceptions and activities, was constituted for the first time as a *centre* in the form of a point at which all the impressions and experiences knit themselves together and fuse into a unity that is conscious of its own organization.'

Two points are to be noted here. Thought is appearing *in an individual* for the *first time*. Teilhard does not shirk the implication of this. He speaks of ' . . . the individual and instantaneous leap from instinct to thought', and says, 'What at first sight disconcerts us is the need to accept that this step could only be achieved *at a single stroke.*'

He considers this need to be inescapable. 'Look at it as we will,' he says, 'we cannot avoid the alternative — either thought is made unimaginable by a denial of its psychical transcendence over instinct, or we are forced to admit that it appeared *between* two individuals.' This is so, he argues, because, though in the human individual we can trace the continuous stages in the development of thought from infancy to adulthood, in the development of the species each stage is carried by a different individual.

He is arguing thus: (a) we have thought, which transcends instinct, (b) the passage from instinct to thought in the *species* can only have occurred as 'a mutation from zero to everything'.

Thought transcends instinct: that is to say, it is a higher (more effective) mode of organization than instinct. We can see in what way it is higher and more effective: it operates *consciously*, giving the organism increased powers of choice, and control; and it is *communicable*, so that what one organism learns from its experience can be passed on as part of a common store of knowledge — it is in this sense that thought is correlative with what we call knowledge. It is in this sense, too, that thought is correlative with language. Here one might aptly paraphrase Kant: Thoughts without words to express them are blind; words without thoughts to be their contents are non-existent.

Thought and knowledge are a unique mode of organization of experience in that they are essentially *conscious, common, and communicable*. These are the three characteristics of the body of thought, the system of concepts, the body of knowledge, that we actually possess, which any account of thought or knowledge must provide for. And it would seem that here the instinctual account of thought runs into difficulties.

Because it is tracing a development from instinct to thought which takes place in the *species*, the successive stages of which are carried by separate *individuals*, it must picture thought as springing fully-fledged from the chrysalis of instinct. But it does not seem that thought, as the sort of thing it actually is, could have arisen in this way.

'When for the first time in a living creature instinct perceived itself in its own mirror . . .'; this pictures, not only the instantaneous birth of thought, but its birth *in an individual*. It is this new manifestation, thought, which has thus arisen in an individual, that is to become *common* thought.

The individual, thus, for the first time in the progress of evolution, endowed with thought, must, in order that his thought may achieve its appointed function, *communicate* it to his fellow men. Thought alone, as some unique fusing of elements into new patterns and new significances within his private consciousness, will not be enough: even for cultural man, the mystic's private ecstasy, to the extent that it is not communicable, is not knowledge.

But the communication of the individual's new-found thought requires language. And language, as the instrument of communication, is necessarily and essentially *common*. It is only as common that it functions as the instrument of communication; it is a system of word-sounds having meanings which are part of the mental equipment of all the members of the cultural group. But language, because of its function as the instrument of communication between individual and individual, is not a self-sufficient 'thing-in-itself'. It is only the thing it is by virtue of its function, that is, by virtue of its content, the meanings that it communicates.

229

It does not seem that we can speak correctly of private thought; thought is essentially *common*, communicable. But to be communicated thought presupposes (necessitates) language.

This seems to explain why language, regarded as a thing-in-itself, without reference to its content, thought, presents itself as 'the most momentous and at the same time the most mysterious product of the human mind', and we are faced with the paradoxical problem as to how that *began* which we now must *learn*. Language, it becomes clear, cannot be accounted for except as the instrument of thought.

And thought, the body of common thought that we are to account for, cannot have arisen, in the absence of language, from an individual, or even a number of individuals severally, having fused the elements of their private instinctual experience into a personal unity of conscious perception, as suggested by Teilhard.

We may put the difficulty this way: Private thought (ignoring for the moment the contradiction in terms involved), to become the common thought that we want to account for, would have to be communicated through the use of language. But the use of language would presuppose common thought, a commonly held system of concepts, words, and meanings.

No more in its beginning than in its present advanced state can knowledge be accounted for in terms of the functioning of an individual consciousness.

41. *Thought and instinct*

It does not seem that thought, as we know it — the body of common thought we actually possess and are trying to account for — could have arisen 'at a stroke'. But it would seem that, if it is to be derived from instinct, it is only in this way that it could have arisen, as 'a critical transformation, a mutation from zero to everything'.

This points to another peculiar difficulty concerning the

attempt to establish an instinctual basis for thought and knowledge. When we consider the development of thought in the species, says Teilhard, 'we have no means at our disposal of evading the problem of discontinuity' — the discontinuity arising from the fact that the successive stages in the development from instinct to thought are carried by different individuals, so that the transition from instinct to (common) thought must occur in the interval between two individuals.

The attempt to derive thought from instinct had the purpose — or at any rate, would have had the effect — of reconciling the two traditionally opposed points of view, that of the transcendentalist, attributing to thought a supernatural origin, and that of the empiricist, insisting that it is 'nothing but' a natural phenomenon to be accounted for in purely naturalistic terms. This reconciliation was to be achieved by showing thought to be both a unique phenomenon as the transcendentalists asserted, but at the same time continuous with other living processes, as the empiricist insisted. But in the outcome, we are to accept, not a continuity, in the sense of a gradual emergence of thought out of instinct, but 'a threshold that must be crossed at a single stride', 'an instantaneous leap from instinct to thought'.

So that, where we set out to demonstrate *continuity*, as providing the solution of the problem of knowledge, we are forced to accept a fundamental *discontinuity*.

Teilhard speaks of 'the need to accept' this 'discontinuity within continuity', as he calls it. But we can see that the need arises from the attempt to treat instinct as the progenitor of thought, the purpose of which was to establish the continuity of thought with other living processes. In the outcome, the argument is taken as forcing us to accept that thought has arisen 'at a single stroke', i.e., discontinuously.

Why does Teilhard feel 'the need to accept' this 'discontinuity within continuity'? 'Look at it as we will,' he says, 'we cannot avoid the alternative — either thought is made unthinkable by a denial of its psychical transcendence over instinct, or we are forced to admit that it appeared *between* two individuals.'

231

But is this the situation confronting us? There is no question of thought's transcendence over instinct; this is the kind of thought we are trying to account for, the thought we actually have. So if we are confronted by an alternative here, it does not concern the nature of thought, about which there is no dispute: we *have* thought, and it is quite other than instinct. So any alternative there is, must reside in the other term of the argument. So the alternative that is raised by the discontinuous passage from instinct to thought poses the question — not 'Does thought transcend instinct?' — but, 'Does instinct in fact give rise to thought?'

The conclusion to be drawn from the inescapable discontinuity where we had set out to establish a basic *continuity* would seem to be that our original assumption was incorrect — thought has not been derived from instinct. Teilhard is reasoning that thought, in its uniqueness, is so different from instinct that one could have arisen from the other only by a break in evolutionary continuity. But this so conflicts with the original premise that it would seem to be simpler to accept the verdict of the facts, that the one has not arisen from the other.

Accepting this, the transcendence of thought over instinct — the uniqueness of thought within the evolutionary process — does not necessitate our accepting this unexpected and disconcerting discontinuity. Rather, it seems that, accepting thought as the unique phenomenon it is, we must find some other account of its origin as continuous with other living processes.

Thought, like instinct, is a mode of adaptation of the organism to its environment. But the closer we look at it the more it appears as an *alternative* mode of organization to instinct. The higher levels of instinctive behaviour seem to be alien to thought, they seem to preclude thought. It is only in man, a creature with the minimum of instinctual equipment that is commensurate with the maintenance of life, that thought has manifested itself. We might say that, far from springing *from* instinct, thought has arisen in the *absence* of instinct. Instinct is one way of meeting the challenge of existence, thought is another way. Thought seems to be a less rigid, a more flexible, and ultimately a more effective mode of attaining, slowly and gropingly, what instinct achieves unerringly within its fixed limits.

Migrating birds have always accomplished, without conscious effort, feats of navigation that the modern airman, after long evolutionary ages, can accomplish only with the aid of an intricate system of delicate instruments. But the principles involved in the airman's instruments can be applied over an ever widening field of activities as part of a general body of knowledge; and — most important — can be taught to other individuals who would not themselves have arrived at such principles. Migrating birds, setting out on their flights with a blind precision, which indicates a most sensitive relationship to their physical environment, are shut off, by that very precision, from knowing anything about the principles involved.

This would seem to be another reason why thought could not have sprung from instinct. Thought is ultimately a more powerful tool, but in its beginnings it must have been a much less efficient, a much more groping and tentative way of meeting the demands and hazards of life.

This draws our attention to another fact about thought: it cannot have sprung into being 'at a stroke'. In fact we know, from the presence of primitive peoples in the world today, that thought has evolved slowly and painfully throughout the ages. The complexity of thought we have today can be seen as resting on the humblest beginnings; men, with the most meagre instinctual equipment to guide them, feeling their way toward some other, unique way of meeting the challenge of existence.

The instinctive creatures are guided, from birth to death, by an innate pattern of behaviour that is so successful because, in the first place, being innate, it is unconscious — the organism is instinctively directed toward goals of which it is itself unaware; the end is pre-ordained, the organism fulfils itself in working blindly toward it. And it is successful in the second place – or perhaps in the first place – because it represents a triumphant compromise with the environment: the organism – more precisely, the species – has struck a bargain with fate, has come to terms with existence, has limited the demands made on it by placing a strict limit on its own demands.

The way of thought was to be quite other than this. Men, who were to achieve thought – or perhaps we should say, who were to be the bearers of thought – must first *create* their world before they could come to terms with it. And to this end – a far distant end, hidden below the horizon of experience – they must create a *common, objective* world out of their *private, subjective* experiential data.

The instinctive creatures were heirs to a life-pattern which was theirs without effort or even conscious acceptance, simply by virtue of their genetic endowment. Man the evolutionary pauper, starting from the barest of equipment, must accumulate his own wealth. And first he must lay the foundations on which to build.

How, from so inauspicious a start, is he to proceed? We know what is to be the outcome of his efforts. He is to produce a complex structure of commonly-held, communicable ideas or concepts, in terms of which the individual may interpret his transient experiential data, thereby raising them to a level to which instinct has never attained, and – even more significant – beyond anything that, left to himself, he could ever have attained by his own individual efforts.

For, as we have already noted, man is essentially a social being. Teilhard has given us a vivid picture of those progenitors of ours who were to lay the foundations of thought, knowledge, language, words and meanings: 'As far back as we can meet them, our great-great-ancestors are to be found *in groups* and gathered round the fire.'

It was out of these intimate social groups, gathered round their fires, that language was to arise.

42. *The evolutionary status of human knowledge*

Social man is the only creature to have achieved knowledge — or, rather, let us put it this way: by knowledge, in the strict sense, we refer to a phenomenon which is peculiar to man, which distinguishes him from all the other animals. There is always a tendency, either to overstate this claim, in the interests of a 'spiritual' or 'idealistic' view of man and his destiny; or, by reaction, to deny it in an attempt to 'debunk' man and his claims. These two opposed attitudes, with their claims and counter-claims, have always bedevilled the problem of knowledge. To meet one claim, man must be equal with the gods; to meet the other, he must be one with the lowliest members of the animal kingdom.

All we are here interested in is the fact: man is, demonstrably, less than a god, but at the same time is a god-like stage apart from the nearest of his animal relatives. That is what we have to account for: a body of knowledge which has lifted man, the animal, to a unique position in the animal kingdom.

Although social man is unique in being the only creature to attain to systematised knowledge, he is, of course, not unique as a social creature. His close relatives, the apes, for instance, are essentially social creatures. But the apes have not attained to anything commensurate with human knowledge. This quite obvious fact is of interest because it draws our attention to the further fact that it is not man's social condition alone that accounts for his possessing knowledge. It is clearly a necessary condition: he is the only one of the social creatures that has made this unique advance; but it is just as clearly not a sufficient condition: no other social creature has made it. Man must have possessed some other characteristic, besides his gregarious nature, to account for his unique achievement.

He was characterized, of course, by his low level of, instinctual behaviour; but this he shared with other social animals, the apes for instance. However, this too would seem to have been a necessary condition for the achievement of knowledge. Any more specialized level of instinctive behaviour is found to be inimical to knowledge in the true sense.

If we use the term 'knowledge' in relation to the precise instinctive behaviour of the social insects, this is only in a secondary and derivative sense, by analogy with human knowledge; and this applies too to many other uses of the term. It is often claimed, as part of the debunking reaction to the claims of the transcendentalists, that man knows in the same way that animals know; that human knowledge is just an extension of animal knowledge. But this really means that, looking back from the level of our human knowledge, we can see that animals 'know' in something the way that we do.

But even this is no more than a not-very-helpful analogy. The fact is that man knows in a way of his own, and that way is quite different from that of the animals. We must avoid here the tendency, which today has become a 'new way of philosophy', of arguing, from our inability to understand a fact, that the fact doesn't exist. But even those who would hesitate to carry the argument to this explicit point, find difficulty in standing up to the challenge of uncomfortable facts. Stuart Chase, in his widely-read *The Tyranny of Words*, says of his famous cat Hobie Baker, 'Hobie can never learn to talk. He can learn to respond to my talk, as he responds to other signs . . . But he cannot master words and language.' And he goes on, 'I find Hobie a useful exhibit along this difficult trail of semantics. What "meaning" connotes for him is often so clear and simple that I have no trouble in following it. I come from a like evolutionary matrix. "Meaning" to me has like roots, and a like mechanism of apprehension. I have a six-cylinder brain and he has a one-lunger, but they operate on like principles.'

But is the difference – the difference between human knowledge and animal 'knowledge', that is – only in the different horsepowers of the brains involved? Do both operate on the same principles? Obviously not. Because when Stuart Chase performs an act of the kind we call 'knowing', what he does is to use a concept, which is common to his cultural community, and which he has learned from his elders by way of language, to interpret his immediate private experiential data. This his cat is unable to do — 'He cannot master words and language' — not only because of the lower power of his brain, but because it doesn't work by the same complex principles that guide his master's act of knowing.

'Meaning', says Chase, 'comes to Hobie as it comes to me, through past experience . . .' But this is incorrect. The meagre 'meaning' the cat has is the product of his own experience, but the system of meaning Chase works with is not drawn from his experience, it is an expression of all men's experience, as taught to him by his elders. (We needn't bother any more about the 'last-ditch' argument that the words he hears are his own private experience.)

Basically, the difference between the cat and his master — the difference between animal 'knowledge' and human knowledge — turns on the use of simple *signs* by animals as against the use of *symbols* by men.

But 'signs' and 'symbols': what is the essential difference between these? There is a concise and useful treatment of this subject in Dr. Susan Langer's *Philosophy in a New Key*, and the best thing I can do is quote from this at length. But first, I would like to make another quotation from Dr. Langer. Having outlined at some length a certain widely-held view of language, the 'biogenesis theory' , she proceeds to submit it to a critical examination, but before doing so she says:

> An interpretation of observed facts that adjusts them to a general scientific outlook, a theory that bridges what used to appear as a *saltus naturae*, a logical explanation displacing a shamefaced resort to miracle, has so much to recommend it that one hates to challenge it on any count. But the best ideas are also the ones most worth reflecting on.

With this gracious apology she then proceeds to reflect on the biogenetic theory — it is essentially an attempt to trace language back to a basis in animal behaviour, thus treating it as continuous with man's evolutionary development (Teilhard de Chardin's was another such attempt, as we saw) — and the outcome of her reflection is to reject it as not accounting for the sort of thing language actually is.

I have quoted Langer's 'apology' because it expresses a difficulty of my own. I want to make use of what Langer has to say about signs and symbols, because I am in her debt for her treatment of this distinction, as in fact for many other ideas on language. But in the long run, I, in my turn, am going to reject the view of language that she substitutes for the biogenetic approach. But I will do so with a diffidence due to my respect for her own attempt to rescue the subject from the confusion into which it has been dragged by the unscientific counter-claims of tender-minded transcendentalist and tough-minded empiricist.

There is a point worth making here. A distinction requires to be drawn between a *criticism* and a *critical examination*. One criticises a writer who is obviously distorting or evading facts in a deliberate attempt to 'smother' a viewpoint he doesn't favour in the interests of a viewpoint which, for some not fully disclosed reason, he does favour. We can't all always get our facts straight, of course, and this may lead to faulty argument, but the philosopher's business is not to be always right — philosophers being human beings — but at least to be honestly wrong.

In the previous section, we drew some useful conclusions from a critical examination of Pierre Teilhard de Chardin's stimulating attempt to derive thought and knowledge from instinct. Presently a critical examination of Langer's view of language will yield other useful results.

What we are actually doing in such a case is, not *criticizing* a writer's views from a standpoint of superior knowledge, or more profound insight, but reaching out toward such an advanced standpoint on the basis of the difficulties disclosed by the other's discussion.

An essential step — or at least, I have found it to be an

essential step — toward a new insight is to become aware of
the limitations of somebody else's argument. That is why
honest mistakes are to be valued, and dishonest ones deplored.
Honest mistakes are mortal man's stepping-stones to truth.

43. From signs to symbols

Symbol and meaning [says Langer] make man's world,
far more than sensation. . . symbolism is the recognized
key to that mental life which is characteristically human
and above the level of their animality . . . The acquisition
of so decisive a tool must certainly be regarded as one of
the great landmarks in human progress, probably the
starting-point of all genuinely intellectual growth . . .
Man's conquest of the world undoubtedly rests on the
supreme development of his brain, which allows him to
synthesise, delay, and modify his reactions by the
interpolation of *symbols* in the gaps and confusions of
direct experience, and by means of 'verbal signs' to add
the experiences of other people to his own.

So much for the advantages of using symbols. She goes on:

There is a profound difference between using symbols
and merely using signs . . . The use of signs is the very
first manifestation of mind . . . It arises as early in
biological history as the famous 'conditioned reflex',
by which a concomitant of a stimulus takes over the
stimulus function.

This was the sort of thing that Pavlov demonstrated in his
famous experiments, in which he caused his dogs to salivate,
not only in the presence of food, but on hearing a sound (a
buzzer or a bell) which, by repetition, they had come to
associate with food. The sound became, for the dog, a sign of
forthcoming food; it acted, that is, as a substitute stimulus for
the food itself.

Obviously signs are a most valuable part of animal
behaviour.

R

As soon as sensations function as signs of conditions in the surrounding world, the animal receiving them is moved to exploit or avoid those conditions. The sound of a gong or whistle, itself entirely unrelated to the process of eating, causes a dog to expect food, if in past experience this sound has always preceded dinner; it is a sign, not a part, of his food. Or the smell of a cigarette, in itself not necessarily displeasing, tells a wild animal that there is danger, and drives it into hiding. . . Even animal mentality, therefore, is built up on a primitive semantic; it is the power of learning, by trial and error, that certain phenomena in the world are signs of certain others, existing or about to exist . . .

Man's superiority in the race for self-preservation was first ascribed to his wider range of signals [signs], his greater power of integrating reflexes, his quicker learning by trial and error; but a little reflection brought a much more fundamental trait to light, namely his peculiar use of 'signs'. Man, unlike all other animals, uses 'signs' not only to *indicate* things, but also to *represent* them.

This brings us to the distinction between *signs,* the use of which constitutes the typical 'mentality' of animals, and *symbols* which are peculiar to man.

To a clever dog, the name of a person is a signal [sign] that the person is present [or is about to appear]. You say the name, he pricks up his ears and looks for the object. If you say 'dinner', he is restive, expecting food. You cannot make any communication to him that is not taken as a signal of something immediately forthcoming. His mind is a simple and direct *transmitter* of messages from the world to his motor centres. . .

The difference here is that between the cat, Hobie's, system of 'meaning' and the meaning that his master works with. The animal's 'meaning' is limited to a direct relation between his sensation and an immediate state of his environment.

With man it is different. We use certain 'signs' among ourselves that do not point to anything in our actual surroundings. Most of our words are not signs in the sense of signals. They are used to talk *about* things, not to direct our eyes and ears and noses toward them. Instead of announcers of things, they are reminders. They have been called 'substitute signs', for in our present experience they take the place of things that we have perceived in the past, or even things that we can merely imagine by combining memories, things that *might* be in past or future experience . . . They serve, rather, to let us develop a characteristic attitude toward objects *in absentia*, which we call 'thinking of' or 'referring to' what is not here. 'Signs' used in this capacity are not symptoms of things, they are symbols . . . An object is a form which is at once an experienced individual thing, and a symbol for the concept of it, for *this sort of thing*.

I think we can say, bearing in mind Hobie the cat and his master, Stuart Chase, that the animal by his dependence on signs, with their immediate reference to specific things and events, is confined within the limits of his own individual experience. What he 'knows' is not knowledge in the sense of which we use the term in regard to human knowledge, because it is personal and private, a direct relationship between him and the thing or event.

Stuart Chase seems to realize this difference, without having any clue as to the nature of the difference. 'Most children do not long maintain Hobie Baker's realistic appraisal of the environment. Verbal identification and confused abstractions begin at a tender age . . . Language is no more than crudely acquired before children begin to suffer from it, and to misinterpret the world by reason of it.'

This is why Stuart Chase calls his book *The Tyranny of Words*. It is a very dashing thesis, evidently meant to shock simple-minded folk who innocently thought that when they used words they were saying what they meant. But, of course, it is a mistaken thesis. Chase, in his desparagement of language, with its system of indirect knowing through a system of symbols, in favour of the direct 'sign' way of 'knowing' by

241

the animal, overlooks the fact that the child finishes up by knowing much more than the cat, on Chase's own showing, could ever begin to know. The reason for this is that the cat is confined to his simple, personal sign-'knowledge', whereas the child is in the process of being initiated into a complex body of common symbolic knowledge. This doesn't betray him into misinterpreting the World; it permits him to enter into the common concept, world, by participating in which he is able to transcend the limits of his own individual experience; he is able to pass from the *sign*-language, to which his animal relatives are confined, to the *symbol*-language that is the unique possession of his own kind, man.

We might represent the difference between the two ways of knowing, thus:

SIGN (Buzzer)	THING
whereas	
SYMBOL (Word)	KIND OF THING

Or we might get a more accurate picture of the situation by presenting it purely in terms of experience, thus:

INDIVIDUAL EXPERIENCE (Sound of Buzzer)	INDIVIDUAL EXPERIENCE (Food)
whereas	
INDIVIDUAL EXPERIENCE (Sound of Word)	COMMON EXPERIENCE (The kind of thing symbolized by the Word as participated in by others.)

The difference between these two modes of knowing — between Hobie Baker's 'meaning' and his master's meaning — raises peculiar difficulties for the standard 'biogenetic theory', which would reduce human knowing to terms of animal knowing, and animal knowing to a mere matter of meeting the organism's simple physiological needs, such as food, sex, survival etc.

Having made this simple reduction, in which human knowledge is distinguished only by a more advanced and so more effective way of meeting the organism's basic needs — on such a purely practical view of knowledge such activities as art, literature, religion, become mere superfluous accretions — the holders of the biogenetic theory seem inevitably to fall into a trap they have laid for themselves. They proceed on the lines demonstrated by Stuart Chase to emphasise all the fallacies, follies and futilities of man's way of knowing, through the symbolic system, language, as against the animal's direct and simple 'realism', which keeps him in immediate and successful contact with his environment — though not, it might be mentioned, as immediate and successful as the way of knowing of the instinctive creatures such as bees and wasps.

Dr. Langer draws our attention to the difficulties that lie in wait for the naive biogenetic theory, which seems to be having it both ways by insisting that human knowledge is only an *advanced* mode of animal knowledge, which, however, puts the human knower at a *disadvantage* as compared with the animal. Dr. Langer aptly remarks:

> A cat with a 'stalking-instinct' or other special equipment, who could never learn to use that asset properly, but was forever stalking chairs and elephants, would scarcely rise in animal estate by virtue of his talent. Men who can use symbols to facilitate their practical responses, but use them constantly to confuse and inhibit, warp and misadapt their actions *and gain no other end by their symbolic devices,* have no prospect of inheriting the earth.

> But man has inherited the earth, so obviously there is something basically wrong with an account of knowledge that makes this impossible.

> Such an 'instinct' [Dr. Langer goes on] would have no chance to develop by any process of successful exercise. The error-quotient is too great. The commonly recognized biological needs — food, shelter, security, sexual satisfaction, and the safety of young ones — are probably

better assuaged by the realistic activities, the meows and gestures, of Hobie Baker than by the verbal imagination and reflections of his master. The cat's world is not falsified by the beliefs and poetic figments that language creates, nor his behaviour unbalanced by the bootless rites and sacrifices that characterize religion, art, and other vagaries of a word-mongering mind. In fact, his vital purposes are so well served without the intervention of these vast mental constructions, these flourishes and embellishments of the cerebral switchboard, that it is hard to see why such an overcomplication of the central exchange was ever permitted, in man's 'higher centres', to block the routes from sensory to motor organs and garble all the messages.

It is for these reasons that Dr. Langer feels the need to find some other account of human knowledge than the 'nothing but' theory of the biogeneticists. And in this we must agree with her.

44 *'The need to symbolize'*

'Symbolism is the recognized key to that mental life which is characteristically human and above the level of sheer animality.'

But what is it that makes man, like any other animal, use signs, but also and more importantly and specifically as a human animal, use symbols? Why and how has he achieved this unique and paradoxical habit? Why, if the habit of translating his experiences into symbols serves no obvious purpose in the furtherance of his basic biological needs, and in fact, if the biogenetic theory is right, obstructs and confuses the furtherance of those needs, did man adopt in the first place a habit so inimical to his evolutionary development? And — even more paradoxically — why, having adopted it, did he proceed to outdistance on the evolutionary scale those other creatures who were so much better served by their simple devotion to the immediate, practical concerns of daily existence?

The moral of this long critique [says Dr. Langer] is, therefore, to reconsider the inventory of human needs, which scientists have established on a basis of animal psychology, and somewhat hastily set up as the measure of man. An unrecorded motive might well account for many an unexplained action. I propose, therefore, to try a new general principle: to conceive the mind, still as an organ in the service of primary needs, but of *characteristically human needs;* instead of assuming that the human mind tries to do the same things as a cat's mind, but by use of a special talent which miscarries four times out of five, I shall assume that the human mind is *trying to do something else.*

. . . This difference of fundamental needs, I believe, determines the difference of function which sets man so far apart from all his zoological brethren; and recognition of it is the key to those paradoxes in the philosophy of mind which our too consciously zoological model of human intelligence has engendered.

. . . I believe there is a primary need in man which other creatures probably do not have, and which actuates all his apparently unzoological aims . . . Despite the fact that this need gives rise to almost everything that we commonly assign to the 'higher' life, it is not itself a 'higher' form of some 'lower' need; it is quite essential, imperious and general, and may be called 'high' only in the sense that it belongs exclusively (I think) to a very complex and perhaps recent genus.

We are reminded here of Teilhard de Chardin's attempt to establish thought as a unique phenomenon, which is at the same time continuous with the evolutionary process. Teilhard tried to establish this by deriving thought from instinct. Langer is proposing to attribute to man a unique need, to account for this unique achievement, the achievement of raising the level of his experience by refracting it through the medium of a symbolic system.

This basic need, [she says] which certainly is obvious only in man, is the *need of symbolization*. The symbol-making function is one of man's primary activities, like eating, looking, or moving about. It is the fundamental process of his mind, and goes on all the time.

This raises an interesting question. We know that man is the only creature to adopt this procedure of representing his experiences to himself through the intermediary of symbols. The question is: Why should men feel this need to symbolize that which originally they experienced directly with all the impact of an immediate experience? This reminds us of the problem raised by Mill's lone individual, which we met earlier. We then asked if such an individual would have either the impulse or the capacity to conceptualize his experience. The answer, we saw, was No; but in any case logical analysis has already shown us that the concepts we actually possess, concepts, that is, which are characterized by the fact that they are common to all the members of a given cultural group, have not been derived from the experience of any one individual.

This, too, is the characteristic of symbolism, for what man represents by his unique word-sound symbols is, not individual things, but, as noted by Langer, 'kinds of things'. Words, as we saw earlier, do not 'mean' by naming the things they denote. Langer says in this regard, 'symbols are not proxy for their objects, but are *vehicles for the conception of objects* . . . it is the conceptions, not the things, that symbols directly 'mean' . . . a word is a symbol associated with a conception, not directly with a public object or event.' The word 'fire' does not *mean* the fire I am now looking at, otherwise when the fire was out the word would have no meaning. 'Fire' *means*, not by referring to this fire, but by reference to a class of experiences of which this fire is an instance.

Words are symbols for concepts, and concepts are something more – much more – than direct records of simple reflexes; and analysis, to repeat, has shown that there is no direct route from reflexes — individual experiences — to concepts — common experiences. That is what gives conceptualized experience its power. The concept stands for *kinds* or *forms* of possible experiences; it is an open cheque on experience which may be cashed for the value of any given experience. Having been inducted into the use of the established system of concepts, the individual, by bringing his immediate and purely private experience under the appropriate common form, can raise his experience to a level of meaning which, in its own right, it cannot achieve.

This is the *outcome* of the procedure of symbolization. But could we say that it was the *purpose* of symbolization? This would seem to be going too far. But this seems to raise the question, Did men symbolize their experience in response to a *need* to symbolize?

But let us first see what Dr. Langer has to say further regarding the symblic process. She is commenting on the statement of another writer, that 'the essential act of thought is symbolization'. Dr. Langer remarks '. . . if the material of thought is symbolic then the thinking organism must be forever furnishing symbolic versions of its experiences, in order to let thinking proceed.'

There are three points to be noted about this account of the origin of symbolism: If men had to reduce the immediate flow of their experience to symbolic form in order to keep thinking going, this would seem to suggest that it was thinking, not symbolism, that was the primary need that men were responding to. Urged on by the inner need to think, they would seem to have found that they could only accomplish this by conceptualizing, i.e., thinking about, their experience.

There seems to be a difficulty here, and it draws our attention to another aspect of this account of what Teilhard de Chardin called 'the birth of thought'. To keep his thought-processes going, the individual must continually transform his immediate experience from the level of direct sign-material to the level of symbol-material. The symbolic process is seen as being applied directly by the individual to his own experience. Langer, for instance, speaks of 'the real world construed by the abstractions which the sense-organs immediately furnish'. That is to say, in effect, that the concept is derived by the individual directly from his own experience. We may recall that this was what the phenomenalist tried to prove, and failed.

However, it is of interest that Langer also says, regarding 'symbolization' as 'the essential act of thought', 'As a matter of fact, it is not the essential act of thought that is symbolization, but an act *essential to thought* and prior to it.' I think we can take this as meaning that the procedure of symbolization is not something that takes place here and now in my act of thought; the symbolization which is essential to my present act of thought is something which has already taken place. In other words, my act of thought does not involve an immediate act of symbolization, it involves my making use of an already established symbolic system.

This seems to bring us closer to the view that our own inquiry has repeatedly led to, that in my act of thought I am not deriving or inferring concepts directly from the data of my own experience. I am subsuming my immediate data under an already-established conceptual system into which I have been inducted by my elders.

But this raises a difficulty. On the one hand, this 'prior' system of symbolization, which the individual uses in his act of thought, is clearly the established system of concepts which is common to the cultural group, or what we have referred to as the common world-picture – the real 'world' of traditional pre-analytic thought. On the other hand there is the reference to 'the real world construed by the abstractions which the sense-organs immediately furnish', which seems to picture the individual abstracting his own symbolic system, his own concepts, directly from his own experiential data.

This reminds us that the thought-situation involves two complementary factors or aspects. On the one hand, there is the established body of common concepts, a historical growth having its roots in man's pre-cultural past. On the other hand, there is the individual's act of judgment: these immediate data belong under that experiential form. Langer has noted these two aspects of the thought situation and the relation between them. 'So, the two most controversial kinds of meaning – the logical and the psychological – are distinguished and at the same time related to each other . . .'

Unless we make this distinction, and keep it clearly in mind, we are liable to find ourselves switching from one standpoint to the other as our argument seems to require emphasis on one factor or the other in the thought-situation.

Perhaps at this point we had better take a closer look at this procedure of symbolization which is so distinctively and uniquely a human activity that it seems like a need of man's nature. However, it would be more satisfactory, if instead of explaining symbolization as arising from a need to symbolize, we could get a clear view of the nature of this 'need'. Perhaps we could do this if we could get a clearer view of the nature of man's procedure of symbolization.

Chapter V

THE ORIGINAL SYNTHESIS OF EXPERIENCE

45. *A dialogue concerning language*

A. 'As far back as we can meet them, our great-great-ancestors are to be found in groups and gathered round the fire.' These were the men who were to produce the symbolic system, language, that we now want to know more about.

B. What puzzles me is, why men *should* have gone to the trouble of setting up a set of symbols to express — well, what? — their experiences. A man's experiences came to him direct. If he hit his head on a rock when he was climbing into his cave, well, that experience meant for him precisely what it felt like; he didn't need to symbolize the rock in order to feel the pain — and even less did he need to symbolize the pain, which was the most direct possible kind of experience with its own immediate 'meaning'. His nervous system recorded the meaning of that rock-bumping experience for him in the simplest and most unambiguous way. Then why should he have given up this unambiguous 'sign language' and gone to the trouble of setting up a string of sounds to symbolize his experiences, so that from now on he took his experiences at second-hand, so to speak? He sacrificed the directness of experience in order to get an indirect kind of experience filtered through his symbols. Why?

A. But the fact is that by using symbols to stand for experiences men have vastly increased their capacity for experience. While they stuck to the 'sign language', as you call it, they were still at the animal level. It is by the use of symbols that they have raised themselves onto what Teilhard calls 'a new biological level'. By the use of symbols, men transcended their animal limitations and became human.

B.   Agreed. But that only makes it more puzzling. Because men couldn't have known — Well, let us bring it down to cases. I suppose I had an ancestor among that group sitting round the fire. Why did 'I' — my pre-language counterpart in the group around the fire, I mean — put 'myself' to the trouble of working out a set of symbols in which to express 'my' experiences? I can't imagine that 'I' had any 'need' to do so. I don't think 'I' symbolized because 'I' had some inner urge to symbolize. As things turned out, this business of symbolization has proved to be a great advantage, but — this is the point I've been trying to get at — I had no means of knowing that that was how it would work out. I hadn't a clue — how could I have? — that symbols would work so much better than my original direct signs. I can see how the idea of a 'need to symbolize' has arisen. Men *did* symbolize, and there couldn't at that stage have been any practical reason why they *should* symbolize — quite the contrary in fact — and so the only explanation seems to be that they must have had some inner urge to symbolize; a sort of inborn disposition or instinct for symbolization. But somehow that doesn't seem a satisfactory account of why 'I' gave up my highly successful 'sign language' in favour of a very speculative and uncertain symbol language. I'd like a better explanation if it was available, though I admit I can't imagine any better.

A.   Let's take it a step at a time. There are two interesting points raised by what you've just been saying. There is the difference, for instance, between what you call 'sign language' and the symbolic language that we are trying to understand. The advantage of the 'sign language', as you say, is that it is direct and unambiguous, it means precisely what it is experienced as meaning. But its corresponding disadvantage or limitation is that it means only for 'you'.

B. Yes. But it does mean directly and unambiguously, and that meets all my requirements, doesn't it?

A. Let's leave that question for the moment. The advantage of the symbol language as compared with the 'sign language' — or let us say simply the difference between them — is that symbol language is not just confined to you, it is a mode of communication.

B. But why should it be?

A. Well, let's just stick to the facts for the moment, and the fact is that symbol language — the sort of thing we *mean* by 'language' — does act as a medium of communication. And, noting that fact, we come to the second interesting point. The symbol language acts as a medium of communication, it acts as a means by which the members of the group can communicate with one another, because the peculiarity of the symbols is that they have the same value — the same meaning — for all the members of the group.

B. Isn't that rather a leap in the dark? *How* do they come to have the same value for everybody? Isn't that just the problem?

A. Yes, that's precisely the problem. But let's get back to the rough ground, as a noted philosopher once said. The symbols of language have a common meaning, a meaning common to all the individuals in the group. So evidently the account you were giving of the transition from 'sign language' to true symbol language, wasn't correct.

B. How so?

A. You found difficulty, you said, in explaining the setting up of symbols to represent 'your' experience, in place of 'your' original and quite satisfactory sign-language. But if, as we now see to be the case, the symbols in question have the same value for all the members of the group, then they weren't the sort of thing you have

253

assumed that they were, i.e., something set up by 'you' for the interpretation of 'your' own experience. So your account of the origin of these symbols was mistaken.

B. I see what you mean. But that doesn't improve matters. It makes it even more difficult to understand my adoption of symbols.

A. I don't think you've quite got my point. Wasn't the difficulty you found in the transition from 'sign language' to symbol language due to the fact that you were treating symbols as deriving from 'your' own experience? — whereas, as *common* symbols, valid for all the members of the group, they can't have been derived in that way. You couldn't understand why or how 'you' made the transition from 'sign-language' to symbol-language. But the difficulty in explaining this, don't you see, was due to the fact that this was not what had happened; symbols couldn't have arisen in that way.

B. So the problem really is, why did the members of the group as a whole, why did all men, adopt symbols instead of their original sign-language?

A. Yes, but let us go slowly. The symbols that were adopted were not originated by 'you'?

B. No.

A. By the same token, then, they were not originated by any other individual in the group?

B. No, that would be so, I suppose. But then —

A. Yes?

B. They haven't been originated by anybody. But we *have* them; we have the set of symbols we call language, so they must have been started by somebody. It doesn't make sense to say the group started them, because 'the group' is only the collective name for all the separate individuals crouched around the fire. So the situation seems to be that nobody *could* have started the symbols, but somebody *must* have. That doesn't look a very promising problem to try to solve.

A. Well, let's stick to our method of taking things a step at a time. What are symbols *for?* — the sort of symbols that constitute language, that is. What do they do? What *are* they?

B.   Well, *what* are they?

A.   The answer I would suggest is this: symbols are essentially modes of organization of experience. Signs are modes of organization, too. To the chap who came face to face with a tiger, when walking down a jungle path, this was a sign to organize his experience in such a way as to exclude the presence of the tiger. In other words, he ran for it. Signs are simple modes for the moment-by-moment organization of individual experience. As Langer puts it, 'signs are something to act upon or a means to command an action'.

B.   Yes, that seems to be an accurate enough description of them.

A.   Symbols are different from signs. And the difference is, according to what we said just now, that symbols are *common* modes, or say forms, for the organization of experience. This is the most obvious respect in which they differ from signs, which are the individual's private way of organizing his experience. Symbols are not just valid for the individual using them, they are valid for him and for all the other members of the group. That is what they *are* — that is how they *work*. We can go as far as that safely, without indulging in any speculation, I would say.

B.   Yes, that's all straightforward enough.

A.   That being so, we can see another characteristic that symbols possess. As common modes for the *organization* of experience, they are not just valid here and now, on this occasion of their use. Once they are established they are available for use by any member of the group on any relevant occasion. Symbols are *permanently* and *commonly* valid.

B.   I'm not sure that I know what you mean by 'any relevant occasion'.

A.   Do you remember what Langer said about symbols standing, not for individual things, but for 'sorts of things'? If we translate that into our present terms of experience, we would say that symbols stand for 'kinds of experiences'. Or as we just said, they are modes or forms for the organization of experiences. And that means, we can see, they are *common* modes or forms for the organization of *individual* experience, an individual's moment-by-moment experiences; what the individual was originally content to organize here and now in terms of his private 'sign-language'. Symbols, once they are established, function as permanent, common forms. The individual can organize the transient flux of his private experience according to the relevant common and permanent form. The symbols or forms work for the individual by his bringing the relevant experiences – the right *kind* of experiences – under the appropriate common form – the kind of experiences that that form is a symbol for. If, meeting the tiger, he interprets the experience under the form, say, large rock, the form and the experience are not mutually relevant, and he makes his (negative) contribution to the development of the symbolic system by not living to perpetuate his mistake.

B.   Yes, I see what you mean by the symbols, the forms, being permanent, being available for use on the relevant occasion. That's all right as a *description* of them, that's the sort of things they are and the way they work, when we come to take a closer look at them. But that still leaves us with the question, Why did men symbolize in the first place? In fact it adds to the difficulty, because it's not now a question of why *an* individual set up a private set of symbols for the organization of his own experience, but why the group set up a system of symbols, a common symbolic system, for all individuals to organize their experience by.

A.   Well, 'why' questions are always a bit troublesome – they're always inclined to lead the earnest inquirer into deeper waters than he finds himself comfortable in. However, if we stick to facts and their immediate implication and go a step at a time, we shouldn't fall over the edge without knowing that we're doing so.

46. *Dialogue continued*

A. The question we are asking is, Why did men symbolize their experience? What caused the group gathered round the fire to set up a symbolic system common to all of them?

B. Yes, and to set it up without having any possible knowledge that it was going to work out to their advantage — it wasn't *that* that caused them to do it. So why did they do it?

A. Perhaps, as a preliminary to asking *why* they did it, we should ask *how* they did it. As you pointed out, we can't say the group did it; 'the group' is only a collective name for the individuals gathered around the fire; 'the group' is an abstraction. And in any case, such an answer only begs the question. So we would have to say that it was the individuals constituting the group, who set going the process that was to lead to common knowledge.

B. But doesn't that set us back where we were? Didn't we come to the conclusion that the individual, left to himself, wouldn't have either the urge or the opportunity to develop symbolized knowledge?

A. Yes, but we were talking then about a solitary individual. Now we are talking about an individual who is not a solitary being, he is a social being, a member of a group. That's the first fact we've got to keep in mind. And the second fact is that, if we are to give an experiential account of knowledge, we must recognize individual experience, the experiences of independent individuals — independent experiential units, we may call them — as its necessary basis. If we stick to the actual conditions that governed the beginnings of knowledge, we are dealing, not with a solitary individual and his private experience, but with social individuals who are to construct a body of common knowledge out of their private experiences.

B.   Yes, but how could they, without having some common form of communication to start with, so that they could compare their experiences? And isn't that just what we are trying to account for?

A.   Yes, that's the obvious, traditional difficulty. But you see, we shouldn't ask, How *could* they manage this? because we know that they did manage it. The question we are trying to answer is, How *did* they manage it? — how did they transform private individual experience into public common knowledge; something that was valid only for the individual, into something that was valid for all individuals? We know that is what they did produce — that is what we mean by 'knowledge' — and on consideration we can see that, as social beings, this is what in the nature of the case they would produce, what they would necessarily produce.

B.   In the nature of the case? — necessarily?

A.   We could put it in a nutshell, this way: Left to himself the individual necessarily wouldn't produce knowledge, but as a social being he isn't left to himself, he is constantly rubbing up against the other members of the group; it is out of these conditions that knowledge has arisen, and in the nature of the circumstances out of which it has arisen it would necessarily be common knowledge; and this is what, as a matter of fact, we know it to be. Taking the nut out of the nutshell, we could say it would be that or nothing; or better, nothing or that.

    The fact is that the main difficulty about the problem of knowledge consists in getting to know what the problem *is*. Once we have succeeded in doing that, the solution begins to force itself upon us. The natural and naive approach is to treat the knowledge any individual possesses as being derived directly from his own experience. But the knowledge he possesses isn't just his own private possession. It is only knowledge because he shares it with others, because it is a *common* knowledge. And common knowledge can't have been derived directly from any one individual's experience — in any case, logical analysis has disposed of that account of the matter. And it is equally obvious that, man being not a solitary creature but a social creature, his common knowledge is an expression of his communal condition.

To repeat, being a social being, it would necessarily be common knowledge that he would produce, if he produced knowledge at all; and he *has* produced knowledge, and it *is* common knowledge. There is one point that emerges here that we should take note of. Social man is the only creature to have produced knowledge and language. But it is clear that though his social state is a condition, and a necessary condition, of his having done this, it is not in itself a sufficient condition. This is so because there are other social creatures, the apes for instance, who have not produced anything in any way commensurate with what we call knowledge and language; if we use these terms in relation to them it is only an analogy with human knowledge and language — at best they display 'something like' what we mean by knowledge and language.

So, the fact of man's being a social creature, though it clearly provides *a* necessary condition for his achieving knowledge and language, does not provide the *only* condition. In answer to our original question, our group around the fire did not symbolize their experience because they were a social group. That, we might say, provided the suitable conditions, but something else was required to cause these men to take advantage of that condition: to cause them to pass from 'sign'-language to

symbol language, from individual experience to common
experience; in fact, to cause them to construct a body
of common experience out of the elements of individual
experience.

B. But isn't that just the problem: *how* did they transform
individual experience, valid only for the experiencing
individual, into symbolised common experience valid for
all individuals?

A. Well, obviously they didn't suddenly become aware of a
deficiency in their social set-up, they didn't call a
meeting of the elders and say 'Let us establish a body of
common knowledge and a symbolic system to represent
it, on the basis of our experience.' They didn't set out to
establish knowledge; it is *we* who know, in retrospect,
that that is what *they* were doing, and it seems to be
that that stands in the way of our knowing *what* they
were doing. As far as they were concerned, they were
merely getting on with the day-by-day business of living,
just sitting around the fire and getting on with one
another as best they could.

B. Yes, they couldn't have known in advance that they
were laying the foundations of a body of common knowledge; but that seems to raise the question, how could
they have proceeded to do just that without having any
inkling that that was what they were doing?

A. I think that we can go to the other extreme and say
that if they could have known in advance what they were
setting out to do, they would never have done it; the
thing would have overwhelmed them. But luckily — for
us and for them — they couldn't at that stage have had
any such idea. Without any theory and without any
consciousness of what was involved, they proceeded to
create a permanent body of common knowledge, a
common system of conceptualized experience, out of the
transient flux of individual experience.

Knowledge, and the language that expresses it, isn't
a theoretical structure. And it isn't a conventional

system either, if by convention is meant a set of rules and counters, like a game of chess, that men have agreed to abide by. It's neither a theory nor a convention, it is a form of life, as a noted philosopher once sagely remarked — and then proceeded to squeeze the life out of it in the interests of his own philosophical requirements.

B. So now we want to know what caused our group around the fire to set about building up common knowledge and language.

A. Yes, but I think it's worth while reminding ourselves here that we set out from the problem confronting modern philosophy, that though analysis had shown that what we call the world is a construction from the data of individual experience, no individual's experience was able to account for the world-picture he actually possessed. And that was — or seemed to be — so paradoxical a conclusion that it precipitated first a 'crisis' and then a 'revolution' in philosophy. But now that we have a calm cool look at the 'problem of knowledge' that frustrating paradox can be seen to have been a product of the way in which the problem was stated. Once we have realized (a) that we are talking about, not an individual's knowledge here and now, but an *established* body of *common* knowledge, and (b) that man is a social being, the 'problem of knowledge' is 'dissolved', to use the current expression, and the 'paradox' is seen for what it was, just a by-product of the failure to take account of how the word 'knowledge' was actually used. In fact what looked like a frustrating paradox was actually, we can now see, the first step toward the solution of the 'problem of knowledge'. Because, as you will remember, analysis had shown that what we call the world was a construction from individual experience which had not been constructed from the experience of any one individual.

So now let us take a look at the genetic cause of knowledge and language as a 'form of life'.

47. *Foundation of the common world-picture*

But if we are to answer our question as to why men symbolized their experiences, if we are to really understand knowledge and language — and that, it seems clear, is what the present stage in the development of thought faces us with — we want something more than a neat description of them as 'a form of life'. We want to fill in, if we can, the picture of our group around the fire transforming the indeterminate flux of their separate experiences as individuals into a common determinate world-picture.

We have agreed that, though man's state as a social being was a necessary condition of his arriving at a common world-picture, something else was necessary. His social state provided the opportunity, but, when we think of other social creatures, we can see that there must have been something peculiar to man, over and above his gregarious instinct, to make him take advantage of the opportunity.

We may not feel satisfied with 'a need to symbolize' as this other condition peculiar to man, but let us recall a point we noted just now about the system that man did in fact arrive at. Symbols differed from the individual's signs in that they referred, as Langer points out, not to an individual's immediate experiences, but to *kinds* of experiences. And this was not a reference to some kind or class of experiences peculiar to the individual using the symbol; symbols stood for kinds of experiences that were common to all the individuals in the group. This is the essential difference between signs and symbols: signs stood for *private individual experiences,* symbols stood for *kinds of common experiences.*

It is in this fact that the power of symbols clearly lies: in place of a private sign, valid only here and now within the confines of the individual's own experience, you have a public symbol valid for all individuals.

When men, hitherto content with the use of signs, turned to the use of symbols, it is clear that they did not merely set up a new kind of language. The function of language is to express something. More precisely, its function is to express experiences. Symbols didn't express individual experiences, the private experiences of the individuals forming the group — signs already did that quite satisfactorily. It is obvious that symbols arose to express some form of experience that was not expressed by signs. And the new kind of experience that symbols expressed was, we know, common experience, or what we call knowledge. So, looking closer, we seem to see, behind men's 'need to symbolize', a need to create common experience.

But that, of course, isn't the solution of our problem. It merely brings us a step nearer to seeing what the problem is. Something happened to cause man, alone of the social creatures, to superimpose upon individual experience this new kind of common experience. What was it that happened? What were the biological conditions that pushed men along the pathway of this adventure of thought?

Teilhard de Chardin has taken both a paleontologist's and a poet's look at this question. Here is what he has to say:

> It is true that in the end, from the organic point of view, the whole metamorphosis leading to man depends on the question of a better brain. But how was this cerebral perfectioning carried out — how could it have worked — if there had not been a whole series of other conditions brought together at just the same time? If the creature from which man issued had not been a biped, his hands would not have been free in time to release the jaws from their prehensile function, and the thick band of maxillary muscles which had imprisoned the cranium could not have been relaxed. It is thanks to two-footedness freeing the hands that the brain was able to grow; and thanks to this, too, that the eyes, brought closer together in the diminished face, were able to converge and fix on what the hands held and brought before them — the very gesture that formed the external counterpart of reflection. In itself this marvellous conjunction should not surprise us. Surely the smallest thing formed in the world is always the result of the most

formidable coincidence — a knot whose strands have been for all time converging from the four corners of space . . .

The outcome of this concatenation of biological circumstances is an increase of what Teilhard de Chardin calls 'psychism', but what we may call simply consciousness or awareness. And with the increase of consciousness goes an increase of individuality. The individual, hitherto, 'narrowly subject to the phylum', as Teilhard puts it, comes increasingly to live in terms of his own capacities and responses; he is becoming an *experiencing* individual rather than a merely *reacting* one.

The increase of psychism or individuality has its own significant effect. As Teilhard puts it, 'The more highly each phylum became charged with psychism, the more it tended to "granulate". The animal grew in value in relation to the species . . . '

Teilhard is here giving us an account of the conditions out of which, we know as a matter of fact, thought, knowledge, common experience, language were to arise. He has drawn his own picture of how these facts were to lead to thought, by way of a leap, in the individual, from instinct to thought; we have found that picture unsatisfactory, and it is the facts alone that here interest us.

We must remind ourselves that those ancestors of ours around the fire were not looking out on our familiar world of things and events seen within a fixed framework of space and time. They were each looking out, or rather *in*, at the momentary flux of their private experiential data. It was out of such discontinuous (as between individual and individual) and indeterminate (as not yet determined within any conceptual system) data, that they were laying the foundations of that familiar, determinate world.

Each individual, as an independent experiential unit, was a sort of recording instrument with its own sensitivity, its own reactions. These private and peculiar reactions did not in themselves yield a determinate picture. They were simply the raw material out of which such a picture was to be constituted.

Two questions present themselves here: What precipitated the movement by which these diverse and disparate individual experiential data were to come together to produce a common world-picture, the picture of a world of things in time and space, common to all the members of the group? And, how were they, diverse and disparate as they were, so combined?

Specifically, we want to know what it was that caused the individual to grope his way out of the closed circle of his own experience, with its simple and unambiguous 'sign-language', toward a strange, abstract, second-hand world, no longer of direct experience, but of *kinds* of experiences, with which he can make contact only through the instrumentality of a specially devised symbolic system, in the setting-up of which he was to create a new kind of non-natural experiential data? And he was to do all this without any foreknowledge that in the outcome he was to gain immeasurably by his strange adventure into the unknown; or rather, not that he, but that later generations, were to gain thereby.

To these questions the conditions outlined by Teilhard suggest the answers. To get a clear view of the answers, let us draw a diagram of our group crouched around the fire:

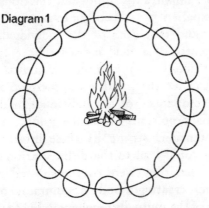

Diagram 1

THE GROUP AROUND THE FIRE 1st Phase

Each circle is to represent an individual, a self-contained experiential unit. The diagram has been drawn so as to emphasize this self-containedness. In this, of course, it gives us a false picture of the actual situation: no creatures, or at any rate no social creatures, are absolutely self-contained experiential units. They have some contact and interaction with one another. They reproduce together, for one thing, and in other ways they affect one another. However, for clarity's sake, let us picture them as shown, each enclosed within the circle of his own reactions. We could think of each circle as a 'field', an *experiential field*.

This is the group that feels, however vaguely and unconsciously at first, the upsurge of the new 'psychism', and with it a growing awareness and consciousness, a tension of individuation.

Hitherto the group, whose members have been rather members of the species than individuals in their own right, has been bound together by a sort of biological inertia. Each experiential unit 'knew its place', though not with the unambiguous rigidity of the instinctive creatures. But with the development of the individual psyche, the growth of individual consciousness, the separate 'fields' constituting the group begin to expand. And in doing so they are brought into closer and, more importantly, quite new relationship with one another: the experiential fields begin to react on one another.

Bearing in mind that each of the individuals who is the experiencing centre of a field is, as we have said, a unique recording instrument with its own sensitivity and its own reactions, we can see that, with every increase of 'psychism', the different 'resonances' of the individual fields set up tensions and mutual repulsions within the group.

Unless the tensions set up by these interactions can be overcome they could lead to the disintegration of the group. But we know that they were overcome, and that this was achieved by men creating a body of common conceptualized experience out of the mutually repellent individual experiential fields. If we reconstruct our original diagram we can see, better than any verbal description could tell us, what was taking place:

Diagram 2

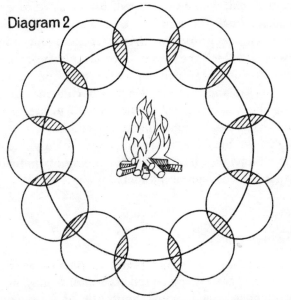

THE GROUP AROUND THE FIRE 2nd Phase

The shaded sections represent (crudely) areas of conflict between experiential standpoints. If the group is not to disintegrate under the strain of its growing tensions it must transform these areas of conflict into areas of mutual understanding. This is not any deliberate procedure of discussion and agreement, of course. It is a mere rough-and-ready process of 'getting on together' as they go about their daily affairs.

But however groping and blundering and unconscious this process may be, in its outcome it is not simply an overcoming of these tensions, it is a *transcending* of them, and in the transcending, a transforming of the whole way of life of the group. For they have set on foot a movement, the combining and co-ordinating of their individual experiential capacities, which is to open up new horizons of being in the same way

267

that the combining of single cells to form an individual organism did.

The individual, who had escaped, by virtue of his growing individuality, from the bondage of the species, has done so only to re-engage himself with the species, but now in a relationship in which the resources of his own being are to be drawn upon and magnified by being paid into a fund of common understanding from which — such is the cumulative power of the new psychism — the individual may then take out more than he or any individual has paid in.

Thought, we may say, is the increment of psychic capital which the individual has gained by paying his individuality into a trust fund of common understanding.

48. *Why men symbolized*

The process of compromise and reconciliation between diverse and disparate experiential standpoints may be called, for convenience, the Original Synthesis of Experience. By presenting it diagrammatically, we have been able to picture something that might otherwise have eluded us. Nevertheless a diagram has the disadvantage of giving an appearance of tidiness and simplicity to a procedure that must have been untidy, because groping and unconscious, and highly complex because of the multiplicity and diversity of the factors involved.

Not only did men differ in their temperaments and their consequent reactions, but different situations brought different temperaments into play, and generated their own peculiar reactions which in turn gave rise to new attitudes and new reactions. And in different circumstances individuals of different temperaments would take the dominant role, and so influence the final outcome in a particular direction, in favour of their way of looking at things. There would be emotional situations, and practical situations, times of re-laxation and idle comfort, times of urgency and stress. To each situation, individuals of a different capacity would be adapted, and others would accept their leadership. And out of this, *kinds of situations* would come to be recognized, a whole variety of reactions would have crystallized to constitute a commonly-held point of view.

And our forebears weren't always crouched around the fire. They had other matters to attend to as well. They may have squabbled, bickered and 'made it up', or just sulkily given way, as they shared their food around the fire, but first the food had to be obtained. And that, mostly, would mean co-operation rather than antagonism.

Picture, for instance, three men going hunting. Three, though in other respects it is a 'crowd' rather than 'company', makes an ideal hunting team. The three hunters are sure to be of different capacities and temperaments: one is an expert tracker of game, another is a sure shot with a throwing stick or other weapon, probably, too, a specialist at choosing or even *shaping* — a preliminary by some thousands of years to *making* — such instruments. The third is fleet of foot and cunning in manoeuvring the game into position for the marksman.

By nods or half-silent grunts or murmurs — for stealth and silence are the essence of hunting — the three hunters co-ordinate their movements. Once the quarry is sighted, one man, the marksman, is to stand stock still, like a mere bush or tree, while the others, going opposite ways, circle and converge so as to drive the quarry towards him.

All this means a merging of their different individual temperamental points of view in the interests of a common end — food for the group around the fire. And — here's the interesting point — this manoeuvring of theirs, this standing, circling, converging to a common point at the same time, all these actual practical actions, dictated by the immediate needs of day-by-day living, involve the ideas of Time and Space: it is in terms of these concepts that these men organize the chase. But it will be many long ages before what is implicit in their actions will force its way into consciousness and become a commonly held explicitly formulated concept.

When this happens, such concepts are the expression of the original act of compromise — co-operative compromise in this case — of the three hunters engrossed in providing food for the group. They do not yet see themselves as moving through a determinate world of things and events in Time and Space. If we were to describe their condition, we would have to say that they are part of a continuum, of which things and events, including themselves, are momentary configurations, which are functions of their immediate tensions of consciousness. What we called earlier the Projection of Experience is yet to come into operation, detaching from them the world they have constructed, to be seen as a thing-in-itself 'independent of all experience', independent, that is, of the experience of any of the individuals who participate in it.

But the immediate point of interest is that concepts such as Space and Time, because of their abstractness, their remoteness, by progressive abstraction, from the raw material of experience on which they ultimately rest, serve to indicate the answer to the question from which our present discussion started: Why did men symbolize their experience? What caused the group around the fire to set up a symbolic system in place of their original direct and simple 'sign language'?

Langer emphasizes that 'the step from mere sign-using to symbol-using marked the crossing of the line between animal and man: this initiated the natural growth of language.' But she speaks of the 'spontaneous abstraction from the stream of sense-experience, elementary sense-knowledge.' This sounds like the individual abstracting directly from the data of his own immediate experience the concepts which are to be expressed by means of symbols. And that this is what is meant is confirmed when she then speaks of the procedure which 'makes symbols for thought out of signs for behaviour'.

And then she says, later, 'Our response to a sign becomes, in turn, a sign of a new situation; the meaning of the first sign having been "cashed in", it has become a context for the next sign. This gives us that continuity of actual experience which makes the sturdy warp of reality, through which we draw the connecting and transforming woof-threads of conception.'

For 'our' and 'we' I think we can read 'my' and 'I'. Langer is thinking of the symbolic system, in terms of which we all interpret our experience, as having been derived directly by each one of us from our own experience, reality, on this view, being the individual's own personal construction. It is this view of a direct step by the individual from signs to symbols that raises the question, Why symbolize? Why did the individual take this step? And to this question there seems to be no answer but by postulating a 'need to symbolize'.

But when we turn from the symbols themselves to their content, to what is being symbolized, we see that what is involved is not a direct step from signs to symbols, but an *indirect* movement, a groping and tentative transition – an unconscious process of abstraction and correlation – from individual experience to common experience.

Once we have seen how men, as social beings, were combining and reducing to a common essence of significance their diverse individual experiences, we can see that what was emerging was the *concept* as a common *form* or pattern of experience: not yet itself an experience, but rather a new way of experiencing.

It was not yet what we mean by a *concept*. In the first place it was an *experiential pattern*. When we speak of concepts we think of these as concepts of determinate things or events. But we must keep in mind that what these primitive men around the fire were doing was, creating, or we might more correctly say *determining,* things and events out of the flux of immediate individual experience. And primitive individual experience must have been largely, even predominantly, emotional. In the same way as a child does, the primitive individual experienced, not a determinate thing or event – a stone against which he stubbed his toe, or a thunder-clap above his head – but simply a cause of pain or fear; or,

T   271

more directly, he experienced, not a thing or event, but a pain or a fear.

It was out of these private and purely subjective pains or fears, together, of course, with other sensory elements of sight, sound, touch, that determinate concepts were to emerge as new, and more significant, *common* modes for the organization of experience. It is clear that concepts, growing in this way out of the living tissue of experience, could only gradually be clarified and defined. We are not dealing with any 'instantaneous leap' to thought, nor with a direct transition from signs to symbols.

In their first emergence, as crude abstractions from the indeterminate flux of subjective experience, they must have carried with them a surplus or overburden of adventitious meaning, the trace of their origin and of the manner of their birth. Even in the more primitive languages in the world today — and these, of course, are highly sophisticated and developed compared with the simple beginnings we are talking of — concepts still show signs of their origins in the raw material of experience. There will not be, for instance, a simple and clear-cut concept *eating,* but the idea of eating will still be embedded in the context of day-by-day living from which it arose. There will be a concept of 'a lot of men eating', 'one man eating', 'women eating', 'eating greedily', 'eating meat', 'eating fruit', etc., but no single concept *'eating'.*

This is quite understandable, and it throws an interesting light on the genesis of concepts out of experience, as referring, not to things or events, but to *kinds of experience.*

So when we speak of our primitive group deriving concepts by abstraction and correlation from the indeterminate flux of individual experience, though we are thinking of concepts as determinate common patterns of experience, we must not think of them emerging from the experiential matrix in this pure and polished form.

In the first place, they are no more than vague and shifting attitudes of mind, mere dispositions to respond to a given set of circumstances in some common way. Gradually these

attitudes define themselves by the same simple abrasive process of give-and-take, of getting on with the other fellow.
And an important part of this process of abstraction and
correlation, as we have called it (thereby rendering it understandable by stating it far too precisely) is the fashioning
of a sound-symbol to 'stand for' the emergent common attitude of mind. For, in the very act of representing – representing – the nebulous attitude, the symbol serves to
define it, to fix it and formalize it and give it a permanent
shape and significance. We might say that the concept was only
such by being symbolized. It is because concept and symbol –
symbol and content – are so closely allied that it has seemed
possible to treat language as a system of symbols, though to
get at its true nature, we must see it as a system of symbolized
experiences.

The growing inter-subjective tensions within the social
group, resulting from the increasing 'psychisms', brings about
– if the group is not to disintegrate under the strain of the
new pressures – the sharing and merging of individual
experiences, and this gives rise to a new form of common
experience, which, for its clarification and definition, calls
for the use of some form of representation, a symbol.

And there is still a further point to be considered concerning the nature of this form of representation, the symbol.
It is in the nature of the concept which is the content of the
symbol that, as the expression of the essence, the common
denominator of significance of a range of individual experiences, it is an *abstraction*.

It is not, as we have said, an experience in itself, it is a *way*
of experiencing, a *form* of possible experiences. And as an
abstraction, it cannot function fully until it is (as it were)
translated back into terms of experience, into terms of
sensory experience, the kind of experience to which the
individual can make a direct response. The concept which has
been abstracted *from* individual experience must be represented in a form which makes it available *as* individual
experience.

273

To be fully functional, the concept requires not only to be given form, and, as we might say, being, by being represented by a physical symbol, a sound, but it must be represented or symbolized in such a way as to render the concept *communicable*. It is only by being communicable that the concept functions effectively as a common form for the organization of (individual) experience.

To be effective as an instrument of communication the symbol which is to represent the concept must be a simple, ready-to-hand piece of sensory experience. And it must be a form of sensory experience that, though it has the same *quality* as the individual's natural data — the 'natural' data which he experiences involuntarily as he goes about his ordinary affairs — must have a unique value of its own which at once distinguishes it from all other data.

Briefly, the symbol that is to represent the common concept which is emerging as an abstraction from the data of individual experience, must itself, to be available to the individual, be a kind of individual experience, but of a kind that marks it off from all other natural data as possessing its own value and meaning.

The symbol — we are talking, of course, about the sound-word — is an instrument of communication by which the concept, given permanent form by being symbolized, can be used to store up man's growing heritage of common knowledge, and to transmit this common store, as a new kind of experiential data having its own unique common value, from one generation to another.

Briefly, then, our ancestors grouped around the fire set up a body of common experience because, as social beings, with a growing experiential capacity, their circumstances pushed them progressively in that direction. And they symbolized this new kind of abstracted common experience because, as the essence of *everybody's* experience it was *nobody's* — no single individual's — experience; because, as such an abstraction, it could be experienced only by being symbolized.

274

49. *How the meaning got into the word*

Our discussion has now brought us face to face with the Word, that unique, non-natural sensory experience, devised by man to give permanent form and significance to the new kind of common experience which has been abstracted from the transient flux of the individual's experiential data.

We have found reason to reject Teilhard's account of 'an instantaneous leap from instinct to thought'; any account of thought that doesn't start by emphasizing its essentially *common* nature may be assumed to be treating it as a direct function of an individual's own experience, and is consequently wrong from the outset. Nevertheless, his view of the consequences to man of the acquisition of thought is worth quoting. He speaks of 'a harmonized collectivity of consciousness equivalent to a sort of super-consciousness . . . Man's possession of it constitutes a radical advance on anything that has gone before.' This hardly fits the picture of thought as resulting from the individual's turning *in* on himself, but it fits the picture we have been brought to of a body of common experience resulting from the individuals of the group turning *outward* toward one another. Teilhard is, in fact, describing common experience. This is clear when he goes on:

> Now the consequences of such a transformation are immense, visible as clearly in nature as any of the facts recorded by physics or astronomy . . . In reality, another world is born. Abstraction, logic, reasoned choice and inventions, mathematics, art, calculation of space and time, anxieties and dreams of love . . .

— these are the far-reaching consequences the possibility of which was released when men took the first blind and groping step toward bringing their diverse experiential outlooks into a common focus of meaning. Teilhard, however, goes on, 'All these activities of the *inner life* are nothing else than the effervescence of the newly formed centre [of the individual's psyche] exploding onto itself.' (The italics are Teilhard's.)

275

Teilhard's attempt to show thought as both the unique phenomenon that it demonstrably is, and at the same time continuous with the whole evolutionary story, by deriving it from the individual's instinctive behaviour, has necessitated his postulating 'discontinuity within continuity'. But the Word as the vehicle of a body of common experience, derived by abstraction and correlation from the experience of all the individuals of the group, is, at one and the same time, something unique in the evolutionary story, and yet directly continuous with that story.

We might say, indeed, that the Word with its meaning is part of man's natural history, though it is utterly different in its origin and functioning from such natural functions as breathing and walking; and it is at the opposite pole from such instinctive activities as the migration of birds or the hiving of bees: it is, in the evolutionary scheme, not simply the antithesis of these activities, it is an alternative and infinitely more powerful and varied mode of organization of experience.

When the hotel porter shouted 'Fire!' in the night-time stillness of the hotel corridor, he tapped a vein of human experience reaching back through man's cultural history. All human experience went into that cry, and the reaction it caused was the releasing of that deposit of experience, bound up in the word-sound, 'fire', in the sensory systems of all those who, through the instrumentality of the Word, had been made beneficiaries of that fund of common experience.

What happened when the cry 'Fire!' was uttered was that the word 'fire' exploded (as we might say) on the stillness of the hotel corridor. The single word-sound fragmented on being uttered, and these sound-fragments, radiating outward from their point of origin — the hotel porter's mouth -- struck on the nerve-endings of the sleeping guests. We can present this series of happenings diagrammatically (see opposite).

Then something happened which, by any theoretical account of knowledge, is impossible. All the hotel guests within hearing

276

Diagram 3

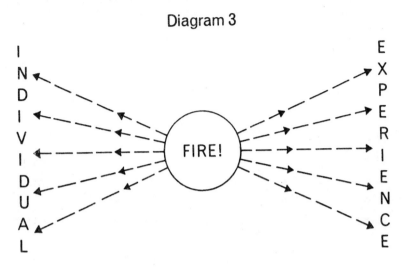

HOW MEANING WORKS

sprang out of bed, and with one common impulse, made for the head of the stairs. And this was impossible because, theoretically, each of these, as an individual, was a closed experiential unit, imprisoned within the limits of his own experiential resources.

However, though, theoretically, no communication took place, they in fact all acted as though communication had taken place. Indeed, we can be more precise and say that the word 'communication' is used as meaning just such a reaction as here described. So in using the word 'communication' to say that communication didn't take place, we are expressing the possibility of such a reaction as above described. So it would be simpler and much more sensible to say, 'In the situation described, what we call communication did in fact take place.' We are then led to ask, 'How did communication take place when the hotel porter shouted "Fire"?'

In the light of what we now know as to the genesis of knowledge out of experience, we can answer that question, How did communication take place in the hotel corridor? by reversing the arrows in Diagram 3.

Diagram 4

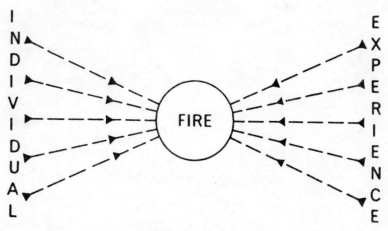

HOW MEANING GOT INTO THE WORD

Here we have the answer to a question that we asked many sections back: How did the meaning get into the word? This reversed diagram illustrates a specific instance of the Original Synthesis of Experience. It pictures the procedure — better called a process, perhaps, because of its groping, unconscious nature — by which the diverse and disparate experiences of individuals, who were, by virtue of their individuality, self-contained experiential units, were brought to a focus of common significance, to constitute the concept Fire.

What the hotel porter has done is, to cash in on this common fund of significance. In detail, experiencing certain sensory data either auditory, visual, olfactory, or all of these – the crackle of flames, the smell or sight of smoke – he has recognized these as belonging under the established conceptual system, and under the specific concept *fire;* and, assuming that the guests will be familiar with this concept – this piece of conceptualized experience – and that (other than foreigners) they will also be familiar with the symbolic sound-word system he employs, he has uttered the appropriate sound-symbol.

This sound-symbol, radiating outward, becomes a series of independent stimuli in the nervous systems of the guests. Each guest, in responding to his own private stimulus, is in effect responding to his own version of the common concept, *fire;* so that each, reacting independently to his own private stimulus, reproduces, in doing so, the reaction of the other guests, which is the reaction intended by the porter.

It can be seen that the stimulus experienced by the porter who discovers the fire, and the various, but identical, stimuli experienced by the guests, though similar in their outcome – the realization that the hotel is on fire – are not of the same order. The porter experienced direct sensory data; an animal that had once been burnt might have reacted in the same way that the porter did, with a sense of danger. But this would have been for the animal, as it was at first for the porter, a purely personal experience. But here the two reactions diverge.

The animal accepts the sensory data as a simple *sign,* a sign of the need to run away. The porter, experiencing the same data, first mentally translates these data into appropriate terms of the common conceptual system. Then, having formed the judgment, 'These data belong under the common experiential form, *fire*', he physically translates this judgment back into terms of sensory experience by uttering the cry 'Fire!'. This new form of sensory experience, the word-sound 'fire', then becomes available to the guests as evidence for a state of affairs, the fact of the hotel being on fire, of which they themselves have no direct sensory evidence.

There is another point to be considered. The porter does not necessarily experience all the sensory data associated with a fire, the smell of burning, the sound of crackling flames, the sight of the flames. By making use of the established body of conceptualized experience — abstracted, as we have seen, from the data of all men's experiential capacities — he is able to know more at any given moment than the data available to him at that moment account for. He knows, for instance, that the guests in the hotel have come from various parts of the world. The concept *world* is perfectly familiar to him, although he may never have been outside the city in which the hotel he works in is situated, and so he has insufficient data of his own to justify his knowledge and use of the word 'world'. He accepts without question that 'the world' is a real entity — real as distinct from a product of his own fancy; he accepts it as part of reality, thereby accepting, too, the even more embracing concept *reality*, for which he has less sensory evidence than he had for the concept *world*.

Amplifying our two diagrams, we can see the source of his confident acceptance of concepts such as these, although they go far beyond anything that he, or in fact anybody, has full sensory evidence for:

Diagram 5

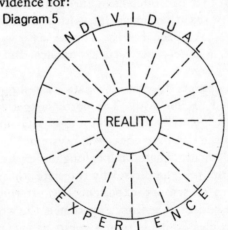

THE SUM OF HUMAN EXPERIENCE

280

Reality, or the World, or Nature, or in another sense, Truth or Knowledge — these concepts stand for the sum of human experience; or, more precisely, the sum of abstracted human experience — the common denominator or the common point of convergence of all human experiential capacities. There can be no precise term for something that precedes, and is the basis of, all terms.

(This inescapable imprecision in the language we must use to give an account of the conditions out of which precise language arose has provided free scope for those of a 'nothing-but' turn of mind, who have enjoyed undermining the ordinary man's faith in his meanings. But the difficulty is that if you pursue any concept back far enough, it brings you, not simply to 'nothing-but' but to *nothing* — nothing that can be expressed in precise language. This is why thinkers of the 'nothing-but' school feel that, as one of them expressed it, 'there is no need to go as far as all that'. Likewise, they feel that only certain words should be submitted to this destructive analysis, other chosen parts of language being kept inviolate.)

No concept is a direct abstraction from any one individual's experience, not even the simplest, resting directly on its relevant experiential data. It might be thought that a concept such as pain, expressing what is essentially a private subjective experience, had been drawn directly from the experience of the individual using the concept. But actually, the more subjective in its reference a concept may be, the more abstract, the further removed from subjective experience, it is. This is so because, for the primitive, the more intimate an experience is, the less need is there, the less possibility is there, of communicating it. He may grunt or ejaculate 'Ouch' when a thorn penetrates the sole of his foot, but this is not an act of communication, it is merely an involuntary exclamation.

Ernst Cassirer, who has written extensively on the problems of symbolism, remarked, in his *Essay on Man*, 'For how can pleasure — the most subjective state of our mind — ever be objectified?' But the answer is implicit in the question, for the question concerns the *subjective* experience which is *objectified* in the common concept, pleasure. But it must have required an advanced capacity for abstraction for men to externalize experiences having a purely private subjective origin, and to submit them to the same conceptualizing procedure by which they had raised private experiences having an external origin to the level of common communicable knowledge.

But this raising of the most intimate of individual experiences to the level of common experience did not only involve an advanced capacity for abstraction. Other factors were involved too. With the elaboration of the system of concepts, men are brought into new relationships, not only with their physical environment — for with each enlargement of the range of concepts, as these are abstracted from the data of individual experience, the individual's own experiential capacities are enlarged and enhanced by a sort of compound progression — but they are brought into a new relationship with one another.

Out of a relationship of common understanding, there must arise other unique relationships, such as *sympathy,* emotional understanding, fellow-feeling. And it is at this level that the abstractive procedure would begin to operate in the realm of the purely private and subjective experiences, such as pain, fear, awe; and meantime, of course, men's capacities for such experiences would become increasingly sensitive.

Men don't live only in a world of things, they live as much in a world of feelings. By the time they have conceptualized the private experience of pain, the texture of their lives, both their private and their common lives, has reached a point of intricacy and mutuality that is expressed in the concept of sympathy with its connotation of something that I not only feel, but feel for you, so that your pain is quite literally my pain, and my sympathy is yours as much as mine.

At the ultimate point of this conceptualization of experience stand comprehensive concepts such as Reality, Nature,

Truth, the epitomization and imaginative limit of all men's capacities for experience. These are abstractions from abstractions in a complex structure of abstractions, the apex of a pyramid of conceptualized experience, the base of which rests upon the discontinuous and indeterminate elements of primitive individual experience.

Chapter VI

THE STRUCTURE OF MODERN THOUGHT

50. *Meaning*

What is meaning? A philosopher has remarked, wistfully, that 'it is doubtful if we shall ever know what meaning is'. And yet it is a most curious fact — a fact for which I can see no possible explanation — that the word, quite literally, expresses its own meaning.

Meaning is, or means, *mean*–ing. It is the mean point of a whole range of individual experience, the experiential data of independent individuals. It is the point of convergence of these disparate data as they are brought, by a procedure of statistical correlation, as we might say, toward a mean of common agreement.

'Meaning' expresses what it means; and yet, when first the concept *meaning* arose in men's minds — at a very advanced level of abstraction, we may remind ourselves — men had no conception of the real nature of meaning. We can be sure that this is so, because it is only during the present century that the development of thought has reached a point where the nature of meaning could become clear to us.

We defined meaning earlier as the power verbal symbols have to cause *different* individuals to react to them in the *same* way, as in the case of the fire in the hotel corridor. This 'power', we then explained, had no mystical or metaphysical significance. It was simply a convenient shorthand way of referring to the observed fact that words do cause people to act in this way. All we were doing was, fixing in our minds this essential characteristic of words, as a preliminary to getting to know more about it — getting to know what was the nature of this 'power' and how it got into the word.

We now know the answer to these questions: A word-sound has the power — its 'meaning' — to cause different people to respond in the same way, by virtue of the fact that it is the symbolization of — it 'stands for' — the abstracted essence of all such responses; having been abstracted *from* individual experience, it is available to the individual as a pattern for the organization *of* his experience.

As the expression — the *ex-pression* — of all men's experience, meaning places the stamp of permanence and universality on the subjective data of individual experience. The separate individual data, acting and reacting on one another, are reduced to their common element or essence, which, as meaning, carries the whole weight of significance of the relevant area of human experience.

The metaphysically-minded, impressed by the observation that the words I, as an individual, use, carry a greater content of significance than my use is capable of bestowing on them — indeed, they saw that it is *because* of their surplusage of significance that they serve my purposes of communication — the metaphysicians, impressed by this aspect of words, saw Meaning as a sort of aureole that the word carried with it.

But — the question then arose — whence this unique character the word possessed? Not from the experience of the individual using the word, because the power of the word, as an instrument of communication, transcended the individual's experience: the word was able to *say* more than the individual, from his own experience, *knew*. The conclusion from this seemed to be clear: meaning, as the word's accompanying 'field of force', transcended the experience of any of the individuals who used the word, and therefore it transcended *all* experience, it derived from some source *outside experience*.

On the face of it, this seems to be perfectly sound reasoning. Nevertheless, we now know that it is wrong; — not wrong, as the empiricist thought, simply because of its transcendental tinge, but in the specific sense that meaning transcends any individual's experience by being an expression of *all* experience.

Its essential character is that it is, not independent of all experience, but a function of all experience.

The very fact that seemed to point to its transcendental character actually indicates its purely experiential character. And indicates, not only *that* it is drawn from experience, but *how* it has been so drawn: by abstraction from and correlation of experiential data which, as peculiar and private to the individual, were not capable of anything more than a limited subjective and, as we might say, local value. Meaning is the universalization of this local subjective value.

Language, as the system of symbolized meanings which have been abstracted from experience, is a man-made structure. It is a conventional system, devised by man for the recording and communication of his experiences. But this account of language requires to be amplified to be fully understood.

Language is a man-made symbolic system. It is a system of arbitrarily appointed symbols, together with a set of rules for their manipulation. Man alone is responsible for the system and its rules. Only man has produced such a system. It is an alternative mode for the organisation of experience, as compared with instinct. It is not a development from instinct; it is the antithesis of instinct as a way of bringing order into experience. Social man, less adapted to his environment than the instinctive social creatures, was, at one and the same time, more in need of some pattern of behaviour, and more adaptable, more capable of achieving such a pattern.

The instinctive creatures had no choice in the formulation of their pattern of reactions, it was imposed upon them. Man is the author of his own pattern of reactions; it has not been imposed upon him 'by some power independent of us'. Must we say, then, that man, or to be specific, the men composing our primitive group around the fire, as compared with the instinctive creatures, exercised a choice in the formulation of their pattern of responses, the common world-picture they were proceeding to build up? We have seen the conditions under which the behavioural pattern was produced, and the answer must be, No. Because, to exercise a choice involves a consciousness of means and end. In laying the foundations of knowledge, and language and its symbolized system of meanings, men were aware neither of what was to be the outcome of the means they employed, nor that these were means to any end other than the moment-by-moment one of 'getting on' together.

A philosopher of language has said that the term 'meaning', though 'useful enough at the level of everyday analysis, does not have the precision necessary for scientific analysis'. However, the purpose of a scientific analysis would be to give the term the desired precision. And when it is so analysed, we see that the answer to the question, What is meaning? is, *'Meaning is a relationship between experiences.'*

As a relationship between experiences — the diverse experiences of disparate individuals — meaning is a conventional system. It is the expression of agreement among men. The agreement is, in fact, twofold. Men have agreed that a certain sound shall symbolize a certain meaning. This is an agreement in the sense that the decision as to what sound shall represent that meaning is fortuitous and arbitrary. In English, the sound h-o-r-s-e represents a certain (common) experience, a certain experiential *form*. In French, a different sound represents the same experiential form. The further a form stands, in the abstractive hierarchy, from the raw material of experience, the less precisely can it be equated with a form in a different language: it is easier to translate a book on the management of dogs from French into English, than to translate a treatise on *Etre et Néant*.

But meaning is a conventional system, a product of agreement, in another and more significant sense. This concerns, not the symbols that stand for the meanings, but the meanings themselves, as the expression of the relationship between the disparate individuals' diverse experiences, the discontinuous and indeterminate experiential data out of which the determinate world of continuous phenomena is to be constructed.

This common, objective picture of a world of things and events in time and space, which men have determined out of the transient flux of subjective individual experience, is a conventional system in the sense — the quite precise sense — of being an expression of agreement among men. But, though it is an expression of agreement among men, it cannot correspondingly be said that it is something that men agreed to. Much less can this be said of meaning than it can be said of the symbols in which meaning is expressed. The symbols are conventional in that they are fortuitous and arbitrary. But are the meanings they express as agreements between diverse experiences, similarly fortuitous and arbitrary?

As we have seen, an element of fortuitousness enters at an advanced stage of abstraction, a stage where we are dealing with abstraction, not from the raw material of sensory or affective experience, but from abstractions themselves, the level of what we might call mental experience. Or perhaps we might better say, an element of *creativeness* enters at this point, and creativeness is not arbitrary; if it were arbitrary, it would be capriciousness, not creativeness.

The procedure — better, process, because of its unconscious and intuitive nature — by which a common world-picture was achieved on the basis of all these diverse experiences, was essentially creative.

We have two senses of the word 'create'. The concept of 'Divine Creation', the bringing into existence of something out of nothing, we reserve for the otherwise inconceivable 'beginning of things'. At the level of human effort, we mean by 'create' the bringing together of already existing elements, in a new relation and significance. The process, to repeat, is not arbitrary. It follows, as we might say, the inherent law or principle of the original elements, in such a way as to discover or elicit what was already implicit in them.

Man's formulation of a common world-picture out of individual experience, his eliciting of permanent *meanings* out of the transient flux of the experience of individuals, each experiencing in terms of his own temperament and capacities, was the generating point and paradigm of all human creativity. It brought existing elements together in

289

new patterns of significance which, embodied in the symbolic system, language, were to be the starting-point of ever new acts of human creativity.

Each meaning, abstracted from the flux of experience, becomes a nucleus around which new experiences form themselves. Every meaning abstracted *from* experience provides men with a new experiential *point d'appui,* thus enlarging their capacity *for* experience. New centres of meaning arise, experience crystallizes around these, and the whole horizon of human experience is progressively pushed outward in all directions in a continuously compounding creative activity, each individual paying his experience into the common fund of meaning, and in the process enriching both himself and others beyond the limits of any of their individual powers of experience. As men build up their common world-picture through successive levels of abstraction, they are *creating* the determinate world which they are presently to get to *understand,* by tracing it back to its discontinuous and indeterminate basis.

It has been claimed that 'partly by means of the study of syntax, we can arrive at considerable knowledge concerning the structure of the world.' This idea leads to difficulties when meaning is taken as a function of the experience of an individual confronting an independently-existing World-in-itself. But it takes on a different significance, once we know that language refers, not to 'the World' as something independent of human experience, but to the common world-picture as an expression of men's co-operative effort of creativity, as a construction by mutual (if unconscious) agreement for all their diverse experiential standpoints.

51. *Universals*

The 'Problem of Universals' has been one of philosophy's most troublesome concerns since Plato, following up the brilliant insight that the individual's own experience was

inadequate to account for the knowledge he possessed, postulated a system of Divine Ideas, or Universal Forms, as the
legislative principles of all experience.

The Greeks, as Emerson remarked, 'anticipated all our
originalities.' Whitehead had the same idea when he said, 'All
Eurpoean philosophy is a footnote to Plato.' Today, however,
we look at things differently. We are inclined to be 'sensible'
about such matters, and say that to keep on asking a question
that has constantly been asked throughout the centuries
without any answer being arrived at, is nonsensical. And the
problem of Universals is just such a question.

In fact, brilliant as the insight was, it gave trouble almost
from the start. To provide a complete account of knowledge,
it seemed necessary that these universal forms that Plato had
postulated must constitute a Realm of Pure Ideas of which
the things of our everyday world were the humble counter-
parts. On the one hand was the world of things, shot through
with error and flawed by the fallibility of our mere human
capacity for knowledge. On the other hand, the world of
Eternal Forms, the dwelling-place of Perfection and Truth
and the Good.

This was a noble and inspiring conception — but that was
just the trouble. One could conceive of a Divine Form of
Beauty, paralleling the ordinary mundane beauty of daily
life. There was no difficulty about setting up Divine Universal
Forms for things that, even in their humble mundane existence, were essentially noble. But must we, to complete the
picture, accept the presence in the Realm of the Pure and
True, of Forms for ignoble things, such as nail-parings, excre-
ment, etc.?

Briefly, Plato's difficulty was: Are there Universal Forms
for ignoble things? Today, as a result of the modern movement of thought, the whole question would be dismissed as
otiose and not worth an answer. And yet the fact is that today,
as a result of the modern movement of thought, we know the
answer, and it is a highly significant answer.

Are there forms for ignoble things? The answer is, No.

But this is not because the things in question are ignoble, but because there are no forms *for* things; things *are* forms.

That there *are* forms, in terms of which the individual organizes his moment-by-moment experience, nobody disputes. And yet, curiously enough, this has been regarded as so persistent a matter of dispute, that today philosophers have turned their backs on the whole subject. Admittedly, it is said, there is a gap in our account of knowledge, the gap between experience and knowledge that the Platonic forms were devised to fill in; rejecting the forms, we are left with the gap; very well, let us take the gap in our stride; I do make inferences from experience to knowledge; these inferences can't be justified: but they are none the worse for that; they 'work', so why not just accept them on their face value?

But even if we accept the working principle that, when a problem looks too difficult, the philosopher's job is to provide us with reasons for not bothering about it, a closer look at this particular difficulty, which is *the* problem of knowledge itself, shows that it arises from the assumption that the knowledge *I* possess is the result of an *inference* made by *me* directly from *my* experience. Whereas, in fact, the knowledge I achieve results from my subsuming my private experiential data under the categories of a common world-picture, which, as an expression of the common cultural heritage, is not a direct inference from my experience or from the experience of any of the other individuals who participate in it. A misstatement of the problem has led to difficulties which are then taken as justifying a repudiation of the problem.

Meantime, the idea of forms having been rejected, the dispute about forms goes on, obscured by changes in terminology. Philosophically, we may take the gap between experience and knowledge in our stride, but this only means that the doubts that the philosopher has failed to face up to, spill over into our ordinary human affairs, and begin to infect all our doings and thinkings.

The difficulty regarding the idea of forms seems to be that Plato got in first — and of course somebody had to get in first, and Plato's was a brilliant achievement at that stage in the development of thought. He not only saw that there must be some forms or principles of organization, governing the step from the individual's immediate experience to knowledge; but he then saw further that the individual, any individual, did not derive from his own experience the governing principles that transformed that experience into knowledge. So he argued — and we have already seen the argument to be a perfectly good one — that if the principles were not derived from *any* individual's experience, they were not derived from experience at all: they were independent of *all* experience, they transcended human experience, and hence they had their source in some supra-experiential realm of Pure Ideas.

And what happened next was, that the empiricist, to whom all such Transcendentalism was uncongenial, repudiated the Platonic idea of forms. But he didn't simply say, *Forms are not transcendental;* he felt the need to make his repudiation more emphatic than that. He said, *There are no forms.* And in saying this, he not only threw the baby out with the bathwater, but he threw the bath after them.

But the fact is that any *thing* of our common experience is a form for the organization of experience.

Consider the 'tree' outside my window. I may regard it naively as a thing-in-itself of which I have a picture — 'we make to ourselves pictures of reality'. The next man, more sophisticated philosophically, may regard it as the permanent substantial thing it is because it is an Idea in the Mind of God. Another may see it as a space-time structure which I 'see' by virtue of certain intuitions which are inherent in the nature of the human mind. You may regard it as a construction which I make from the data of my experience.

That there are difficulties in all these standpoints doesn't at the moment concern us. The important point is that, whichever of these ways of looking at the 'thing' we may prefer, or whichever may ultimately be accepted as correct, the 'tree' functions as a form towards which each of us must orient ourselves if we are to render our private experience communicable and not just the expression of some private quirk of our own.

For one it may be a natural form, a piece of external nature, for another a form stored up in heaven, for another a function of experience. But for each, no matter what account he may give of its ultimate nature, it is an accepted pattern against which to evaluate his private experience.

So the real disagreement between philosophers has all along been, not as to whether there *are* forms, but as to the nature of the forms, and, consequently, how they worked as organizing principles for human experience. The real dispute was not as to whether there were forms, but as to whether they were divine, natural or experiential.

Today, thanks to Plato's brilliant preliminary insight, which opened up the whole subject, we know that the answer is: *the common forms which govern the organization of the individual's experience have been drawn from individual experience.*

The brilliance of Plato's insight consisted in his seeing, not only that the individual organized his experience in terms of given forms – his own experience, Plato saw, was otherwise inadequate to produce knowledge – but that these forms were not drawn by any individual from his own experience. The next step in his argument, that the forms were thus independent of all experience, was none the less brilliant because we now know it to be mistaken.

When the Platonic forms were thrown over, with them went the insight that the individual's own experience was not competent to account for the knowledge he possessed. The empiricist had to discover this again, for himself; with this advantage, however, that in re-discovering it, he at the same time discovered that the forms were experiential constructions which had not been constructed from any one individual's experience.

Only one step more was required to arrive at the answer to

Plato's problem concerning forms for ignoble things. The difficulty arose for Plato because the forms had been thought of as Divine. But that the real difficulty lay elsewhere is shown by the fact that there was also a difficulty, which Plato faced but never solved, as to how things participated in the forms. The technical nature of the difficulty needn't detain us.

Once it is seen that the term 'thing' refers, not to some independently-existing thing-in-itself, but to a piece of common experience, a public pattern of experience, Plato's problem no longer exists. For him, the thing the individual was found to know was the thing it was only by virtue of its participation in a Divine Form or Universal. But now we see that the thing is — the term 'thing', as used in the symbolic system we call language, refers to — a form or universal, the abstracted essence of a given range of individual experiences, in terms of which the individual interprets his private experiential data in order to give it coherence and meaning.

Things, whether noble or ignoble, do not participate *in* forms which transcend all experience; they *are* forms which have been abstracted *from* all experience. What Plato saw as a procedure in which the individual gave meaning to his otherwise chaotic experience by recognizing the Divine Form to which the thing he was experiencing belonged, we can recognize as the individual's act of bringing his immediate experiential data under the appropriate form or universal or category of the common world-picture.

The forms which Plato saw as supra-experiential, because they transcended any individual's experience, we can see as transcending any individual's experience because they are the abstracted essence of all individuals' experience.

The purpose of Plato's Universal Forms was to bridge the gap that was found to exist between the knowledge the individual possessed and his own experience, which was found to be inadequate to account for this knowledge. With the repudiation, by the modern empiricist, of the whole conception of forms governing the organization of the individual's experience, the 'gap' reappeared, in the form of the question,

How does the individual, confronting an External World, infer knowledge from his experiential data?

This question proved to be unanswerable. There seemed to be nothing for it but to take the 'gap' 'in our stride', accepting our 'inferences' from data to knowledge as incapable of justification, 'but none the worse for that'. Finally the whole problem of knowledge was dismissed as an insoluble pseudo-problem. And, in the form in which it was being formulated, this it in fact was. Once we realize that the forms, which Plato (quite naturally, at his stage in the development of thought) attributed to some supra-experiential realm of Divine Ideas, have been abstracted from the whole range of human capacities for experience, neither the 'Problem of Universals', nor the problem of a 'gap' between individual experience and knowledge, any longer exists. We see, instead, that the present development of thought faces us with an entirely new conception of the nature of knowledge, and so of the relationship between experience and knowledge.

We may summarize the two stages in the development of the Problem of Knowledge as follows:

1. Plato observes that the individual, any individual to whom one may turn, possesses knowledge which his own experience is incompetent to account for. He asks, How has this knowledge come about? and finds the answer in Divine Forms, replicas of which the individual carries in his soul.

2. In the light of the modern movement of thought, we ask: How has the body of knowledge we all possess been derived from the data of individual experience? The answer that emerges when this body of knowledge has been traced back to its foundations in experience, is: By all men pooling their *subjective* individual experience to constitute a fund of *common* experience, our common world-picture or, simply, our world.

This does not change in any way *what* we know, but it changes in the most fundamental way our ideas of *how* we know. For its implication is that it is not men who know, but Man who knows.

52. *The Word: its 'kingly role'*

Today we have outgrown the Abstractions, with a majuscule to indicate their transcendental status, with which the nineteenth-century philosopher liked to bedeck his pages; though frequently this new stance of ours is no more than an uneasy compromise, in which we retain the abstraction as part of our intellectual tool-box, but reduce it to lower-case as a sort of vague gesture of emancipation. But the intention is clear — the Age of Abstraction is over.

And now we find ourselves faced with a conclusion so far-reaching and revolutionary in its nature that it requires an abstraction with a capital letter to express its full import: *it is not men who know, but Man who knows.*

Not only does the conclusion conflict with our accepted formulation of the problem of knowledge — in which formulation, however, the problem has proved to be insoluble — but it goes directly against the grain of our present thinking. The present mode of thought is that Man is a meaningless term; there are only individual men, each going about his own affairs in his own individual way. That this contradicts the observed facts is regarded as of less importance than the avoidance of all abstractions, with their lingering taint of metaphysics.

It is a relief then to know that the abstraction Man, as the creator of knowledge, carries no such metaphysical stigma. Knowledge, as an observed fact, is common knowledge, or, more precisely, the term 'knowledge' is used, in our ordinary acts of communication, as referring to this fact of understanding between men: the fact that if somebody cries 'Fire!', everybody heads for the stairs.

Investigating this fact, we find that this phenomenon, knowledge, is characteristically human. Nothing comparable to it is found below the level of social men. But further, as our investigation showed, the phenomenon of knowledge does not occur, even among social men, at the level of the individual and his experience.

The thing we call knowledge, what we mean by 'knowledge', is not a simple function of any one individual's experience. It is only at the level of this complex experiential construction that the phenomenon we call knowledge arises; the body of abstracted, conceptualized, common experience that transcends the experience of any of the individuals who participate in it.

It is in this sense that it is Man who knows, not men who independently and individually know. So Man had better be unashamedly allotted an initial capital to help us keep in mind the sort of thing we now know knowledge to be.

We have already noted the fact that this abstracted, conceptualized essence of all men's experience, just because it was an *abstraction,* could be made fully functional only by being symbolized. Only in this way could this new kind of abstracted experience be itself transformed into something capable of being experienced, and so communicated between individual and individual.

The abstracted meaning — mean-ing — of men's sensory data is not itself the same sort of thing as the sensory data from which it has been abstracted. These original sensory data were reactions in the nervous systems of various individuals. The new, abstracted essence of these data is in itself no more than an 'attitude of mind' (for lack of any more precise term). As a point of 'agreement' between the various individuals, it is a disposition to respond in a certain way, which is present in each one of them.

It is these *subjective* dispositions to respond that must be symbolized to make them *objective* as common meaning. This symbolization, as we know, consists in representing the subjective disposition to respond by a sound, i.e., by an auditory sense-datum. In this way, the meaning which has been abstracted from the original sense-data is reconverted into sense-data, and thus made available to the individual in the ordinary way, through the receptors of his nervous system.

This new kind of auditory verbal sense-data is unique in

that it has been created by man himself to serve a specific purpose. The individuals' undiscriminated subjective data, the sights and sounds that come unbidden to them as they go about their daily affairs, have been translated into a new kind of data, a new kind of experience, the sole justification and function of which is that they are to be the vehicle of Man's objective meanings. They are to give fixed and permanent form to the universally accepted experiential forms, in terms of which the individual, once inducted into the symbolic system, will be able to organize his private data in such a way as to raise them to the level of communicable knowledge.

The individual can enter into this symbolic system only by learning it: 'he will not say even the first word by instinct.' Langer had in mind the problem of how language originated. How did the art *begin,* she asks, which now we all have to *learn?* We now know the answer to that question: it began by our primitive forebears, in response to the tension set up by their increasing 'psychism', pooling their individual experiences to constitute a body of common experience. The problem has always been, how could men arrive at the sort of agreement we call language, without first possessing language? But the agreement that is the essence of language – the moment-by-moment business of getting-on-together – was of a kind that did not require language for its establishment. But, once established, it required language, a system of verbal symbols, for its expression and communication.

But another problem has always arisen as to how the art of language, having been (somehow) begun, could be learned, for each one of us is, by virtue of our physical individuality, a closed experiential unit, experiencing only our own private data. Even the words which my elders address to me must reach me as data that are private to me. How can such purely subjective data give rise to common objective knowledge?

When we examined this 'last ditch' argument earlier, we found it necessary to accept, without trying to explain it, the observed fact that the words of my elders do produce common knowledge; they have the effect of causing me to build up in my private consciousness my own replica of the common world-picture. We then saw that my data, private as they must necessarily be, are not all of the same order or value. The verbal data, through which the instruction of my elders reaches me, have a different value from 'natural' data. They have the 'power' to cause in me a disposition to react in a pre-determined way.

This is the focal point of the whole problem of knowledge — of *our* problem, that is; which is *not* the problem of how I, here and now, build up knowledge from my experience, but the problem of how our proto-cultural forebears laid the foundations, on the basis of *their* experience, of the body of knowledge I now enter into as part of my cultural heritage.

Once we know the origin and nature of the Word — a specially devised kind of sensory datum plus a meaning — the fact of the individual being confined to data which are private to him, no longer raises any difficulty regarding his acquisition of common knowledge. It is precisely the nature and purpose of these specialized data that they are the individual's private equivalent of the common meaning.

To the infant in his cot, one sound is at first as good as another; he starts, in effect, where primitive men started. But where primitive men had to *achieve* the agreement that was to be expressed in language, our infant inherits it.

Throughout the ages his predecessors have been at work extending and enriching the system of symbols that he is now about to enter into with unconscious ease. The 'strategy' of these developers of language — an unconscious strategy, of course — has been to use each area of experience conquered as a *point d'appui* for the conquest of a still further area of experience. One area of experience having been symbolized and fixed as a commonly-held 'picture', other peripheral experiences can be brought into the system by being related to the established picture.

In this way an ever more elaborate structure of interrelated common experiences has been built up, surpassing in its complexity and power anything that could have been achieved by the individual himself, confined within the limits of his own experiential resources. The Word is the magic formula that gives him entry to this treasure-house of accumulated human experience.

At first, for the infant, the barking of a dog, the crowing of a rooster, the sound of a motor horn, the voices of those around him, are all of equal value. They are all, for him, natural data. But gradually the special kind of data which are the words of his elders begin to take precedence. They are more persistently presented to him, and are more intimately related to his own enlarging experience.

But the child does not at first *learn words*. He imitates noises. Words are still to him no more than a particularly interesting kind of natural noise, one source of interest being that he gradually learns to make some of these noises himself. Next he discovers that certain noises go with certain movements or happenings. These noises, which were at first mere chance natural sounds, have now become *signs* of those movements or happenings.

And then, perhaps gradually and unconsciously, perhaps in a sudden burst of illumination, the idea *meaning* dawns. The verbal sounds *mean* what they are *signs* of. They are not just signs of the presence of the thing, they are guarantees of the *being* of the thing; in a peculiar way they *are* the thing.

The child has now established the relationship between the two kinds of data, say certain visual, auditory and tactile data (a tree) and certain other auditory (later visual also) data, the vocally produced sound which symbolizes that particular kind of conjunction of data. He is then able to form the judgment which he expresses in the form, 'That is a tree', i.e. these present data belong under the established experiential form, Tree, (here, again, it is methodologically useful to use an initial capital to make the distinction between the permanent common form and the individual's momentary instance of that form).

This is the problem that Plato so brilliantly foreshadowed

over two thousand years ago. He asked: How do things participate in their Forms? Today the development of thought has reached a point where we can see, not the answer to Plato's question, for in that form it was unanswerable, but the answer to the question that was implicit in Plato's problem. We now ask: How does the individual experiencing certain data which are private to him, bring these under the appropriate common experiential form? He is not, as Plato thought, bringing a *thing* under some supra-experiential Form; he is bringing an experienced instance of a form — a thing-form — under the appropriate experiential form. And he is able to do this through his gradual induction into the established system of common meanings.

This tremendous achievement, the awareness of meaning, has taken place in the individual at an unconscious level, just as the creation of meaning out of the diversities of individual experiences did in the first place. The child has been building into his growing consciousness the foundations of the common world-picture. As his faculties have developed, they have developed around (as we might say) the established system of categories and experiential forms. As his capacities for experience have taken shape, they have taken the shape of these experiential forms. The individual's whole system of responses has been conditioned to the patterns of meaning which Man has abstracted out of experience.

This so far has been a purely unconscious process. Once the Word, as the vehicle of meaning, has been grasped by the individual, the whole process takes a leap forward. Under the instruction of his elders he is now proceeding to build up in his growing consciousness his own replica of the common world-picture. With the mastery of the categories of this universal system of experiential forms, his capacity for experience is infinitely enlarged. He is now able to know, not only what he as an individual knows, but what Man knows. He is able to experience in terms of all men's capacities for experience.

It is, of course, an ever-growing structure of knowledge,

302

this body of common experience. The individual is contributing to it while he uses it for the organization of his own momentary experiential data. Because of his unique individuality, because he is the person he is, his data, his ways of experiencing, never quite fit the given forms. There is always a modicum of strain. The fit is never perfect. This is the point of growth, where within the established forms, under the irritation set up by the tension between the given experiential pattern and the individually-experienced instance of it, new overtones of meaning are secreted, laying the basis of new forms of experience.

It is at this point of growth, where our involuntary acts of creativity pay back into the common fund some small meed of what it has bestowed on us, that the critics of language see its 'failure' to meet the demands we make on it. It condemns us, they tell us, to live in a 'second-hand world', it 'bewitches' us by imposing its 'pictures' on us, it cuts us off from our own true individual insights into Reality as it really is.

As it happens, the experiment of leaving the individual alone to draw up his own picture of Reality has been involuntarily carried out in the several authentic cases of 'wild children' who, abondoned in infancy, have been reared by animals. Langer, in *Philosophy in a New Key*, gives an interesting account of the pathetic but highly significant result. For these children were found to be little better than animals. Left to themselves, they had not been able to take the first step toward conceptualized knowledge, and were found to be incapable, at the age at which they were captured, of entering into a conceptual system — the limited number of words they were able to achieve under intensive instruction were no more than signs for things, not symbols for kinds of things.

The story of the Wild Children should be compulsory reading for those critics of language who yearn to break free from the conceptual scheme which our forebears, around their communal fire, have bequeathed to us, and to make their own individual and idyllic contact with Reality-as-such.

The fate of these children left by chance to their own experiential resources serves to bring home the truth that it is Man who knows.

53. *The uniqueness of knowledge*

With the harmonization of the reactions of independent organisms to constitute a body of reaction-patterns which shall be valid for all of them, a new mode of organization of experience enters the evolutionary story. Indeed, we might say that it is in this way that the phenomenon we call experience for the first time manifests itself.

We would not speak of the purely instinctive creatures experiencing. They merely follow the dictates of a genetically determined pattern of behaviour. Experience implies an element of conscious choice. Even at the level of the animals, where a greater level of choice and freedom may be said to prevail, we still would not speak of experience because there is no *conscious* choice.

This suggests that even at the level of social men — our group around the fire — though there is even greater freedom and conscious choice, there is not yet experience in the proper sense. Man is still closer to the animal world than to the distinctively human world. He is a superior animal. His reactions, as an individual, are perhaps more diverse and more spontaneous — in any case we know, from the outcome, that they were potentially so — but some new impulse or power is wanted to finally lift him above his animal nature and transform him into a human being, capable of developing knowledge, culture, reason, logic, art: a whole undreamt-of complex of new delicately-structured reactions.

Out of individual 'experiences' is built up a body of common experience, and strictly speaking it is only at this level that the term 'experience' applies. With men's procedure of pooling their individual 'experiences' something entirely new has come into the world; something that is only conceivable because it has actually happened, and which can be seen to have represented a decisive evolutionary advance. One member of the animal kingdom has taken the step that is to initiate a new biological phenomenon: thought and knowledge, an abstract conceptualized body of common experiential forms.

Hitherto men have simply *reacted* to their environment. But by pooling their reactions, and abstracting from these a common core of significance, they have, however blindly and blunderingly, set themselves up as the *interpreters* of their environment. At the animal individual level they merely accepted their world as it presented itself to them from moment to moment. At the level of common experience they have *created* their world: they have created, as a thought-structure, the world that in time they will come to know and control.

Man's world is, in this sense, a purely man-made structure, it is 'just the way man happens to look at things'. This relativity to human experience necessarily characterizes language, too, with its symbolized concepts in terms of which we all must experience if our subjective data are to have the value of common knowledge.

Does this argue, then, that human knowledge is 'no better than a fiction', merely a sort of total delusion from which we all suffer, but from which we might recover if we could only break free from the tyranny of our system of concepts and confront reality – more precisely, in this case, Reality – face to face? Couldn't man then become the master of his own destiny, shaping his own concepts out of his own direct and unmediated experience and so building for himself a world of experience to meet his own hopes and desires?

Such questions express the modern 'indictment' of knowledge. They rest on the assumption that knowledge, as a creation from man's experience which has come down to us through the ages, is a fiction with no better guarantee than that, until the modern thinker took the matter in hand, nobody had ever thought to question it.

But the outstanding fact about this 'fiction', the foundations of which were laid in all innocence by our group round the fire, is that it has 'worked'. It has worked in the specific sense that it has been the instrument of man's advance from that original state of nescience, to our modern state of knowledge and insight where we are able to stand apart from knowledge and look at it objectively as — well, as what? As an ancient mistake which we, with our modern techniques of thought, can now correct; or as the unique procedure of funding human experience, which was the basis and starting-point from which these present-day techniques have evolved?

The significant fact would seem to be, not that the world-picture man created for himself out of the disparities of individual experience was a 'fiction', but that, as such a 'fiction' or 'creation' or whatever we may like to call it, it has worked, in the precise sense that it has led to a progressive enlargement and enrichment of human experience.

And we can see in what way it has worked. We have already glanced at the conception of our primitive proto-cultural forebears as a group or system of recording instruments, each delicately adjusted (by virtue of his individuality, his own kind and degree of 'psychism') to register its own response to the stimuli impinging on it. And then, by virtue of the overall increase of psychism, the progressive development of individuality, these recording systems or experiential units begin to resonate in response to one another. And finally to achieve — if 'achieve' is the correct way to describe a mere mutual reaction of psychic stimulus and response — 'arrive at' would be better — a harmonization of responses, a common, unified response, which then has the effect of immeasurably increasing the 'recording instrument's' capacity to register and react to the stimuli coming to it; an important part of this reaction being a new and unique capacity to *devise* stimuli, the stimuli we call words.

When, as during the present century, we are confronted by the fact that what we had thought of as the World, an independent 'something out there', whose structure we have

been investigating, is after all a man-made creation, a construction from the data of experience, the force of this new
and unexpected piece of knowledge has two effects on us.
On the one hand we close our eyes to the fact, and go on
talking about the World as the subject of our studies, appeasing our conscience by now depriving it of its capital W. On
the other hand, we assert ourselves in the face of this disconcerting new piece of knowledge, which challenges all our
ideas of what we know and how we know it, by boldly
announcing that 'the world is a mere fiction', that 'it doesn't
exist', and that human knowledge is 'merely relative' in the
same way as that of a dog or a fly. This curious duality of
standpoints will no doubt provide an interesting study for
future philosophers, concerned with the steps by which
'modern thought' has emerged out of man's evolutionary past.

Man, when he set up his system of common concepts,
didn't sever the umbilical cord that bound him to his animal
beginnings, but by his act of pooling his individual experiences,
he did something and achieved something that had not been
known in the world before. It is difficult to get at the significance of this fact in the confusion of disputation that has
arisen around it. On the one hand, there are those who see the
uniqueness of human knowledge as lifting man onto a level
with the gods. By reaction, others have insisted that the
relativity of knowledge to human experience shows it to be
mere delusion, cutting us off from Reality. It is of interest
that those who espouse the latter view mean by 'relative to
human experience', 'relative to the experience of *an* individual',
and as no individual's experience is capable of accounting for
the body of knowledge in which he participates, the case
against the uniqueness of knowledge seems to be established.
So one mistake comes to the support of another mistake.

In fact, it almost seems to be the case that once a mistake
is made, it proceeds to proliferate by spontaneous generation.
For instance, though it is, as we have seen, of the very essence
of the knowledge that is to be accounted for that it differen-
tiates man at a stroke from his animal beginnings, it has been

said: 'our psychology of belief' — (note that at the outset 'psychology' involves an assumption that conflicts with the facts to be accounted for) — 'while it must be able, at its conclusion, to embrace the refined abstractions of the logician, must, at its outset, be applicable to animals and young children, and must show logical categories as a natural development out of animal habits.'

And again, 'in the matter of language, as in other respects, there is a continuous gradation from animal behaviour to that of the most precise man of science, and from pre-linguistic noises to the polished diction of the lexicographers.'

We need not wonder that, with these stipulations laid down as a starting-point, it has been said that 'the problem of theory of knowledge remains very obscure and very difficult to deal with'; or, as another philosopher plaintively put it, as he gave the whole problem up as a bad job, 'Mental processes just are queer.'

The idealist was impressed by the fact that knowledge is a *unique* phenomenon and so attributed to it a transcendental status. The empiricist was impressed by the fact that it was a *phenomenon* and so attributed to it a purely natural or animal status. Each was emphasising a different aspect of the same fact. Thought, as we now see, *is* a natural phenomenon, a part of our biological history. It is also a *unique* phenomenon, constituting a decisive break in the biological story.

But we can see the sort of significance knowledge has by contrasting it again with instinct. In the instinctive creatures the dominant role is played by the species. The function of the individual in relation to the group is that of an organ performing an appointed function, rather than an independent organism.

The distinguishing character of the new phenomenon, thought and knowledge, is that the individual does not abdicate his own individuality by paying it (as it were) into a common fund. He does not lose his initiative: he gains in initiative as his own initiative is now reinforced by that of all the members of the group.

It is out of these reinforcements of in-themselves-local and limited initiatives that knowledge arises. The unique situation is thus established that, though it is Man who knows, the individual can know more through his participation in this common knowledge, and his enhanced capacity for knowing increases the contribution to the progressive growth of knowledge, that he is able to make.

It is an interesting fact that, with the harmonization of individual experience to constitute common experience, a new biological principle comes into operation. At the animal level, as just remarked, the organism must adapt itself to its environment as best it can. In the extreme case, failure to adapt means failure to survive: that organism has no further contribution to make to the development of the species. If he succeeds in adapting himself, the characteristics that he represents have been 'selected' by 'nature' for transmission to future generations – and future processes of natural selection.

Herbert Spencer's phrase 'the survival of the fittest' gives a clear-cut dramatic picture of this aspect of the evolutionary story; those who survive are thereby shown to be the fittest to survive. But this of course means they are the fittest to survive in the given condition. No moral considerations enter, no criterion of fittedness to survive, other than the fact of survival, survival under the given conditions. The survivors are those who have won out in the competition for food and mates. It is a rough-and-ready, wasteful, but in the long run effective process. At any rate, we must pronounce it effective in that it has produced the unique creature, Man. And Man is, as we have seen, unique in that, by a hitherto undreamt-of act of creativity, he has produced the unique phenomena, thought, knowledge, and language.

And, these being produced, Man has raised himself, by his own act – his own unconscious and groping act – onto a new plane of being. He has brought himself into a new relationship with his environment. And that environment now includes as an important element or factor, the New Individual (as we may call him) who, under the guidance of the common experience — quite literally, a common consciousness — is translating his environment, the 'given condition' of the original selective process, into a thought-structure, expressing the essence, or significant core, of his total experience.

The interesting fact is that this significant core of all these diverse experiences is itself the expression of a kind of natural selection. By a process of give-and-take, of mutual adjustment and reconciliation and 'agreement' between these diverse experiential standpoints, that standpoint has survived which is the best adapted in the given conditions, the conditions set up, that is, by the tension between these experiential standpoints.

This is 'natural selection' and 'the survival of the fittest', but now under conditions generated by man himself. Or let us put it differently, to bring out the peculiar features of this new biological principle.

Out of the blind evolutionary process of natural selection has arisen a process of selection by which the fittest to survive — the fittest standpoint — shall be not that best adapted to a given set of conditions, but that best suited to the *creation* of a certain set of conditions, namely, those in which the organism shall achieve an increasing independence of, and finally control over, its environment.

But even that is not quite correct. The standpoint that survives and finds expression in language, is not just some one chosen standpoint out of all the individual standpoints available. It is the chosen *essence* of these various individual standpoints, their core of greatest significance as an instrument of experience.

The individual does not survive, as in Natural Selection, to propagate itself and its selected traits. In the new form of what (for lack of a better term) we may call psychic selection, the individual — the individual standpoint, that is, the reactions of a single organism to the stimuli coming to it from this environment — does not survive *as* an individual. In the mingling and merging of itself with other individual standpoints, it abdicates (as we might say) its own unique subjectivity to

310

receive it back enriched by its contact with all the other standpoints. It is a process of selection in which the interacting elements do not eliminate one another, but reinforce and enrich one another.

Once this new biological principle is established, a new mode of transmission, not only of inherited characters, but even more importantly, of acquired characters — characters acquired by the organism during its lifetime — comes into operation. Indeed, it is a principle, not only for the transmission of newly acquired characters — new experiential standpoints and dispositions to respond — but for *generating* new characters.

In common experience, man has created a world for himself, and in his symbolic system, language, he has created an instrument for the *perpetuation* and growth of his world, as the body of common experience is passed on from generation to generation, surmounting the innate privacy and subjectivity of the nascent individual's sensory data by the power of the Word.

54. *The rationale of philosophical analysis*

Even while, in the first quarter of the present century, the analytical movement was going from success to success, certain peculiar features of its method presented themselves. G.E. Moore, for instance, very early pointed out what came to be called the Paradox of Analysis. An analysis — in the logical as distinct from the physical sense — consists (putting it baldly) in substituting for a given sentence another sentence or sentences having an equivalent meaning. Now the peculiar feature of this procedure to which Moore drew attention is that your analysis is correct only if your second sentence or set of sentences says the same thing as the original sentence; but in that case you have told yourself nothing that you didn't already know. On the other hand, if your second sentence or set of sentences is not equivalent to the original sentence, if it tells you something different, your analysis is incorrect and so worthless. Or, as it has been pithily expressed, 'a statement of equivalence is, if correct, a tautology, if incorrect, a contradiction.'

And there was another peculiar feature of the procedure of analysis, associated with the 'Paradox'. Analysis was not just a capricious substitution of one sentence for another; the substituted sentence was not only to be equivalent to, it was to be *truer* than the original sentence — truer in the sense that it was to reveal the actual conditions underlying the original statement, its experiential justification, as we might say.

This aspect of analysis was expressed in the technical form 'wherever possible, logical constructions are to be substituted for inferred entities'. Stated more fully and less technically, this amounted to saying: the things of our everyday world are inferences from experience; the purpose of analysis is to reveal the experiential basis and to talk about this instead of about the inferred entities.

'A complete application of this method', said Bertrand Russell, 'which substitutes constructions for inferences would exhibit matter wholly in terms of sense-data, and even, we may add, of the sense-data of a single person, since the sense-data of others cannot be known without some element of inference.'

But it was this view of analysis that was to lead to the other peculiar feature above referred to. For it gradually emerged that there was no 'language of sense-data' in which to refer to the sense-data into which the 'inferred entities', the things of our everyday world, were to be reduced. Language, as we know it and use it, is the language of *public things,* but sense-data, the reactions in an individual's nervous system, are *private happenings,* they are essentially incommunicable. You can talk about, say, a desk, but when you reduce the desk to its equivalent sense-data, you seem to be under the necessity of talking about 'deskish sense-data'. Well, that being so, why talk about the sense-data as accounting for the desk, when, in fact, you must talk about the desk to account for the sense-data?

And there was a still further and final and, it had to be admitted, fatal objection to the reduction of the things that I was said to know, to my sensory data, and that was that my sensory data proved to be inadequate to the task that was expected of them, they couldn't be made to account for what I 'knew'.

It was at this point that the War placed a long and painful moratorium on philosophical thinking, a period which provided opportunity for some second thoughts − (or perhaps they were really first thoughts − at any rate they were new thoughts) − on the subject of analysis. Young philosophers returning eagerly to their studies after the enforced break were not as inclined as were their seniors, to whom 'analysis' meant 'philosophy', to try to make the analytic procedure work in the face of its increasing difficulties. The irreverent question began to be asked, 'Why analyse?'

But even these doubts might not have proved decisive if, at this time, the 'new way of philosophizing' had not presented impatient young philosophers with a new direction in which to turn their thinking. From this it was a short step to the conclusion that 'there is no longer any *reason* to believe in the exclusive efficacy of old-style analysis', and, 'there is, accordingly, no guarantee whatever that our analysis, even if it could be convincingly formulated, would alleviate our philosophical troubles.' The next step was that 'the belief in the exclusive efficacy of this method is just the troublesome legacy of discredited theories.' This was the final answer to the question 'Why analyse?'

But this was rather too cavalier a treatment of a discipline which so recently had seemed to be the ultimate pathway to philosophical truth − and which, too, in the process of proving itself unworkable, had played havoc with our habitual ways of thought and the certainties that (however mistakenly) went with them, without putting anything better or even anything at all in their place. It isn't sufficient, having pulled down the family mansion, on the grounds that you can build a far better one, only to find that you are incapable of building one at all, to then shrug off the whole enterprise, with the comment that it was all an unfortunate mistake, the sooner forgotten the better. In the meantime honest folk must conduct their lives exposed to the full force of the elements!

So let us take our own look at the debacle of philosophical analysis — a summarizing backward glance, really, as we have already glanced at these various points in the course of our inquiry. But now, at the end of our inquiry, we have the advantage of an overall view of what, seen from within, was a confused and confusing situation.

It will be most convenient to back-track along the path of those difficulties which we have just seen to have been the chief cause of the analyst's difficulties.

The first difficulty we come to, once so paradoxical and frustrating that it brought about the *volte face* which has been called 'the revolution in philosophy', no longer presents a problem. We know why the individual's sense-data wouldn't add up to the knowledge he possessed: the individual was not doing what he was assumed to be doing, and knowledge was not the kind of structure it was assumed to be: knowledge couldn't be derived from sense-data in this way because, though it had been derived from individual sense-data, it had not been derived from the data of any one individual.

This brings us to the difficulty that in reducing the things of our everyday world to the data of sense, it was found that there was no language in which to talk about these sense-data; the every-day thing-language had to be used to talk about the data into which the things had been reduced.

But we can see now why there was no language of sense-data, but only of things. There are in fact two reasons for this. In the first place sense-data are private and personal to the experiencing individual; at that level they are incommunicable. It is only when, by a procedure of correlation and abstraction, they have paid the essence of their significance into a common fund of understanding that they become, through the power of the Word, part of communicable knowledge.

Language *is* the language of *common things* as these have been abstracted from *private sensory-data*. There is no language *of* sense-data because language is an abstraction from sense-data. If you trace the public language of things, as the analyst was doing, back to its pre-language basis in the data of experience, you necessarily cannot apply language to this pre-language basis except in terms of the things from which your analysis started.

This brings us to Moore's famous 'Paradox of Analysis'. that if the statement your analysis finishes with is equivalent to the statement you started from you have a tautology, if not, a contradiction. If this is what analysis is doing it raises in an acute form the question 'why analyse?' And we may ask, why *did* anybody bother to analyse if this was to be the result of their efforts?

But of course this was not how analysts really looked at their activities. They were urged on by the conviction that, somehow, this reduction of thing-statements to sense-data statements carried them a step nearer to their philosophical heart's desire, which was certainty.

If I say 'I see a ghost', I may be mistaken, it may only be the family washing on the line. I have misinterpreted my sense-data. But if I say, 'I am having certain sense-data which seem to me to be of a ghostish character' then I can't be mistaken (though I may be lying).

This is an extreme example, but it illustrates the fact that sense-data statements, if they could be arrived at, would be more certain than thing-statements. *If they could be arrived at:* there's the rub. It transpired that they couldn't be. But that after all didn't really matter, because the mistake was being made, in any case, of trying to trace the thing I 'saw' directly back to my own immediate sense-data, and the thing was not a thing of that order, it had not been derived from experience in that way.

But this at once throws the analyst's 'paradox' into a new light. The thing he was trying to reduce to its basis in the data of sense was an abstraction from all men's sensory data. That is why his analysis could not show how it had been derived from *any one* individual's experience. But, this being so, the sense-data statement, to which he reduced his original thing-statement, was not a mere tautology. It was not saying the *same* thing in a different way. This indeed was evident from the fact that the one statement could not be made equivalent to the other, the individual's sense-data wouldn't add up to the thing which was said to be inferred from them. This was attributed to there being something amiss with the theory of analysis, without inquiry being made as to what this theory was.

And what was wrong with the theory, of course, was the assumption that knowledge was a simple function, here and now, of the individual's own experience, whereas it was a complex function by abstraction and correlation of all men's experience, a procedure reaching back into men's pre-cultural past.

The sense-data statement was not the same statement as the thing-statement, because the sense-data to which the thing-statement had been reduced were – not my sensory data here and now – but, the discontinuous, indeterminate and incommunicable data of primitive individual experience.

The analyst's sense-data statement was not just saying – or failing to say – the *same* thing in a *different* way, as the Paradox of Analysis assumed: the sense-data statement was a statement *about* the thing-statement: it was a statement to the effect that the thing-statement was a statement about something which was a complex experiential construction, having its roots in man's past as a social being.

These considerations throw an interesting light on the dictum that 'logical constructions are to be substituted for inferred entities'. That this is a reference to entities or things as inferences made by the individual from his own experience is clear from the further statement that 'the complete application of this method would exhibit matter wholly in terms of sense-data, and even of the sense-data of a single person.'

But logical analysis has shown that these entities themselves are constructions from sense-data, and we now know (as indeed analysis indicated) that they are not *inferences* from data, they are *constructions* by an unconscious procedure of abstraction and correlation, and not from an individual's experience, but from all men's experience.

So what the analyst is actually doing is, not substituting logical constructions for inferred entities, but showing entities to be experiential constructions. The analyst was not constructing things from sense-data, he was reducing already-constructed things to their experiential basis.

The fact that the discontinuous, indeterminate and incommunicable sense-data, to which analysis had reduced the things of our familiar everyday world, were not the sense-data of any individual here and now, does not mean that they were unreal, fictitious or purely theoretical entities. That they were not of this order is guaranteed by the 'Egocentric Predicament' which, as we saw earlier, did *not* apply to cultural man, but did apply to pre-cultural man (though not, then, as a 'predicament').

When placed in its proper historical or evolutionary context, it was seen as indicating the conditions governing the emergence of knowledge out of experience. It was out of the experience of men who were independent experiential units that knowledge, a commonly held body of ideas or world-picture, was to be abstracted. The original data are absorbed into, we might say lost in, the emergent common picture of a world of determinate things in time and space. So that when, in time, in the 'search for certainty', these determinate things are traced back by methodical analysis to their experiential basis — the basis of our ideas, our language and our meanings — they are found to have 'no basis in any known experience'. (This is a peculiar inversion, because it is 'known experience', our common world-picture, that is being traced back to its experiential basis.) And this catastrophic outcome

— catastrophic as the outcome of a confident search for a certain basis for knowledge — *seems to be confirmed* when it is found that no individual's experiential data will account for the knowledge he possesses. Until we know what the analyst is really doing, the search for certainty seems to have disclosed a fundamental *uncertainty* underlying all knowledge.

We are told that, as a result of the philosopher's analysis, he 'can find no Archimedean point outside our given habits of thought, he can do no more than study and expound these habits and criticize the illusions and pretences of those who would step outside them and above them'. The 'philosopher's pen' becomes 'an instrument of deflation', poised ready to prick the bubble of thought whenever it gives signs of rising above the ever-more-minute dissection of the language forms in which our 'habits of thought' find expression; a dissection which shows human knowledge to be 'no different from that of a dog, a fly or a sea-urchin'.

And meaning? This provides a peculiarly instructive case. For, at the point where analysis has shown us what meaning *is*, how it has arisen *out of* individual experience and how it functions in the organization *of* an individual's experience, we are persuaded by 'echoes of the dimly understood debates of the modern logicians' to doubt that 'we all know what something means, or even that we know what meaning itself is'.

The real paradox of analysis is that, just when it has brought us face to face with the experiential justification of meaning, it is interpreted as telling us that meaning is without justification. It is here that the seemingly remote debates of the philosophers begin to impinge upon our daily lives in the pervading theme of contemporary literature, 'the impossibility of communication between one human being and another'.

The contemporary denigration of meaning is part of the general claim that there is no one function that words perform, they perform *countless* functions. The seeming plausibility of this claim is due to the obvious fact that men, having an infinite capacity for experience, use words in a great variety of ways to give expression to this variety of experiences: the claim expresses an obvious truth.

But the objection to the claim is that it persuades us to accept what is in fact a partial truth concerning words and meanings as though it were the whole truth. The whole truth is that men are able to use language in these countless ways because of the one function that language performs: *it embodies our common experience.* It is because it does this that the individuals, you and I in our multifarious circumstances, are able to use words in a countless variety of combinations and applications, for the communication of our otherwise private and incommunicable experiences.

Because of these common meanings, expressing common experiential forms, as these have been abstracted from the flux of individual experience, and because of the system of rules (grammar) governing the combination of words to express complex experiences, the inherent egocentricity of the human state has been transcended and everyman's capacity for experience thereby enhanced and enriched.

When I communicate with you across the physical and psychical gap that was man's original condition, behind me stand my parents and teachers, passing on to me the common fund of inherited experience, the human counterpart of the patrimony of instinctive behaviour of the lower creatures, but the more flexible and powerful because of the manner of its emergence out of experience. And behind my parents and teachers stand their parents and teachers and theirs, and theirs, reaching back to our original group around the fire, transmuting their disruptive psychical tensions into common and communicable understandings.

EPILOGUE

At the outset of our philosophic adventure, we left on one side the question, What is philosophy? on the assumption that the answer might emerge as we proceeded. But after all, the journey has proved to be longer than expected and the answer hasn't emerged, though it may have begun to suggest itself.

But even as far as we have gone, though we cannot say precisely what philosophy *is*, we can say pretty precisely what it is not.

Philosophy is not the finding of temperamentally congenial reasons for adopting one view instead of another. It is not the finding of reasons for adopting any view at all. We are doing our thinking at a stage in the development of thought where what is demanded of us is that we cease trying to place our own interpretation on facts, but look directly at the facts as we find them, to see as honestly as we can what they have to declare to us. And this means, of course, that philosophy is not the finding of reasons for abandoning problems that begin to look too difficult for us, and then laying down as a directive for all future philosophizing, that only *our* chosen problems shall be philosophically respectable.

Finally and above all, philosophy is *not* modern man sitting in judgment on the thinkers of the past and showing up their frailties and failures. The very term 'modern' has unsatisfactory overtones about it. This may seem a strange accusation to make when the present book has been called *The Structure of Modern Thought*. But the title was — as most titles are — a compromise. It was a compromise, for one thing, concerning the content of the book, what it was about. No title seemed satisfactory, and so the least unsatisfactory had to be chosen. And in the outcome the present title was the least unsatisfactory simply because it took up less space.

321

A title such as *The Structure of Thought During the First Six Decades of the Twentieth Century* might have been more precise, but it would have been less convenient.

So, having apologized for the use of the term, we can ponder on the strong suggestion of intellectual arrogance that goes with its usual use. We hear of 'modern ideas', 'modern techniques', 'modern methods', and capping all, Modern Man, the daring and self-sufficient author of all these innovations.

This picture of the 'modern' situation is based on the assumption that all our achievements are due to our having cast off the shackles of the past with its burden of inherited ideas and values. We have examined, with the calm objectivity of 'modern' thought, the traditional ideas which have descended to us from 'the prehistoric metaphysicians to whom common sense is due', and have found them to have no foundation in any known experience. It is hardly to be expected (so the argument runs) that our primitive forebears (this refers, of course, to our group crouched around their communal fire) would have made much of a success of their groping efforts to devise a theory to fit the complex world of things and events in time and space that they found themselves moving about in. Even less likely that inferences made in this way by the primitive individual from the data of his own experience, shot through as it was with emotional overtones and false assumptions, would stand up to the analytical techniques of 'modern' thought.

This standard picture of modern man and his achievements, as he shakes himself free from the lingering remnants of his past and stands erect as the master of his own destiny, is so gratifying to us that we never think to question it. But the facts, as it turns out, fail to support it. The primitive individuals around the fire didn't, as assumed, devise a world-theory, each by inferences from his own experiential data; the body of knowledge that was arrived at was of an utterly different nature from this: men *created* their world − our world − of things in time and space, by pooling their individual experiences to form a body of common understanding.

And it is not that, after all the intervening generations when these ideas were accepted without question, *we* have shown them to be empty of meaning. These ideas have not been found, under logical examination, to be without justification. On the contrary, in our procedure of logical analysis, we have been justifying them. We have been tracing them back to their basis in experience, and showing, not that they are without meaning, but how they came to have meaning; more precisely, how they emerged as the meaning of experience, how meaning itself emerged out of experience; how primitive men, without benefit of theory or blueprint, transformed the potentially disruptive diversities of their individual experiential capacities into an instrument of unity and understanding, the very diversities becoming, in the outcome, a source of richness and power.

It is to be expected that so complete a divorce between what we picture ourselves as doing – undermining meaning and showing its meaninglessness – and what we actually are doing – disclosing the nature of meaning and its origin in experience – that so drastic a divorce between our theory and our practice would have its own effect on our thought-processes. And this is found to be so.

The peculiar fact is that we hold two different and irreconcilable pictures of our current intellectual situation. On the one hand, we see ourselves, as above, as initiators of an entirely new way of thought and, by virtue of it, masters of our own intellectual destiny. On the other hand, we complain – and justly – that this picture of ourselves as repudiators of the past and architects of the future doesn't work. The dream fades and then spills over into nightmare. Before we can lay the foundations of the future we must solve the problems of the present. But these problems multiply and threaten to overwhelm us. The very effort to deal with them seems to accentuate them. To build the future of our choice, we must choose the sort of future we want. But this at once brings us up against the diversity of human interests. The very effort to choose our future plunges our present into chaos.

The fact is that if man is to be the master of his own destiny, then one man's or group's idea of that destiny is as good as another's, with no means of deciding between them except by the appeal of force. The path to our chosen future – if only we *could* choose it – seems to lie across a waste land of violence and destruction.

But surely (we plead) in this extremity, reason must prevail. But reason, too, seems to have failed us. Knowledge itself, that realm of all our great achievements, seems to contradict our dream. Our efforts to shape a rational world for ourselves seem to be frustrated by an element of 'irrationality' and 'meaninglessness' at the core of things. Every increase of knowledge seems to be accompanied by a decrease of understanding. The more we know, the less we seem to understand what we know or how we know it. Life becomes not more, but less, rational with every new application of our new knowledge.

What is the reason (we ask ourselves) for this divorce between our efforts and their outcome, between promise and fulfilment? And the answer seems to be: We are defeated by the 'irrationality' and 'meaninglessness' at the heart of things, which forever comes between what we are trying to achieve and what we actually do achieve . . .

There is no need to pursue this picture any further. We are only too familiar with the details of the modern psychosis. We are now familiar, too, with its etiology, which has been the subject of our own inquiry. And the symptoms of the disease – we have only glanced at the more obvious of them, of course – are just what would be expected, once we know the peculiar and complex nature of their cause.

Under analysis, meaning and our familiar world of things in time and space dissolve into the conditions, the discontinuities and indeterminacies of individual experience, out of which they arose. But if our assumptions as to what we are doing prevent us from recognizing these conditions, or cause us to judge them in advance to be 'trivial' and irrelevant to our inquiry into the foundations of knowledge, all we can see is that meaning has dissolved into 'meaninglessness'. While we are, in fact, showing how meaning and rationality arose out of experience, we see ourselves as showing that 'there is no such thing as meaning', and that there is 'an inescapable element of irrationality at the heart of things'.

While we are in fact turning back to the past and making contact with the original synthesis of experience which is the source of all our certainties, we see ourselves as sitting in judgment on the past and repudiating it and its ideas. It is a highly significant fact that, *with every step we have taken back toward the foundations of knowledge in experience, new sources of knowledge, new ways of experiencing, and new insights and powers have opened up to us.* But these powers and insights, the result of bringing up into consciousness the basic elements and constitutive principles of knowledge, have seemed to us to be the result of our *repudiating* those elements — 'freeing knowledge from its anthropomorphic elements', we call it — and showing those principles to be without rational foundation.

In this divorce between what we are actually doing and what we regard ourselves as doing, can be seen the cause of our 'modern crisis of feeling and of thought', and the source of those problems which seem continually to rise up between us and the new world of our hopes and desires.

Once we had adopted the role of critics of the past, we had cut ourselves off from any understanding of the present as it has issued out of the past — as we ourselves have related the present to the past by feeling our way back to the foundations of knowledge in experience. We complain — and how right we are — that every advance we have made has yielded an increase of knowledge and power without any corresponding increase of understanding. We thought that knowledge would open up to us the gates of freedom; instead it seems to enclose us in a prison of fear. Physical science, following the logic of ideas wherever it might lead, has gone from one success to another, giving us an ever-increasing insight into and power over our environment. To some the only cure for our ills seems to be more physics, more science. To others this seems to be precisely and frighteningly the cause of the trouble – and so yet another ill besets us: the spectre of 'the two cultures', an irreconcilable split in the modern psyche.

But in the light of the facts, the source and the nature of this imbalance between power and understanding is clear. Once the 'crisis in physics', expressed first in Relativity Theory and then in Quantum Theory, was passed – and it was passed, to repeat, by the physicist's adherence to the logic of his ideas – 'the heavens began to open as though according to a plan', to adapt a phrase of Whitehead's.

The essence of these theories has been expressed by Max Born, a noted contributor to the Quantum Theory: ' . . . quantum mechanics does not describe an objective state in an independent external world, but the aspect of this world gained by considering it from a certain subjective standpoint.' It is of interest that this reference to 'a certain subjective standpoint' implies the mistaken individual-experience view of knowledge, but it is the general intention, rather than the exact statement, that interests us. What Born is pointing out, and what Einstein first made clear in the Restricted Theory of Relativity, is that the world which is the subject of the physicist's investigation and which in classical physics had been accepted as existing independently of the observer, is in some way, a function of the act of observation; i.e. that what had been regarded as an Absolute which was the *cause* of experience, is, in fact, *relative to* or a *construction from* experience.

For the physicist's specialized purposes, it was not necessary to ask in what way the world was an experiential construction. The fact itself, once accepted, was good enough for his needs. But it can be seen that it was precisely this question, In what way is what we call 'the World' an experiential construction?, that presented itself to the philosopher as a challenge when the attempt failed to account for knowledge as a direct inference by an individual from his own experience.

Here the philosopher was faced with the same 'crisis' as the physicist. The physicist, whose business was knowledge as power, accepted the challenge and went from triumph to triumph. The philosopher, whose business was knowledge as understanding, threw in his hand and brought to a halt the development that should have counter-balanced the revolution in physics.

While philosophers, during the period of the War, 'quietly assimilated and developed these new ideas' that were to relieve them from the need to face up to the challenge of their 'crisis', the physicists were busily at work producing their atomic bomb, the lineal descendants of which today provide our lives with a perpetual backdrop of fear. All the philosopher was able to provide in compensation of the physicist's ultimate insight, was the pronouncements, Don't ask for the meaning, ask for the use; and, Every statement has its own logic. The one insight that did present itself, *that knowledge, our common world-picture, is an experiential construction which has not been constructed from any one individual's experience,* became overlaid by the dictum that language and knowledge are just part of our natural history.

And once we have turned our backs in this way on the facts of our situation, we have set up a state of psychic tension which we can neither live with nor escape from, so that our sense of 'meaninglessness' and 'irrationality' as infecting and frustrating all our efforts, seems to be continually confirmed; and, indeed, *is* confirmed, while we continue to misconstrue the facts.

It is confirmed further by our 'philosophy of language' and the 'philosophical method which has been established, and which will, or should, be permanent,' a method which is 'apt to be employed as an instrument of deflation,' giving the philosopher the power to 'criticize the illusions and pretences of those who would step outside or above our established habits of thought.' Language, as we have seen, is an intricate and delicate texture of mutual understandings. It depends for its functioning upon honest dealing and mutual trust. Earlier thinkers were tempted to betray this trust, with the best of intentions no doubt, by inflating honest meanings into grandiose but empty Abstractions. The new philosophy has built its 'method' around the opposite principle. Whereas the first betrayal consisted in *inflating* discourse to the point where it lost any real significance or reference, the latter consists in deliberately *deflating* discourse, with a similar, but more destructive, loss of reference and significance. By this method thought is prevented from ever rising above ground level, and the idea is confirmed of a fundamental 'meaning-lessness' infecting all our thinking processes.

Once we have turned our backs on the facts there seems no escape from a vicious circle in which we go on re-infecting ourselves with the by-products of our original mistake.

But (we might demand, out of the depths of our psychosis) is it all as simple as that? Would we, by merely adjusting ourselves to the fact of our situation, by seeing ourselves as exploring the nature of knowledge by reaching back to its foundations in experience, thereby free ourselves from the eroding effects of our psychosis, and so return to some idyllic state of 'normalcy', in which all would be forgotten and all forgiven, and we would live happily ever afterwards, without any further effort on our part?

In the light of the facts, the answer to this must be, No.

For the facts we are in retreat before are not just the facts of our psychosis. They are the facts of a revolution in our basic thought-processes. Specifically, they are the facts of a revolution in our ideas as to the nature of knowledge.

The alternative before us is not simply between psychosis and some hypothetical 'normal state' of comfort and well-being, from which we have somehow become estranged. It is an alternative between psychosis and a new and challenging adventure of the spirit. When we try to look ahead out of the gloom of our present confusion and doubt, we seem to see nothing but a menacing play of lightning along the edge of an abyss. And yet that same prospect, once we have got our facts right, can be seen as the opening up before of us of a new horizon of thought: not something to 'cure us of all our troubles', but something to make us shed our self-induced troubles in a new effort of understanding, a new sense of our relation, as rational beings, to one another and to that other that we call Reality.

A modern poet has said, in a moment of prophetic exuberance, 'A fine wind is blowing the new direction of time.' But, *the other that we call Reality:* does this introduce a subtle contradiction as the final note of what has been a straightforward empirical inquiry? For, throughout, the burden of our tale has been that we cannot speak any longer of Reality with a capital R — what Eddington called Reality-loud-cheers — we can only speak of a humble lower-case reality which bears no higher status than that of an experiential construction.

But in the course of our inquiry we have learned that, even if we refuse our reality the accolade of a capital R, and treat the term as referring simply to a picture which men have put together from the data of their experience, we have not thereby reduced it to a mere arbitrary make-believe having no better status than the view taken by a dog, or a fly or a sea-urchin, except perhaps that it is more complex and so more shot through with error.

Knowledge presented itself as this sort of haphazard and subjective fiction only while philosophic inquiry was stuck with the task of trying to account for knowledge as a simple function, here and now, of an individual's own experience. When that endeavour failed, this seemed to mean that there was 'no such thing as knowledge' or, sidestepping this rather too drastic conclusion — that knowledge was 'nothing but . . . ', the details filled in according to taste and temperament. To this sort of knowledge, or to the reality that it was still (incongruously) regarded as knowledge of, you could hardly accord an initial capital.

329

But knowledge, as we have seen, is not a structure of this order. And we found that to make clear to ourselves the sort of structure it is, we had to have recourse to an initial capital, for we found that it is not men who individually know, but Man who knows.

And *what* man knows, we also found, has a status peculiar to it because of the manner of its knowing. The 'something' that man knows is not of the same status as that which the individual — the lonely wayfarer of Mill's picture — might be thought of as knowing. For what man knows is an abstraction, not a simple sign of an experience here and now, but a complex symbol of the whole range of human capacities for experience.

And the striking characteristic of this abstracted symbol of all men's experience is that it has *worked:* it has worked in the precise sense that it has enlarged man's capacity for experience. And this enlargement of human experience has shown itself, most obviously and dramatically, as an ever increasing insight into and power over — what? Some purely relative and capricious fiction, a sort of universal delusion, which men have put together out of the chance elements of this experience? — but how would such a structure be made to work in the way that our actual knowledge does work? — or some *other* than our own selves and our experience; something so other that only man could know it, but which man could know only because men were, at the same time, part of, participators in, that which the abstracted essence of their individual experiences was to picture for them? It is this that, in the light of what we now know as to the nature and functioning of knowledge, we can only refer to as the other that we call Reality . . .

And if it should still be complained that in this I contradict myself, I can only reply with Whitman, 'Very well then, I contradict myself.'

INDEX

bliothèque
é d'Ct'

The Library